AGGREGATING THE NEWS

Aggregating the News

*Secondhand Storytelling and the
Changing Work of Digital Journalism*

Mark Coddington

Columbia University Press   New York

Columbia University Press
Publishers Since 1893
New York   Chichester, West Sussex
cup.columbia.edu
Copyright © 2019 Columbia University Press
All rights reserved

Cataloging-in-Publication Data is available from the Library of Congress.

ISBN 978-0-231-18730-5 (cloth)
ISBN 978-0-231-18731-2 (paper)
ISBN 978-0-231-54719-2 (ebook)

Cover image: © Enrico Sacchetti / Millennium Images UK
Cover design: Lisa Hamm

For Dana

Contents

Acknowledgments

There are dozens of people who contributed to this book in ways large and small, tangible and intangible, and I'm deeply thankful for each one of them. This project began at the University of Texas at Austin, where Steve Reese, my doctoral adviser, had a remarkable influence on the ideas in this book, and on my growth as a young scholar. His perceptive questions and insightful suggestions have indelibly shaped this project and served as a superb model for thoughtful engagement with challenging issues. I am tremendously grateful to have had him as an intellectual guide.

Other faculty there also offered extremely useful ideas and advice, particularly Regina Lawrence, Sharon Strover, and Mary Bock. And the early stages of this project would hardly have been bearable without the friendship, encouragement, and good humor of my fellow doctoral students, including Logan Molyneux, Avery Holton, Rachel Mourão, Shannon McGregor, Magdalena Saldaña, and Ji Won Kim. Thank you all for your kindness and generosity of spirit.

At Washington and Lee University, I have been fortunate to have the strong support of the administration and my department, including funding for travel for this research, as well as for writing and revising this manuscript. Thanks especially to my two department heads, Pam Luecke and Toni Locy, for their encouragement and their help in securing the time and resources to do this work.

Two other friends and colleagues, Nikki Usher and Chris Anderson, have been essential sources of practical advice and moral support throughout this project, gladly answering my hopelessly naïve questions about gaining access to field sites, writing book proposals, and framing conclusions, and providing much-needed gut checks and reassurances at key points along the way. Many thanks to you both, as well as to Jake Batsell and Seth Lewis, who also offered valuable suggestions during the project.

I am extremely grateful for the opportunity to have worked with Columbia University Press on this book, and with Philip Leventhal in particular. Philip has shown interest in this project since its embryonic stage, and has a knack for asking the exact right questions at the right times to patiently draw out clearer, more precise versions of the things I've meant to say. This book is far better for his role in it.

I've also been fortunate to have two outstanding anonymous peer reviewers of this manuscript, whose suggestions have sharpened this book at several points and have served to substantially deepen it conceptually. Reviewing is often a thankless task, but they did it very well, and I'm thankful to them for their help in making this book better. I'm thankful as well for the other peer reviewers who have read portions of this project as submissions to academic conferences and the journal *Journalism*, where portions of chapters 2 and 3 have been published as part of the article "Gathering Evidence of Evidence: News Aggregation as an Epistemological Practice" (2018, published online before print).

None of this book would have been possible, of course, without the assistance of the scores of people I interviewed and observed. I had little to offer them through their participation, but they gladly gave their time to reflect on their work and allow me to watch them do it. I'm indebted to them for their generosity and thoughtfulness, which formed the backbone of this project. Thanks in particular to those who allowed me to spend time visiting and observing their organizations: Anthony De Rosa at Circa; Chris Krewson and Jim Brady at Billy Penn; and the gatekeepers at SportsPop, VidNews, and Social Post whom I'm unable to name here. Their openness was essential to this project.

My deepest thanks go to my family. My parents, Curt and Joan, have given me more support and encouragement than I could ever have asked. They helped teach me how to think for myself, and they have given me their unconditional love and support no matter where that has taken me. That is an incredible gift, and one I will always be grateful for. My children, Melody, Noelle, and Caleb, have been my inspiration throughout this project. I love you to the moon and back.

Finally, to my wife, Dana: I will never be able to thank you enough for the rock-solid support you've provided, for the deep sacrifices you've made, and for the life-giving encouragement you've given and patience you've shown. You have given so much throughout this project that it's yours as much as it is mine; we made this together. Thank you.

AGGREGATING THE NEWS

Introduction

Understanding Aggregation in Context

Cameron Harris was a twenty-three-year-old aspiring political consultant in Maryland who needed cash to pay for the same expenses that most recent college graduates are preoccupied with: rent, car payments, and student loans. But Harris's plan to pay for them was very different. It was the home stretch of the vicious and absurd 2016 U.S. presidential campaign between Donald Trump and Hillary Clinton, so Harris was hoping to make money writing political news. "News" would be a stretch, though; his plan was simply to make something up.

Harris had already launched an ersatz news site, called *Christian Times Newspaper*, for his creations. For his breakthrough story, he started with the headline, "BREAKING: 'Tens of Thousands' of Fraudulent Clinton Votes Found in Ohio Warehouse." He then fabricated a Columbus-area electrical worker named Randall Prince, who discovered the ballots, and found and sloppily altered a year-old photo from Birmingham, England, to depict "Prince" and his faux find. "Even before I posted it, I knew it would take off," he later told the *New York Times*.[1]

Harris was almost immediately proven right. He published on Friday, September 30, and the story quickly ricocheted through conservative corners of the web—on Facebook, Twitter, and forums. Within hours, it was tweeted by Trump's unofficial Twitter campaign ringleader, Bill Mitchell, who accompanied it with half-hearted skepticism: "Is this story real? Were these merely sample ballots to show 'how to vote'?

What is this about? No idea."[2] A few fringe conservative aggregators with names like *US Defense Watch* and *I Love My Freedom* had begun to repost the story, copying some or all of the text with a small link to Harris's article at the bottom and little else.[3] By late Friday afternoon, Columbus election officials had heard the story was bouncing around online and quickly began investigating.[4]

Within about five hours from the time the story surfaced, Snopes, a website renowned for debunking online rumors and hoaxes, had already published a post declaring Harris's story false.[5] The site had traced Harris's altered photograph to its original source on the website of a British newspaper and linked to four stories by *Christian Times Newspaper* that it had debunked in the previous year. The evidence was clear and the self-correcting mechanism of the online information ecosystem had worked remarkably efficiently. Harris's story had been posted earlier in the day, risen to prominence by the afternoon, and was debunked by an authoritative source by early evening. Its life cycle could have been over.

But, of course, it had only just started. The original story was still being widely shared on social media, and now the aggregators were beginning to run with it. Prominent conservative anti-Muslim commentator Pamela Geller republished the story in full on her website, with a two-sentence introduction.[6] Numerous other conservative sites were running the story, either in full (with a superfluous "read more" link at the end) or an extensive excerpt. Some peppered the story with outraged commentary of their own, while others posted nothing more than Harris's original story and headline with a link.[7] On YouTube, a few commentators with official-sounding names like "Golden State Times" posted videos that depicted simply a screen capture of their computer as they scrolled through the story and read virtually the entire thing aloud, followed by statements like, "God, that makes you wonder how many times stuff like this has been done."[8]

The Franklin County Board of Elections issued a statement the next day asserting that Harris's article "appears to be absolutely fake" and linking to the British newspaper article from which Harris had stolen his picture.[9] Now legacy media was involved as well. The *Columbus Dispatch* published a four-paragraph item dismissing the article as fake, but two local TV stations treated its validity as more uncertain. One published a story under the headline "Franklin Co. Board of Elections Launches Investigation into 'Fraudulent' Ballots" and characterized the board as conducting an ongoing investigation whose preliminary findings indicated the article wasn't true.[10] This misleading report spurred another round of aggregation, now framing the claim as contested. Geller updated her story with a link to the TV report, writing: "Franklin County launches an investigation. The story may have been planted. If so, this is now a pattern and I believe a deliberate attempt by Democrats to muddy the waters."[11]

Over the next two days, aggregators continued to spread the story. Early Saturday morning, October 1, after Snopes had debunked the story but just before the election officials' statement, the story had received 11,513 page views. By Sunday evening, that number had more than tripled, growing to 39,645. By the next weekend, the story had attracted at least 53,229 page views before Harris took it down.[12] Some aggregators continued to quote from and republish the story as if it had not been challenged, while others described its truthfulness as in question or referred to it as a hoax. "Editor's Note: This story has not yet been fully corroborated," one site added above a word-for-word republication of the story three days after the Snopes article.[13] "We warned that this was a developing story," added another in an update the same day.[14] As late as October 5, five days after the Snopes article and four days after the election officials' statement, the story was still being aggregated without a reference to either.[15]

Like a snake whose head has been severed but continues to bite, Harris's story lingered for several days after it had been debunked, garnering several times more readers than it had during the brief period while its veracity was still being determined. It was amplified in part by credulous readers sharing it on social media before they checked its authenticity, aided by professional journalists' he-said, she-said framing of the story that left its truth seeming more ambiguous than it was. But it was also strengthened by aggregators who ensured that it wasn't simply published once and distributed—it was republished again and again. Some aggregators were clear about the story's falsehood and framed it unambiguously as a hoax to be tamped down. Others disregarded questions about its truthfulness, apparently entranced by the way it conformed to their beliefs and those of their audiences. The rigor and conscientiousness of the aggregated versions of Harris's story varied widely, and the consequences of those differences for news consumers were dramatic.

This story isn't as exceptional as it might seem. The content of the news being spread—namely, that it wasn't news at all but false information—was certainly out of the ordinary. But the way this news traveled, and the sources that carried it along, should be familiar to anyone who has consumed news online in the past decade. News is passed along from source to source, altered at each step by a sensationalistic headline or a misleading or irrelevant bit of context. Established and unknown sources produce reports that sit side by side in social media feeds, jockeying for attention, with little at first glance to indicate the provenance or reliability of the information they contain. And underneath it all is a set of events that, if not altogether fictional as in this case, is often hollow and inconsequential compared with the deluge of information it has unleashed. "Fake news" like Harris's story has been rightly pilloried as a threat to citizens' ability to make informed political decisions, but the real news whose processes and flows it mimics can be almost as corrosive to our efforts at robust information consumption.

It is natural to pinpoint social media as a central factor in this frenetically fruitless news environment, and many scholars have adeptly analyzed the role of social media in changing the way news spreads and the way we consume it.[16] But our focus on social media may overemphasize the role of news *distribution* in creating this combination of relentlessness and hollowness in digital news and underplay the role of news *production*. Instead, the way news is distributed can help point us back toward the central role of production. It does this by providing a telling clue to the type of news production that has become so influential: much of our news comes to us from sources other than where it first appeared. We like to think of news as the province of reporters who interview sources, observe events, look at documents, and put that all together into the news stories we consume. And that still happens. But much of the news we read is also produced by repackaging those published stories, summarizing them, combining them, reorganizing them, spicing them up, and making them clickable and shareable. That work is *aggregation*, and almost as much as reporting, it's how our news gets made. But it's not always clear to the public or to journalists what exactly this work is and how similar it is to the work that journalists have been doing for decades. Scholars have also wondered how aggregation fits into the profession of journalism, as journalists navigate massive technological and economic changes, and how aggregation ultimately shapes the quality, accessibility, and depth of the news we consume. Those are the issues that begin to get at the core of how digital news is made and they are the ones that will drive this book.

DEFINING AGGREGATION

First, it's important to define our central term. *Aggregation* is a word that encompasses a wide set of practices across a variety of organizations, platforms, and styles, so it is imperative (though difficult) to establish the elements that unite those practices. I define news aggregation as *taking news from published sources, reshaping it, and republishing it in an abbreviated form within a single place.* This definition draws from a more general definition of aggregation that has been adopted by several previous scholars while adding several components to distinguish it from related newswork.[17] First, this definition is particular to *news* aggregation. There are many other aggregators that collect and republish nonnews information, but those aren't the subject of this study.[18] Throughout the book, I often use *aggregation* and *aggregators* rather than *news aggregation* and *news aggregators* as a way to avoid repetition and cut down on verbiage, but when I refer to aggregation in this way, I'm referring to those who aggregate *news.* Second, the news is from *published* sources, which includes not only print and online sources but broadcast as well, using *published* in a broader sense to refer to information that already has been produced and made available to a public. This distinguishes aggregation from most reporting and pre-publication editing, which do not involve collecting already published information.[19] Third, aggregation *reshapes* the information it draws on and publishes it in an *abbreviated form.* This element is meant to call attention to the work aggregators do in adapting and repackaging information as they republish it, rather than simply reprinting it in total. This definition, then, doesn't include wholesale redistribution of published content (such as hosting wire content or running syndicated videos on a news website). With some automated aggregators like Google News and SmartNews, the reshaping and abbreviation may be minimal—only an organization of several similar sources and an excerpting of a headline, photo, and brief description—but the source information is still repackaged and abbreviated in some way. Fourth, aggregation brings these sources together *within a single place.* This is a fairly straightforward element of the definition, but it does tie the definition into the broader dictionary definition of *aggregation,* which involves collecting varied units into a whole. Aggregators bring together a broad range of information into a single location, whether that location is a single article, an email, an app, or a website. Most of the forms of aggregation that we encounter today (and that this study focuses on) are digital. But this definition is intended to be flexible enough to include both aggregation's historical, predigital forms and future forms that haven't yet been conceived.

Aggregation, then, includes mobile apps like Apple News or the defunct NYT Now and Circa, as well as email newsletters like *TheSkimm* that provide link-laden summaries of the day's news. It includes BuzzFeed articles embedding dozens of tweets to capture the latest social media outrage, and it includes blog posts flagging highlights of a bombshell 5,000-word magazine article. It includes automated services like Flipboard and Google News, and it includes articles summarizing a story that's gone viral, with a quick phone call to confirm the story's accuracy. Aggregation can appear drastically different based not only on the platform on which it appears but also on its level of institutionalization—the degree to which it's tied to the organizational structures and cultural norms of professional journalism. Many of the fly-by-night conservative aggregators that spread Cameron Harris's false news story are extremely disconnected from those structures and norms, while, for example, the *Washington Post's* aggregation teams are deeply embedded in them. As a result, both groups are engaging in similar core activity— enough that both could be defined as aggregators—but their standards, values, and degrees of thoroughness are likely miles apart. Much of this book focuses on the more institutional aggregators who are more attuned to journalism's professional norms and their own professional identity. But the less institutional (and often less scrupulous) forms of aggregation are an important part of our information environment as well. There's nothing exclusively individual or organizational about aggregation, so when I refer to "aggregators" in this book, it can mean either organizations or (more commonly) individuals who do aggregation, depending on the context.

The boundaries around aggregation are not firm. Aggregation work runs up against, and overlaps with, several other forms of journalism, not least reporting. Several major news organizations, from BuzzFeed to CNN to the *New York Times*, have established "breaking news teams" that are predominantly meant to produce quick pieces on stories that are attracting (or are about to attract) significant attention on social media.[20] These teams are often collecting information from published sources on social media and other news outlets but supplementing it with their own interviews—sometimes several of them for a single story. Their work is a little bit of aggregation and a little bit of reporting, and the mix varies from organization to organization or even story to story. These teams are an edge case for aggregation, straddling its boundaries, forming hybrid routines, and showing how fluid a set of practices aggregation is. I've included in this study data from interviews with several members and editors of these teams, but their work (and the work of many other journalists) can't be cleanly divided into categories based on strict academic definitions.

You may notice that I'm not using the term *curation* to refer to this sort of work. Curation has emerged as a buzzword in digital media over the past decade, and it's often used either interchangeably with aggregation or as a more acceptable, honorable alternative to aggregation, to be contrasted with it.[21] *Curation*, of course, is a term borrowed from the art world. Art curators acquire, care for, and preserve works of art to present together in coherent collections in museums and galleries. Some advocates for online curation have compared it to art curation, arguing that both forms involve selecting high-quality materials, organizing those materials around coherent themes, and giving those materials additional meaning by presenting them together.[22] But in practice, the term *curation* often ends up being used simply to refer to manual aggregation or aggregation that is done particularly thoughtfully or carefully. The term tends to be contrasted with "mere" aggregation, with aggregation denigrated as mechanical, parasitic, and unhelpful, and curation held up as purposeful, responsible, and useful.[23] But there is little in any of the characterizations of online curation that falls outside of the definition of aggregation. Curation has thus come to mean, essentially, "good aggregation"—or, as media columnist Mathew Ingram once put it, "it's called curation if you like it, aggregation if you don't."[24] Curation uses the association with the sophistication of art curation to establish distance from the baggage that's been attached to the word *aggregation*. "Aggregator, for some good reasons, has apparently become a dirty word," wrote Sam Kirkland for the Poynter Institute in 2014. "So now it seems there's a tendency to elevate the act of summarizing other people's reporting into an art form that sounds more benign and skillful than aggregation."[25] Indeed, many of the people interviewed in this study didn't refer to their own work as aggregation but as curation or simply editing or writing. But it wasn't because they objected to their work being defined as aggregation; mostly, it was simply because they wanted to avoid aggregation's negative connotations. The term *curation* serves as a shield against censure and a limitation of scholars' ability to examine these practices critically, because it leaves no room for bad curation to exist: if it's curation, it's by definition good, and if it's not good, then it's actually just aggregation. For that reason, I'm avoiding the term *curation* in this book and using *aggregation* to describe this work instead.

WIDELY ADOPTED—AND WIDELY REVILED

It's difficult to say precisely how prevalent aggregation is in today's news environment. This is partly because it's often challenging to peel apart aggregation from reporting. But there are several indicators that aggregation is widespread throughout professional journalism, and that it's more common than it was at the beginning of this century. Several studies have found it prevalent among the news on offer to consumers. A 2010 Pew Research Center study examining the "news ecosystem" of Baltimore, Maryland, found that eight out of ten news stories produced by the city's media sources on major local issues contained no new information but simply repeated previously published news, and another study published the same year found that 40 percent of local news in Dutch communities came from aggregators.[26] More recently, a 2017 study by three Greek scholars found that recycled news content at both elite news sources and popular news sites had increased significantly between 2013 and 2016.[27] Annual studies of global digital news consumption in 2017 and 2018 found that a quarter of iPhone users in the U.S. and Australia reported using Apple News weekly, and Google News was used weekly by an estimated 10 to 20 percent of adults in numerous countries across North America, the EU, East Asia, and Latin America. In Japan, where all-purpose web platforms such as Yahoo and aggregation apps like SmartNews reign, 36 percent of adults said aggregators were their main gateway to news.[28] Other scholars have found aggregation to be a core part of the online news production process. C. W. Anderson, in a study of news production in Philadelphia, described news aggregation alongside reporting as the "two dominant forms of newswork [that] now exist in the digital age."[29] After studying digital journalism in Germany, Dominic Boyer concluded in his 2013 book: "[N]ewsmaking today is as much about managing multiple fast-moving flows of information already in circulation as it is about locating and sharing 'new' news."[30] Other researchers studying digital journalism have made similar observations: organizing and representing secondhand information is making up a substantial part of the news we consume and the journalistic work that produces it.[31]

We might have an image of aggregation as the domain of breezy, social media-oriented news organizations like BuzzFeed and Huffington Post or largely automated feeds like Google News or Flipboard. All of those organizations certainly do aggregation, but it's not limited to them. The *New York Times*, the *Wall Street Journal*, the BBC, NPR—the most iconic organizations in news—do aggregation. They write quick-hit summaries of stories that are trending on social media. They write email newsletters rounding up daily news on specialized topics. Aggregation has reached virtually every part of the news industry, though it hasn't always loudly announced its presence. Aggregators have almost never been given journalism awards, and their work is rarely taught in journalism schools. Aggregation is denounced far more often than it is held up for admiration, often by journalists from the same organizations that are increasingly practicing it. But (mostly) quietly, it has become a staple of news, and newswork, in the digital age.

That's not to say it's new; aggregation has been around far longer than the reporting it's feared to be replacing. But it has been ascendant within journalism for the past two decades. In the U.S. and Western

Europe, the idea of aggregation as a distinct form of news breached the journalistic consciousness in the early 2000s, when discussion of the propriety of automated aggregators like Google News and manual republishing on blogs began to percolate in journalism trade publications and media blogs.[32] It wasn't long before those aggregators were loathed. The animosity peaked in the late 2000s and early 2010s, as media executives described aggregators as parasites, pirates, and plagiarists, at the same time that their own industry was facing unprecedented economic challenges.[33] This was no coincidence. Aggregators and their parent companies were attracting significant investment while legacy news organizations' profits and share prices were plummeting, and they were doing it by building on those very organizations' content. It was easy in that contrast to draw a causal connection between the two—news organizations were flailing because aggregators were stealing their content and audiences—and many people did just that. In the minds of many journalists, and perhaps some of the public, aggregators' ascendance is specifically linked with the downfall of traditional journalism, which has given aggregation's image a stain that remains nearly as prominent today as it was then.[34] In the rhetoric of professional journalism since the late 2000s, aggregation arrogantly hastens journalism's decline, even as it parasitically relies on that journalism for its very existence. But ultimately, journalism holds the influence and the authority. Remove it, and aggregation stands exposed as worthless.

The public has absorbed some of this attitude as well. A 2018 poll found that Americans had less confidence in aggregators to provide accurate and politically balanced news than in cable news, network news, or local or national newspapers.[35] Meanwhile, the term *clickbait* quickly migrated from the insular world of online media professionals to widespread public use as a derogatory description of news that's packaged in order to manipulate readers into clicking on an underwhelming story. It's a term that's often been associated with aggregators like Buzz-Feed and Upworthy.[36] Even though news consumers don't share journalists' motivations (and might not even know what aggregation is), they have absorbed much of journalists' perceptions of aggregators: they're producing low-quality work that's cynically meant to grab attention in a sleazy bid for economic gain.

And yet, aggregation is also becoming simply an accepted, if grudgingly tolerated, widespread part of journalism. Even as it was being lambasted, it was also becoming a simple fact of journalistic life. "Today, pretty much everyone aggregates, at least sometimes," wrote Ezra Klein, co-founder and editor-in-chief of the Vox media empire, in 2015.[37] This is something aggregation's critics have acknowledged as well. In the midst of a widely discussed 2011 critique of aggregation that compared the *Huffington Post* to Somali pirates, former *New York Times* executive editor Bill Keller acknowledged that the *Times* did aggregation, too, and so did he.[38] After a while, attacking aggregation as an existential threat to journalism began to seem naïve at best and hypocritical at worst, as executives realized it was better to join aggregators than bash them.

A mid-2010s exchange between new *Washington Post* owner Jeff Bezos and executive editor Martin Baron, recalled years later by Baron, illustrates the mindset well. "You do this big investigation and you spend months on it, you spend a lot of money on it, and then somebody comes along and in 15 minutes, they've rewritten your piece, they've picked up the best nuggets, and they get more traffic than you do. How do you respond to that?" Baron recalled Bezos quizzing him. "Well," Baron replied, "number one, we should aggregate them, and number two, we should aggregate ourselves." And that's what Baron's *Post* did, developing several teams of journalists who aggregated internal and external stories around the clock, becoming a major source of traffic for the *Post*'s website. As Baron recalled the conversation, he concluded, "I think I gave the right answer, thank God."[39] And so aggregation and the journalistic establishment seem to have reached an uneasy détente. Aggregation's defenders in the late 2000s and early 2010s don't feel as much of a need to stick up for it anymore, but it isn't something that's celebrated, either. To much of the journalism world, aggregation just *is*—a necessary evil of sorts, a rather ugly reality of the news business that isn't going away no matter how much it's railed against. The question of whether or how aggregation was hurting journalism was never resolved; it was simply swallowed up by necessity. But in the process, a thoughtful discussion of what aggregation is, what it means, and how it's changing journalism got short-circuited. That's where I hope to step in.

A HAUNTED PRACTICE OF KNOCKOFF
KNOWLEDGE PRODUCTION

Journalists and media critics have spent much of the past decade debating whether aggregation's impact on journalism is harmful or benign and, it seems, have largely found that argument exhausting and unfruitful. As with almost any subject, the reality of aggregation is much more complex than a simple good/bad or responsible/sleazy binary. Instead, perhaps more than any other characteristic, aggregation is *haunted*. Aggregators' newsgathering methods and values are haunted by reporting; it's the venerated journalistic practice they build on and model themselves after, but they are always secondary to it and removed from it. Their professional identity is haunted by the norms and ideals of journalistic professionalism; they revere those standards, but they can never quite grasp full legitimacy and status as respected journalists. They're haunted by old views of an inert, economically framed news audience that are magnified by reliance on online metrics, despite work that's ostensibly more audience-centric than ever. And they're haunted by journalism's rigid narrative structures built on the inverted pyramid, even as they push to collapse and rethink the traditional news article for a digital age.

Aggregation is always secondary, always chasing something else, always battling inferiority and scrapping for a legitimacy that it can't seem to acquire. It's a set of new practices and values inextricably dependent on old ones, like scaffolding extending from a building under construction. Aggregation is a picture of what happens when journalists develop new practices without requiring much specialized skill, or imbuing them with substantial professional importance, or granting much autonomy to the people who perform them. It's a picture of journalism evolution that's somewhat aspirational but mostly just atrophied. This book is an effort to characterize and understand this hauntedness and malaise of contemporary aggregation, to explain where it comes from and what it means.

The picture of aggregation isn't all dreary, though. The aggregators in this study have substantial skill in processing the torrent of information flowing through the web and in quickly assessing its newsworthiness and piecing it together in a cohesive and engaging way. By and large, they care deeply about the quality of work they are doing. They want to get the facts right. And many of them also want to contextualize those facts in a way that brings new insight to people or present the facts in a way that makes their impact real to wider audiences. They want to add something to the journalistic community to which they belong. Some of them have developed new narrative formats to better fit new mobile devices and news consumption habits. In doing so, they have not only changed how news articles are written but have also begun to alter how they see relationships among news events at a fundamental level. Aggregators have also begun to articulate professional norms in order to define and ensure high standards for their work, adapting and extending principles of journalism to their own distinct conditions. Some of those norms, as we'll see with the admonitions against clickbait, are ambiguous or ultimately toothless at this point. Still, parts of aggregation are mirroring some of the markers of professional journalism more broadly.

It's especially here that this picture of aggregation has implications for the work of digital journalism more broadly. There is a mosaic of forms of newswork that have emerged over the past few decades that are rooted in the capabilities and affordances of new technological capacities—what Matthew Powers calls "technologically specific work."[40] Some of these forms involve specialized and technical knowledge that have been classified by the journalistic profession as extremely valuable, giving these "tech-savvy" journalists an image almost of wizards doing magic. These are the forms documented by Nikki Usher in her study of "interactive journalism," the domain of data journalists, programmer-journalists, mobile developers, and the like.[41]

But much of the work of digital journalism is seen not as magical but as marginal. It's the work of web producers and social media interns, of entry-level employees and displaced former reporters. Digital journalists have always faced an uphill climb to be treated as equals and professionals by their peers, and the ubiquity and establishment of digital news shouldn't obscure the fact that that climb is not yet complete.[42] The state of aggregation is a potent reminder that even as the work of journalism shifts toward a more deeply digital orientation, the profession's center of gravity—its core of what it means to be a journalist—has not shifted as far along with it. Still, as we examine the world of aggregation, we see the "other side" of the transformation of journalism, the side that isn't as innovative or trendy as the areas we like to lavish attention on but is exerting its own pull on what journalism is and means all the same.

In both its hauntedness and marginality, aggregation is similar to other forms of what we might call "knockoff" knowledge creation. It's a process of creating knowledge that imitates more established forms of knowledge production (in this case, reporting) but is ultimately derivative of that knowledge. Forms of knockoff knowledge creation have emerged and grown in recent years, both within and beyond journalism, often as ways to exploit the ease of creating and disseminating digital information. Conspiracy theories are an enduring knockoff form that have been given fresh momentum online. They echo the form of in-depth investigation, amassing archival, physical, audiovisual, and digital evidence as a detective might and using it to give off the appearance of a carefully researched conclusion. But their evidence assemblage lacks the logical rigor and epistemological openness of the true investigations they imitate. Predatory academic publishing is another, newer form of knockoff knowledge. It mimics the format and processes of scholarly research as a means of outright deceit, reaping revenue from researchers in exchange for a knowledge production process that seems just legitimate enough to fool them (or their tenure review committees).[43] Compared with the more established forms it mirrors, knockoff knowledge production is hastier, more piecemeal, and often more preoccupied with maintaining the *feel* of knowledge creation than in refining the particulars of the creation process itself.

Knockoff knowledge is at least as old as the Sophists of ancient Greece, but it has taken on new significance in recent years. Both researchers and the public have been increasingly concerned about the quality of public knowledge about current events, especially since the populist uprisings of the past several years in the United States and Europe and the emergence of "fake news" as a focal point of political and scholarly discussion. This type of knowledge creation doesn't have to be as malicious as false news or predatory publishing—aggregation certainly isn't—but it does play a substantial role in producing an information environment that feels relentlessly churning but ultimately hollow. This book is a study of how one form of knockoff knowledge is produced and the complex ways it interacts with the forms it imitates.

Aggregation is built on established forms of news production but is a derivative imitation of them, without an independent or distinctive means of validating its own claims. Without those robust validation processes, its product becomes at its worst a sort of pseudo-information. It takes on the external qualities of more valuable information, and even contains some of that information's more thoroughly verified claims, but is at its center anemic and minimally valuable. As a whole, aggregation and knockoff knowledge processes ultimately saturate us with information whose primary result is redundancy and confusion. But these qualities aren't inherent in aggregation. Aggregation can be a valuable part of a news ecosystem, making sense of sprawling news stories and complex public issues for hurried news consumers. It can provide another point of entry to news and discussion on important issues for audiences neglected by traditional journalistic approaches. Achieving these characteristics depends greatly on aggregators' abilities to turn their secondhand, makeshift practices into a viable form of knowledge production—one that can form the basis for robust professional identity and authority. To understand how aggregation can be both a constructive and detrimental form of knockoff knowledge, we first need to examine the complex but crucial relationship between journalists' cultural authority, their professional identity, and the ways they create knowledge.

RELATING JOURNALISTIC AUTHORITY, EPISTEMOLOGY, AND PROFESSIONAL IDENTITY

What distinguishes aggregation from other forms of newswork is its process of gathering information, shaping it, and presenting it to the public. In other words, it's a particular form of knowledge production. Aggregation's characteristics as a type of knowledge production have deep repercussions for two particular areas of journalists' social standing: their authority and their professional identity. Specifically, the secondhand nature of aggregation's knowledge production process undermines aggregators' sense of identity as professional journalists and contributes to the erosion of their authority to present reality in ways that are accepted as legitimate. Three concepts—authority, epistemology, and professionalism—have always been tightly connected by theorists, particularly in journalism. Studying aggregation allows us to examine those connections more closely and especially what happens to those connections when at least one of those concepts begins to break down in practice. To understand those connections, let's first look at each of these concepts in turn.

Journalistic *authority* is the ability of journalists to "possess a right to create legitimate discursive knowledge about events in the world for others," as Matt Carlson puts it—or, the ability to characterize their accounts of the world as reality and have others take them seriously.[44] It's more than trust or credibility; it's weightier and more complex, and less oriented toward effects.[45] But it's not as overpowering as authority in the classic sense theorized by Max Weber, which is built around inducing obedience. Instead, journalistic authority is a form of what the sociologist Paul Starr calls cultural authority, which involves defining and attaching meaning to reality in ways that are understood as valid.[46] The brand of authority journalists possess, Carlson says, is at its core about maintaining "a right to be listened to."[47]

That right is crucial for journalists, and it's at the center of every function they claim to serve.[48] To act as a watchdog for government, journalists' accounts of government action have to be understood as accurate representations of reality, and they have to be given weight among both the public and political officials in order to be acted on. To serve as a forum for conversation on public issues, news organizations must be recognized as a legitimate space in which particular issues are appropriately deemed important, the speakers who are privileged have a right to be taken seriously, and the discussion is likely to influence events or opinion in some way. All of these characteristics require substantial authority. Without it, the service to democracy that journalists so eagerly tout is rendered meaningless.

But authority cannot be exercised unilaterally. Each of the characteristics in the previous paragraph requires the assent of people outside journalism. The perception of an actor as authoritative is often defined as legitimacy and the process of producing that perception as legitimation.[49] The necessity of legitimacy for authority means that authority cannot exist as a static object but is always constituted as a relationship—in journalism's case, with audiences, sources, critics, technologies, the state, the market, and other information-producing professions. The maintenance of authority, then, requires constant work in order to negotiate and sustain those relationships.⁵⁰ For journalists, that authority-production work often takes place through discourse, as they articulate their norms and values and seek to justify them before others.⁵¹ But it also takes place through practice, as journalists create and reinforce processes and routines to construct authoritative accounts of reality and serve as the substrate for norms and narratives about their work.⁵² This is where aggregation comes in. It's a practice of knowledge work that has substantial difficulty supporting journalistic authority as other practices, particularly reporting, do.

The second concept, the *epistemology* of journalism, becomes crucial in this respect. Journalists' primary source of authority lies in the practices by which they create knowledge and the way those practices are discursively justified to others, particularly the public. Journalists' claim to authority at bottom is their ability, as Mats Ekström has characterized it, "to present, on a regular basis, reliable, neutral and current factual information that is important and valuable for the citizens in a democracy."⁵³ This claim is an epistemological one; it revolves around journalism's ability to produce a particular quality of knowledge. That claim, in turn, rests on particular practices of producing knowledge, which journalism seeks to refine, defend, and control. By exercising authority over those knowledge-producing practices, journalism can make a case for its ability to provide reliable knowledge through them, thus building a broader form of cultural authority that allows its construction of reality to be taken seriously.⁵⁴

News, then, is fundamentally a form of public knowledge and journalism a set of practices meant to produce it. Robert Park, the renowned early-twentieth-century sociologist of the Chicago School, was among the first to explicitly characterize news this way.⁵⁵ In the 1970s and 1980s, a wave of researchers deepened this notion, going into newsrooms to break down exactly how this knowledge was created. Led by the sociologist Gaye Tuchman, they found that journalists produced knowledge through routines and rituals (like the beat system and objectivity) that were intended to make reality manageable but ultimately elided at least as much as they revealed.⁵⁶

Journalists use various practices in the course of producing knowledge—design, data analysis, editing—but the dominant one for more than a century has been reporting. Reporting is modern journalism's distinctive innovation in knowledge-producing practices and has proven an enduringly effective way to quickly gain practical knowledge about quickly changing events and the actions of officials and public figures.[57] Accordingly, it has taken on immense importance in journalists' ways of thinking and talking about what they do.[58] Aggregation and reporting have a good deal in common as knowledge-producing practices. Both involve gathering information (usually very quickly), evaluating it as evidence, weighing it, distilling it into "the facts," and presenting it in a brief summary. But the crucial difference between the two is in the objects of evidence they use. Reporting employs observation, interviews, and documents, and aggregation largely uses published reports—that is, the fruits of other people's reporting.[59]

This is what makes aggregation a knockoff of reporting. It's a practice built on the principles and practices of reporting, but it is always reliant on it and coming after it in both time and importance. This secondary nature shapes aggregation's epistemological practices at every turn, but it also damages aggregation's claims to authority. If journalistic authority is based on journalists' claim to present knowledge about the world that can be taken as definitive, then shifting knowledge production to a practice that is inherently derivative and further from the events it depicts erodes the credibility of that claim. And when aggregation has difficulty presenting itself as a viable foundation for journalistic authority, the fallout is severe. The value of aggregated news plummets, and beyond that, aggregators' sense of their own value is damaged, and the degree to which they view themselves as a meaningful part of the broader journalistic project is shaken.

This is where the third concept, *professionalism* and *professional identity*, reveals its significance. Professionalism, more than anything else, is the glue that holds knowledge and authority together. As Max Weber conceived of it, the purpose of professionalism is to translate a group's epistemological expertise into cultural authority. Professions seek to monopolize a socially useful body of knowledge (the news, in journalism's case) and convert it to both social status and economic power.[60] For journalism, that means working to validate journalists' epistemological practices as legitimate and reliable sources of knowledge about public events. Journalistic professionalism presents these practices as authoritative by articulating norms, or rules establishing and encouraging particular modes of conduct. It also forms and protects a strong bond between the profession of journalism and its particular forms of knowledge work (i.e., reporting). This link between a profession and its work is, as Andrew Abbott put it in his landmark work on the sociology of professions, "the central phenomenon of professional life."[61]

Ideally for a profession, this link should be exclusive; professions seek to be the only ones capable of performing their work. Many professions have succeeded on this front—doctors diagnosing medical conditions, accountants conducting audits—but journalists have not. The open-ended nature of the work of reporting on current events means that journalists will never be able to claim exclusive control over that task, and the explosion of participatory technologies for gathering and disseminating information quickly, such as the smartphone and social media, has continued to weaken the professional distinctiveness of journalistic work.[62] That's not the only characteristic of a classic profession that journalism is missing: it has no required education, an ill-defined body of knowledge to protect, and minimal power to enforce compliance with its standards. It continually articulates two of the fundamental qualities of professionalism—a purpose built on a broader societal good and a desire to be free from intervention from the state and the market to do its work. In practice, though, both its public-service aims and autonomy are deeply constrained, especially by commercial forces. But as the study of professions has shifted from a trait-based approach to an emphasis on professionalism as a source of meaning and identity, journalism has taken on a more professional cast and become more fruitful ground for professional dynamics.[63] The most frequently posed question by scholars of journalism as a profession, then, is not whether it counts as one, but under what circumstances do journalists seek to turn it into a profession and turn themselves into professionals?[64]

This approach puts professional identity at the forefront of what it means to practice journalism. Professional identity is a form of group identity that extends beyond organizations and is driven by the confluence of individual autonomy, specialized skills, and social affiliation that professionalized groups tend to engender.[65] Journalists have a very strong sense of this identity, especially compared with their lack of conformity to classic professional characteristics. They defend themselves in professional terms—as a group of people who perform a distinct set of tasks, oriented around a high calling of public service, which should imbue their work with great social value and give them broad autonomy to exercise control over it.[66]

Professional identity has a great deal of value for journalists. It provides a central motivation for upholding norms and standards in the absence of forceful mechanisms. It reinforces a sense of community that sustains its members' commitment and buffers their relationships with other institutions.[67] It can also act as a bulwark against demoralizing work conditions. Journalists' image of themselves as savvy and noble, if unruly, guardians of democracy helps them cope with the increasingly routine, constrained nature of newswork.[68] Professional identity can operate along multiple vectors: It is, in one sense, based on a set of ideals and values that define and prescribe appropriate beliefs and actions for journalists.[69] Scholars who focus on this dimension of professional identity often characterize it as professional ideology or professional role conceptions. But it is also rooted in particular routines and practices, and journalists' ability to establish control over them, as well as their sense that those practices are epistemologically viable as a basis for their authority. Professional identity is bound up in journalists' *work*: its conditions, its requirement of skill and expertise, its ability to reliably produce authoritative knowledge.

Journalists' epistemological practices are crucial in this respect to maintaining their professional identity. This is part of a broader connection between practice and identity through which journalistic identity is rooted in the routines and habits of journalism—or, as David Ryfe writes, "being a journalist is closely connected to doing journalism."[70] Those routines and work conditions have a substantial impact on the identity of aggregators and other journalists, but the epistemological components of the work have a distinctive role. Without a sense that their newswork is an effective means of producing reliable knowledge that can serve as a basis for their cultural authority, journalists' identity is damaged. This dimension of the practice–identity link is an important connection between the epistemological and professional realms. It's also a connection that runs in the reverse direction. Epistemologically viable work practices are necessary for professional identity to be sustained, but professional identity is an important component in work practices reaching epistemological coherence as well. When journalists' sense of professional identity is fostered, they are more likely to develop and adhere to the norms that can help elevate the quality of knowledge their work produces. But when professional identity breaks down, work becomes merely rote and hollow, and the commitment and cognitive investment necessary to continually create valid knowledge goes lacking. Journalistic knowledge work and professional identity are mutually constitutive; they continually produce and reinforce each other when they are present, and they erode and undermine each other when they are deficient.

The relationship among journalistic authority, knowledge work, and professionalism is what makes journalism work. Knowledge work forms the basis for journalism's claims to authority over its depictions of reality, and it also forms the cognitive realm that professionalism seeks to protect. Professionalism, in turn, invokes knowledge work in its case for authority by articulating norms around it and protecting it from rivals. Both authority and the practices of knowledge work feed journalists' professional identity, giving them a distinct set of skills and social roles to rally around. There are other factors contributing to journalistic authority, of course: the form of news, journalists' discourse about themselves, journalists' relationship with its audience, journalism's economic capital, and so on.[71] But this study makes the argument that the work of journalism itself—and specifically the degree to which it is effective in producing knowledge that can be taken as a reliable, legitimate presentation of reality—is a crucial component of journalistic authority.

This book is an examination of what happens to journalistic authority and professional identity when the practices of knowledge work are weakened. The consequences are profound: the mutually constitutive relationship between knowledge work and professional identity is undermined, and without a firm epistemological and professional foundation, authority is eroded. The frailty of these relationships is a substantial part of the challenges to journalism's authority and professional status in recent years. The role that the audience's intrusion on the processes of news production plays in those challenges has received substantial scholarly attention, and rightly so.[72] But there is another major factor in play: the work of journalism itself is changing, and its epistemological viability has been become more uncertain. As we seek to understand the nature of journalists' precarious authority in an age of fuzzy boundaries, false news, and declining trust, the shifting work of knowledge production itself and its relationship with professional identity deserve a closer look.

AGGREGATION PAST AND PRESENT

In order to understand how aggregation produces knowledge and justifies it as authoritative, it helps to take a look at how it has evolved and what is shaping its current iteration. Journalists did not come to characterize aggregation, by that term, as a distinct form of their work until the last two decades, but it has as long of a history as any other type of newswork. Most of early American journalism was much closer to aggregation than reporting. Newspapers in the eighteenth and early nineteenth centuries consisted primarily of reprinted letters and columns from other publications interspersed with their own broadsides and short notices of business and political happenings.[73] The Postal Service Act of 1792 encouraged this type of reprinting of others' content, allowing newspapers to exchange copies for free with one another. By 1800, according to one estimate, between one-fourth and one-fifth of all the newspapers mailed in the United States were sent, gratis, from one paper to another. As a result, the nonlocal news that filled the newspaper in the early 1800s came overwhelmingly from other papers, reprinted in full.[74] Literary scholar Meredith McGill describes pre-Civil War newspapers as "a tissue of items copied from other print authorities," and Nieman Journalism Lab editor Joshua Benton has characterized the network as "a system designed to inspire what many people today would consider rampant theft of news."[75]

But this widespread republishing of content was not a matter of shame but of professional pride, as the "exchange editors" responsible for this work saw their duty as sagely separating wheat from chaff. The system played a valuable social role as well. Through the partisan nature of many of the newspapers involved, exchanges also helped constitute national political networks through which policy positions were spread and voters were mobilized. "Exchanges," writes historian Richard Kielbowicz, "were the central nervous system of the press before the advent of the telegraph."[76] Much of the information was republished with credit, and those who violated the norm were occasionally publicly castigated by other newspapers. But the imperative to attribute information couldn't be reliably enforced, and reprinting without credit or with incorrect credit was fairly common.[77]

In Britain, aggregated news took a different path but wound up in a very similar place. Newspaper historian Anthony Smith describes a world in seventeenth- and eighteenth-century Britain in which information for country weeklies came almost exclusively from the larger London newspapers. Even those papers' information came not from their own reporting but from foreign journals, private newsletters, markets, courts, and the like. Most of that information was placed in the newspaper by the sources themselves, often unaltered. Newspapers consequently characterized themselves as carriers of information rather than generators of it. For the British printer of the eighteenth century, Smith writes, the " 'editing' function consisted in little more than checking for obvious libels."[78] To be a newspaper editor in the eighteenth and early nineteenth century was to aggregate. Any other form of newsgathering was virtually unknown.

It was not until the mid-1800s that reporting developed as a practice. Until that point, newspapers had been one- or two-person operations, with friends or travelers obliging as correspondents. The penny papers were the first to employ reporters and foreign correspondents, and by the late 1800s, reporting began to crystallize into a systematic and professionalized form revolving around the use of interviews and observation to gather information that could be distilled into facts.[79] During the next 125 years or so, reporting enjoyed its heyday within journalism, dominating its practice and arising alongside objectivity to form a key part of journalists' professional identity. Reporting's prominence peaked during what media scholar Daniel Hallin has termed the "high modern" period that reigned in American journalism after World War II, when objectivity, political and commercial independence, and investigative journalism were particularly prized.[80] Even during the era of reporting, however, examples of aggregation arise: the Scripps family newspapers developed a writing style called "condensation" in the 1870s and 1880s that consisted of copying stories from rival newspapers or the wire and rewriting them brief, summarized form. In Sweden, cutting and pasting work from other publications remained a dominant form of newswork into the early twentieth century.[81] American clipping bureaus read through thousands of periodicals at dizzying speeds to collect excerpts into reports for clients in business and government as well as the trade press.[82] Rewriting competitors' stories was common enough during the yellow journalism era of the turn of the century that a few news organizations successfully published bogus reports to catch rivals in the act.[83] *Time* magazine launched in 1923 with a promise to read and digest "every magazine and newspaper of note in the world" and reduce that information to "approximately 100 short articles, none of which are over 400 words in length," and it wasn't alone.[84] By 1944, the journalist and activist Oswald Garrison Villard was lamenting that "the most widely read publication of all, the *Reader's Digest*, influences public opinion almost wholly by choice of articles from other publications."[85]

During this era, other journalistic positions and practices developed that bear strong resemblances to elements of today's aggregation. Wire editors were an evolution from the previous era's "exchange editor," and their duties were quite similar to those of aggregators. They monitored newswires, compared the accounts of competing services, selected a mix of stories, then worked to trim them and sometimes reorganize them or combine them with internally produced information.[86] Their work was distinct from aggregation—they were dealing with information that had been published but wasn't already available to their audiences—but it also bore striking similarities. In reporting, too, there was aggregative work. Reporters everywhere can tell stories of being beaten to a big story by a competitor and being forced to "chase" that story, regathering information that has already been published so that their organization can claim their own version of the story. And as researchers have found, particularly since the 1990s, even much of the information in reported stories comes from quasi-published information sources given to journalists like press releases and media kits.[87] Reporting has prevailed in the journalistic imagination over the past century, but aggregation has run right alongside it the entire time.

As an increasing amount of information consumption moved online in the 1990s, though, aggregation began to take on a greater role in the news environment. A 1997 study of newspaper journalists found that they saw their filtering role as becoming increasingly important with the exponentially expanding amount of information available to their audiences. Readers, one journalist said, prefer having someone "give you a short version of all that stuff, digest it, truthfully tell you, honestly, what it means and what it doesn't mean."[88] Meanwhile, modern online aggregation began to develop through two distinct strands. In the first strand, web portals, led initially by Yahoo, emerged as central sites to aggregate all kinds of information, including news, for vast numbers of internet users. Google News was the first of those sites to launch strictly as a news aggregator in 2002, and it was met with a mixture of concern and amazement from news organizations. The French news agency Agence France-Presse immediately sued Google for copyright infringement.[89] Google News grew to become one of the largest news sites on the web by the late 2000s and inspired a wave of portal-style aggregators like Topix, the Examiner, and Bing News.[90] It pioneered and still leads the automated forms of aggregation exemplified by apps like SmartNews and Flipboard.

The second strand grew out of blogging, which was built in the 1990s largely on the simple structure of linking to interesting sites and posts around the web and commenting on them.[91] The Drudge Report was the most popular early aggregator to arise from this model and perhaps the simplest as well. It did away with the "comment" part of the link-and-comment approach, communicating its conservative perspective simply through incendiary headlines. It began in 1995 as an email newsletter and achieved its breakthrough when it broke the news of the Monica Lewinsky scandal in 1998. Elsewhere, other blogs or blog-like sites developed distinctive forms of aggregating the news, some of them becoming must-read sites in particular niches. The aggregator of this kind that caught most journalists' attention was Jim Romenesko's Media News site for the nonprofit Poynter Institute, which he launched under the title Media Gossip in 1999 and ran until his resignation in 2011.[92] Romenesko's site was a constantly updated compendium of links to stories about the news industry across the web with paragraph-long summaries and clever headlines. It became a zeitgeist-defining site for journalists and a standard-bearer for sharp, obsessively focused news aggregation. Romenesko "helped transform aggregation and curation from the pre-dawn avocation of a guy in his jammies to a craft with significant consequence for journalism," wrote Poynter's Bill Mitchell in 2011.[93] At around the same time, another media blog, Gawker, led the way for a form of aggregation that was at once smart, sly, and relentlessly productive and commercial. Founded in 2002 by Nick Denton and Elizabeth Spiers, it covered New York media gossip with a cutting wit and a restless energy fueled by writers who were given bonuses for the amount of traffic their work drew.[94] Gawker was shut down in 2016 after its parent company was bankrupted by a controversial privacy lawsuit by former wrestling star Hulk Hogan.[95] By that time, Gawker had defined the odd combination of sardonic hustle that characterized not only a large amount of aggregation but much of a generation of writing on the web.

Around this time, and throughout the 2000s in particular, various factors began to congeal into the economic forces that would indelibly influence contemporary aggregation. Advertising revenue, journalism's primary subsidy throughout its modern history, collapsed, particularly in the newspaper and magazine industries. It did so because the simple, large-scale distribution capabilities of the internet allowed advertisers to more cheaply and effectively reach audiences there. But those same factors also kept digital advertising revenue from becoming lucrative enough to replace its traditional-media counterparts, as publishers had hoped. The relative ease of distributing information online and accumulating mass audiences there meant that publishers faced a raft of competition for both news and advertising. Fledgling news sites could set up shop quickly and gather and distribute news widely—often through aggregation—flooding the internet's advertising inventory and driving rates down. And advertisers had a whole array of new mediators who could help them find audiences more efficiently than news organizations had (Google was an especially popular choice), and new options to reach those audiences directly, through social media and their own websites.[96]

Those factors combined to keep digital ad rates in the basement. Still, a model based on free content and advertising revenue dominated online publishing through the early 2010s. (It remains one of the primary models in the news business, though the subscription-based model has taken a place alongside it.) But if this model was to work with such minimal advertising rates, it would require massive scale—a torrent of material to sell ads against and as many people drawn to that material as possible. Traffic became king, and the metrics that tracked user behavior online became a point of obsession for journalists and their managers.[97] Social media emerged as a seemingly ideal gateway to those longed-for mass audiences, allowing each story the theoretical potential to be widely shared through interpersonal networks and "go viral." This put publishers at the mercy of social media platforms like Facebook, which drove a large portion of their traffic and controlled their material's placement in users' feeds.[98]

Aggregation solved a lot of problems in this economic environment. Traditional reporting, with its time- and resource-intensive methods, was too expensive to support through this model, and it didn't produce the kind of constant stream of content that the model required. Aggregation, on the other hand, could produce a lot of material very quickly. It didn't require travel, and it could be done by inexperienced journalists, so it was quite inexpensive compared with reporting. And it could be focused on shaping news to draw as much traffic as possible through search engines or sharing on social media.

Aggregation seemed perfectly suited for these economic conditions, but it's more accurate to say that these economic conditions have molded aggregation in order to fit. The dominant form of aggregation that has emerged in the current era has been oriented around quickly and efficiently producing brief, easily consumable content that is precisely tailored to being read and shared on social media. Gawker pioneered this style in the 2000s before the widespread adoption of social media, and BuzzFeed and the Atlantic Wire (the latter under the direction of a former Gawker editor, Gabriel Snyder) adapted it to the social media era through two widely imitated iterations in the early 2010s—BuzzFeed's frothy and breathless pop culture content, and the Atlantic Wire's conversational but pointed news analysis. Not all of today's aggregation has followed this blueprint, but across its varieties, aggregation remains deeply constrained by these economic forces. As a result, aggregation is responding to the flood of information that users encounter online, seeking to quickly make sense of it, but it is in no small part a flood of its own making. The same economic forces have influenced not only the product but the conditions of its production, making a frenzied, metrics-driven cycle dubbed "the Hamster Wheel" by the *Columbia Journalism Review*'s Dean Starkman the standard for today's aggregation work.[99] They have become so deeply embedded into the work of aggregation that they can sometimes disappear, but they are always present and pressing.

EXAMINING AGGREGATION: HOW THIS PROJECT WAS DONE

This is the professional context in which I explore how the work of aggregation is done and what it means to the people who do it. To do that, I employed a combination of observation of aggregators at work and interviews with aggregators and their editors. In 2015 and 2016, I conducted eighty-eight interviews and spent five weeks watching aggregators work in five different news organizations.[100] In all, I observed or talked to aggregators at twenty-eight organizations, ranging from news industry stalwarts like the *New York Times* to up-and-comers like Buzz-Feed to platforms like Twitter to automated app startups like Smart-News. Some of the people I spoke to allowed me to name them and their organizations, but others—usually because of company media relations or nondisclosure policies, but some simply out of concern that candid description of their work might hurt their reputation—did not.[101] The five organizations I observed form much of the backbone of the data for this book; you'll see them throughout each of the next five chapters. Here's a brief introduction to each:

- **Circa** was a startup mobile news app founded in 2012 and shut down in 2015. It was based on the concept of the atomic unit of news, in which users "followed" ongoing stories and were given updates only with new information regarding those stories. Each of Circa's stories was broken into a series of "points," which can be either a single, verifiable statement, a quote, a map, or an editor's note. Stories were conceived as ongoing issues or developing series of events (such as religious liberty legislation, the rollout of a tech product, or a plane crash) and were updated by aggregating from news sources when significant, verifiable events occurred within those issues. Those who followed the stories were sent a push notification for most updates and were shown only the newly added points, while all other readers saw the full story—a set of strung-together points on the entire ongoing story. All of the work of selecting, writing, and organizing stories was done manually, and as of the time of my visit in 2015 the app had a full-time editorial staff of eight, along with several part-time contract workers who helped cover night and weekend shifts.

Circa was based in San Francisco but also had an office at a shared workspace in New York, where I observed. Nearly all of its editorial employees, though, worked remotely. Circa was funded through venture capital, and its business model was always vague. Its leaders planned to sell native advertisements that resembled its editorial content and to license its content management system or to develop a subscription-based financial news product. But none of those ideas materialized. When I visited in January 2015, Circa was attempting to raise a round of Series A venture capital funding, but it announced in April 2015 that it had failed to secure that funding and was exploring a sale.[102] The company was unable to find a suitor and shut down in June 2015. Its name and technical assets were purchased by the broadcasting conglomerate Sinclair, which relaunched it in 2016 a separate, new news organization. Sinclair's Circa shut down in 2019.[103]

- **VidNews** is my pseudonym for a video news aggregator that produces short videos on daily news events using brief third-party video clips, motion graphics, and original narration. VidNews produces its own graphics and narration, but they are based on articles and video clips aggregated from other news organizations. The visual elements of the videos are composed primarily of aggregated video clips, photos, and screenshots of articles, as well as originally produced graphics, text, and anchor stand-ups. VidNews is a former startup now owned by a large media company and has gone through several iterations. When I visited in 2015, these aggregated videos represented the bulk of its work, but by 2016 it had shifted toward more originally reported videos, though it still produces aggregated videos. VidNews' use of video to aggregate is notable among the sites chosen for this study. Though most aggregation is textual, news video drawn from other published sources became more prominent in the late 2010s as social media platforms and advertisers prioritized video.[104] VidNews' offices are separate from its parent company's headquarters. The company had an editorial staff in 2015 of about thirty-five full-time employees and about twenty to twenty-five part-time employees, nearly all of whom worked out of VidNews' offices.

- **SportsPop** is my pseudonym for a social news site that publishes largely aggregated news and short opinion pieces on sports. SportsPop was founded in 2013 as an initiative of a major legacy U.S. news organization. Its business model is based on selling advertising and attracting as much web traffic as possible through sharing on social media. The site publishes content on generally light subjects within sports and pop culture with attention-grabbing headlines. SportsPop's social media-based model and operation within a legacy news organization are its defining features as a site for observation. It allows a closer glimpse at aggregation's relationship with traditional professional journalism, as well as an exclusively traffic-driven model of digital publishing at work. I visited SportsPop for a week in 2015 that included Super Bowl Sunday, its highest-traffic day of the year. At that time, SportsPop had a full-time editorial staff of about ten, with several part-time contributors. Half of that staff worked in a row of desks within the organization's newsroom. The other half worked remotely. Most of SportsPop's writers also produce reported pieces in addition to their primary work in aggregating news. These pieces occasionally appear in the organization's legacy outlet, though they are written primarily for SportsPop. Many of the organization's traditional sports reporters also contribute material to the site either occasionally or regularly, and the site is overseen by the department editor of the parent news organization.
- **Social Post** is my pseudonym for a conservative social news site that covers political and cultural news that's intended to be shared widely by a largely conservative audience on social media. Social Post was founded in 2012 and immediately began growing rapidly. In addition to political news, Social Post publishes an eclectic combination of mostly aggregated cultural news: tabloid-style crime stories from around the United States, "news of the weird" stories, celebrity news, and "inspirational" stories often revolving around faith and family. Its advertising-based publishing model has revolved overwhelmingly around Facebook, where its stories are posted to various pages targeted to particular demographics. Social Post's business model is similar to SportsPop's but untethered from legacy media's influence, and

it is also notable as a conservative social media-oriented news site of the kind that drew widespread concern in the wake of the 2016 U.S. elections. I visited Social Post's East Coast newsroom in June and July 2016, shortly before the formal beginning of the 2016 presidential general-election campaign between Donald Trump and Hillary Clinton. At that point, Social Post had about forty full-time editorial employees, most of whom worked from its newsroom, and only two of whom were full-time reporters.

- **Billy Penn** is an online local news organization covering Philadelphia and aimed at urban millennial readers. Billy Penn was founded in 2014 by former washingtonpost.com editor Jim Brady and employs a hybrid model in which its "reporter-curators" spend much of their time reporting local enterprise stories while rotating shifts of aggregating news from other local news outlets. This allows Billy Penn's small staff (three reporter-curators, plus three other full-time editors at the time I visited) to cover a larger footprint of Philadelphia news. Aggregation, then, is only a secondary part of Billy Penn's strategy, which makes it distinct from the other organizations I visited, but similar to many mainstream news organizations that engage in aggregation. Billy Penn was a venture capital-backed startup at the time I visited in 2016, with most of its revenue coming from hosting events, supplemented by advertising. It shifted toward a membership model in late 2017, and in 2019, it was sold to the Philadelphia public broadcaster WHYY.[105]

These five organizations—plus the other two dozen represented through interviews—give us a varied but detailed survey of aggregation in practice.[106] One (SportsPop) is in a legacy media setting, while the other four are newer news organizations of various types (including one, VidNews, owned by a large media company). Two (SportsPop and Social Post) share a common business model for contemporary aggregation—attracting ad dollars by doing everything they can to maximize social sharing—but the others are built differently. The organizations span several main products: not only websites but also videos (VidNews) and a mobile app (Circa). One (Billy Penn) is local and another (SportsPop) covers sports. One (Social Post) is openly, though not uniformly, partisan. And one (Billy Penn) uses aggregation only as a supplement to reporting, while others use it primarily or, in Circa's case, virtually exclusively.

The aggregation work I examined, then, consists of a broad range of practices and values. That makes for a fuller picture of aggregation as a phenomenon, but it also means that for almost every statement I make about aggregation in this book, there are exceptions and edge cases somewhere. I have tried to note exceptions (in the text or in endnotes) where they are significant, but noting all of the exceptions to every characterization would be tedious and confusing for the reader. I have striven to produce a nuanced and careful picture of the mosaic of aggregation practice, but the range of practice is beyond something that can be fully captured in a single project, and the generalized statements I make aren't intended as absolutes. And even this range is inevitably incomplete. All of these sites, for instance, are within the United States. There is fascinating aggregation work that is eminently worthy of study going on around the world, but covering the breadth of that work, across so many professional and political contexts, and maintaining contextual depth and detail is simply beyond what is possible in a project such as this one. The textured variety of aggregation practice in even one country provides more than enough richness for sustained study.[107]

Nevertheless, it is remarkable that so many practices and values were shared across these sites. We're accustomed to seeing some of these different types of news organizations (like partisan and mainstream news, or new media and legacy media) as fundamentally distinct from each other, and they do differ in substantial ways. But the practices of gathering and producing news were largely similar across these boundaries. The writers at the conservative Social Post were doing much of the same work as their peers at steadfastly nonpartisan sites; they were just putting spicier headlines on their articles and choosing different types of stories to write about. Likewise with the team at SportsPop; they just did their work in the midst of a large legacy media newsroom. Those variations are significant (and I'll cover Social Post's distinctly partisan approach to its audience in chapter 5 and SportsPop's relationship with its parent organization in chapter 4), but it's a testament to the universalizing power of journalism's professional norms and routines that the broad contours of news aggregation take such similar shape across disparate contexts.[108]

LOOKING AHEAD

There's a lot in aggregation to untangle. It's an emerging form of digital journalism but also a centuries-old practice. It's both an everyday, routine part of journalism and a form that's derided as the worst journalism has to offer. In the chapters that follow, I characterize this contested practice by connecting the process of aggregation as knowledge work with the professional world of the people who do it. By examining these two elements together, we see a fuller picture of not only how aggregation is practiced, but how it is embedded in relationships that constitute its legitimacy within its field and among the public.

First, the book breaks down the practice of aggregation itself, detailing and analyzing it as a process of creating secondhand knowledge. Chapter 1 fleshes out the relationship between aggregation and reporting, showing how each are evidence-gathering, knowledge-producing processes, but aggregation is further removed from the evidence it relies on. It conceptualizes aggregation as a secondary form of newswork, something scaffolded on top of reporting practices but marked by a distance from its sources in a way it struggles to overcome. Chapter 2 then walks through the process of producing aggregated news, starting with finding potential stories and evaluating their newsworthiness, and moving through aggregators' verification process. It shows how aggregators develop the news production process in ways meant to mitigate their uncertainty about the reliability and facticity of their stories.

Next, the book examines the two relationships that most deeply shape aggregators' work and values—with their profession and their audience. Chapter 3 looks at aggregators' professional identity, exploring where it comes from, how it affects their work, and how they're attempting to bolster it. It examines the immediacy and monotony of aggregators' work and the way those conditions interact with the perceptions of the rest of professional journalism to produce a deep sense of inferiority among aggregators. But it also examines ways aggregators are developing norms meant to elevate the standards of their work as well as their own professional standing.

Chapter 4 details aggregators' approach to their audiences, showing how they are both somewhat cynically preoccupied with the audience's preferences and also aloof from that audience, which is only known through online metrics. As they navigate this tension, aggregators use norms around the concept of clickbait to delineate and defend responsible behavior regarding audiences.

But aggregation can also be a site for innovation, developing new ways of conceiving and structuring news. Chapter 5 focuses on a notable example of that innovation, in aggregation's relationship with narrative. The chapter looks closely at Circa and its attempt to "atomize" the news by breaking it into discrete units that can be organized in new forms. In deconstructing news narrative to its most granular level, Circa's aggregators paradoxically broadened it into a new way of viewing news events as more thoroughly connected across time and topic. Though they don't share Circa's distinct structure, many other aggregators engage in the same narrative broadening despite their short form.

Finally, chapter 6 provides a bigger-picture reflection of aggregation's place in the news ecosystem and its implications for journalistic knowledge and authority in a digital environment. It brings together the analysis of the epistemological, professional, and economic forces shaping aggregation and lays out a framework for understanding when and how aggregation reaches its most constructive and most worthless forms. Across all of these chapters, you'll see a picture of a practice defined by its secondary nature, marked by what it lacks, and on the edges of what journalists will claim as their own. But you'll also see a picture of journalists working to produce reliable, engaging news and prove to their peers that they can do consistently valuable and innovative journalism. You'll see the tensions and marginality that have plagued digital journalism since its inception on display in an acute way. And you'll get a glimpse of what news production looks like in a journalistic environment that is equal parts precarious and promising. Aggregators sit on the margins of their profession, but their work is central to understanding how journalism functions in the future.

CHAPTER ONE

Gathering Evidence of Evidence

Aggregation as Second-Order Newswork

It's shortly after 8 a.m. when Samantha[1] receives a story assignment from her editor at VidNews: a new British study has found that half of people in the UK will get cancer at some point in their lives. Or perhaps two-thirds. Samantha's editor, Luke, has found a BBC article on the study citing the one in two statistic and a web article by the British newspaper the *Telegraph* citing the figure as two out of three. He sends a message to Samantha on Google's Gchat messenger system noting the discrepancy and asking her to determine the cause: Is one of the organizations misreporting the number, or is there some other difference, like a geographical one?[2]

"interestinggggggggg," types Samantha before pulling up the stories on her computer at a workspace she shares with other producers and editors in VidNews' small, sunlit newsroom, a converted radiology office. She's in her early twenties, two years out of college, having come to VidNews from a stint at a local TV news station. She's in TV-style on-camera makeup today, ready for the "anchor" intros and standups she'll record for several VidNews videos throughout the day. For this assignment, she'll be required to write the script for a ninety-second video on the study with graphics and stock photos and video, then hand it off to a producer to create the graphics and stitch together the visual elements. In this case, Samantha will add the voiceover and on-camera read for her own video.

Samantha reads through both stories and finds generally the same information—a description of the study, background information on cancer rates, quotes from an interview with one of the researchers. She probably needs the original study to adjudicate the factual dispute, so she searches for it on Google News. She finds an article on the tech site Mashable, which links to a press release by the research group that conducted the study. That press release links to a blog post by the group, which has a link to the study as well as a slick graphical explanatory video similar to the one she's been assigned to create. The reason for the high cancer rate, the video explains, is largely because people are living longer.

Samantha watches the video and quickly starts on her own script. Without having read the original study yet, she goes with "half" as the number in her lead because the *Telegraph* used "more than half" in addition to two out of three in its article, and Luke has suggested via Gchat that he thinks the discrepancy might simply be a rounding difference. Most of the other information she needs for her story—the reasons for the rise, the background on survival rate—comes from the research group's press release and blog post. She breezes through a draft and adds links to the press release, the *Telegraph* article, the original study, and U.S. Social Security data she has used to refer to Americans' life expectancy.

As she waits to see if VidNews' graphics editor will be able to create graphics for her video, she decides to finally wade into the study itself to check on the *Telegraph*'s two-thirds figure. She finds the number, 53.5 percent, and keeps "half" in her lead. "I mean, it's 53.5," she says. "That's pretty much half." This raises questions about why the *Telegraph* is using two-thirds and whether the story should now be that the *Telegraph* is misreporting cancer statistics. "I don't really just want to call out the *Telegraph*," she says. We're both scouring the *Telegraph*'s article for the origin of its two-thirds claim when I find it: the 53.5 percent figure in the study is for people born in 1960, and the two-thirds number comes from an interview with the researcher, who estimates that two-thirds of children born today will get cancer. Samantha's concerns are immediately assuaged. She adds a quote from the *Telegraph*'s interview and moves on toward the editing process, where she'll add background and links to Mayo Clinic and the World Health Organization based on Google searches for cancer survival rates and early detection.

Samantha produced a brief, explanatory report on an important new scientific study by comparing sources, evaluating them, and following a trail of evidence back to the original source to resolve differences between them. But many journalists wouldn't consider her work reporting—she didn't contact anyone, she didn't do anything to check the veracity of the *Telegraph*'s quotes from the researcher, and her sources were largely the published reports of other journalists, as well as a press release. Much about her newsgathering process is quite similar to reporting, but those subtle differences are telling. The processes of aggregation and reporting—and the work that other aggregators do to find and validate information and present it as news—not only shape the veracity and credibility of the information we receive as news consumers each day, but they also form very different foundations for journalism's authority to present news as valid. For all their overlap in practices, aggregation's shift to gathering news secondhand from others' reporting undermines aggregators' authority, as well as their own confidence in the reliability of their accounts. It is in this respect that aggregation's difference from reporting is pivotal in determining its value for journalism.

HOW REPORTING AND AGGREGATION TURN INFORMATION INTO "THE NEWS"

If aggregation has a competing form against which it is measured in the journalistic world, it is reporting. Aggregation and reporting are certainly not the only forms of work that go into producing news: there's also editing, design, and distribution. But aggregation and reporting are often set in opposition as the two primary means of gathering and organizing the information that becomes news reports. Scholars have described them as the two dominant forms of newswork in the digital age, and they have noted the shift from reporting as a means of newsgathering toward, as one researcher put it, "the filtration, selection, and gatekeeping of already existing content."[3] Journalists are keen to set them against each other as well, often drawing a sharp boundary between aggregation and the work of creating original news, often valorized as "shoe-leather reporting," "boots-on-the-ground reporting," "original reporting," or simply "real journalism."[4] In the discourse and mythology of professional journalism, reporting involves going to the scene of major events, knocking on doors, cornering public officials, unearthing hard-to-find documents, and uncovering scoops that drive public discussion and official action.[5] In actuality, of course, reporting is often much less adventurous: getting a press release and making a couple of phone calls to flesh it out or making a quick call to an organization's spokesperson to confirm details of a competitor's story.

Aggregation and reporting are tangled both in practice and in history. As we have seen in the introduction, aggregation predates reporting throughout U.S. and UK journalism history and has existed alongside it for more than a century through news organizations' digests of news and opinion and their interweaving of staff-written and wire copy. For decades reporters have done only minimal rewriting and information-gathering to produce their own reports from press releases or competitors' accounts.[6] Even when reporting is at its most ambitious, it is a process of pulling together information from disparate sources, both published and unpublished, and compressing it into a summary for busy audiences—which is essentially what aggregation does, too. And in today's digital news environment, many journalists are doing aggregation and reporting within the same job. It's important, then, not to conceive of aggregation and reporting as cleanly divided binaries. Still, there are important general distinctions between the two practices, which begin to emerge as we examine them as forms of journalistic knowledge production.

The fundamental difference is that aggregation is a step further removed from the evidence on which both practices rely. It is, as journalism scholar C. W. Anderson has described, second-order newswork—a process of piecing together bits of firsthand (and secondhand) information that have been published already, often gathered by journalists through reporting—and repackaging them into new forms.[7] This derivative, second-hand relationship to reporting colors virtually everything else about aggregation. At the narrowest level, it indelibly shapes aggregators' techniques of gathering and verifying information. But more broadly, it's a key to the fundamental dynamics examined in this book: because aggregation is a knockoff of reporting, it has difficulty serving as a foundation for journalistic authority the way that reporting can.

The ripple effects are dramatic. The relative lack of journalistic authority makes it more difficult to build a sustained audience around aggregation. It makes aggregation less economically valuable to advertisers and subscribers than reported work.[8] And it undermines many aggregators' sense of their own value and identity as professionals, which in turn can erode their commitment to doing aggregation for long enough to make substantial improvements to their work. To understand the magnitude of this difference, though, it helps to start with reporting and aggregation's shared epistemological roots.

The core commonality between reporting and aggregation is their orientation around gathering evidence to build claims of knowledge regarding news events—often through what journalists conceive of as *facts*—and authoritatively presenting those claims to the public. This is a process that is fundamentally epistemological—that is, it's a process of producing and publicly justifying knowledge. Media scholar Mats Ekström distinguishes between philosophical epistemology (theories of the nature of knowledge and possibility of scientific truth) and sociological epistemology (the routines and procedures that determine how knowledge is produced, expressed, and justified).[9] The latter is the main object I'm concerned with here. Journalists are hardly philosophers (to say the least), but they do spend their days analyzing information in order to produce knowledge. They evaluate sources of evidence, weigh competing pieces of information, organize that information, and then present it to the public in ways that appear justified enough to be considered news facts. That's epistemological work—the work of knowledge production. Those knowledge-oriented routines and procedures are what provide us the news and determine whether it's trustworthy.

Journalists' main claim to cultural authority is their ability to provide reliable information on current events. That claim rests on the public's acceptance that the information is factual and the means of its production validate that factuality.[10] If journalism's democratic function is to provide people with the information they need to effectively self-govern, then the epistemological questions of how that information is produced, and whether the public accepts those production methods as valid, are crucial to journalism's democratic value as well.[11] Public acceptance has withered in recent decades, as trust in the media has dropped to some of its lowest levels in numerous countries around the world.[12] This mistrust has political roots, of course; it's shot through with ideology and tribalism. But it's also deeply epistemological. One 2016 poll of Americans found that one of the top two reasons they cited for losing trust in a news source—running neck-and-neck with perceptions of bias—was that they "found facts that were wrong."[13] At a deeper level, the news media have faced increased skepticism of whether they can find facts at all—a shift in which "the notion that journalists or anyone else can arrive at a truthful account of things or follow an objective method of verification has been eroded in the public mind," as former journalists Bill Kovach and Tom Rosenstiel lamented in their 2007 classic, *The Elements of Journalism*.[14] Journalism's knowledge-producing practices, then, are particularly important *and* imperiled. Aggregation's derivative nature provides a further challenge to the legitimacy of those practices, but aggregation also represents a possible avenue for those practices to adapt to the digital information age.

Modern American reporting's knowledge-producing process starts with the belief that there is a reality "out there" that reporters should strive to depict, and that they can do so using a set of methods meant to gather information with minimal subjective interference.[15] This approach to knowledge has much in common with science. Indeed, many journalists of the early 1900s, led by the political commentator Walter Lippmann, expressed an admiration for science and invoked scientific language as a rationale for their own reporting methods. Lippmann advocated a form of "objective" reporting based on scientific methods of evidence-gathering, and even through the 1960s, several strands of journalism, both mainstream and niche, explicitly emulated science's techniques of knowledge production.[16] In practice, of course, journalism does not engage in anything resembling a formal scientific method. Journalists' hypotheses take the form of hunches and common-sense assumptions rather than theoretically grounded propositions, and their evidence-gathering techniques are born much more out of organizational and time constraints than out of systematic attempts to measure reality. Journalists have long acknowledged these shortcomings: even Lippmann famously declared that "news and truth are not the same thing, and must be clearly distinguished." Objectivity was seen as an unattainable myth by many journalists as early as the 1930s and became a term of abuse within much of professional journalism by the 1960s.[17]

In practice, today's journalists tend to be circumspect about the extent to which they can claim to have captured the truth in news accounts and operate from a more pragmatic mindset that, in the words of Watergate reporting legend Carl Bernstein, strives for "the best obtainable version of the truth."[18]

One of the main constraints limiting reporters' efforts to gather and validate reliable information is time. With the exception of extensive (and expensive) investigative reporting projects that constitute a very small portion of journalistic work, reporting takes place on extremely tight time schedules, typically on the scale of hours or days. These constraints mean that journalists don't have time to rigorously confirm all of the knowledge they produce, so they're forced to rely on "an established network of sources who deliver information that is assumed, a priori, to be justified," as Mats Ekström has put it.[19] When the mayor says that five city employees have been laid off to help resolve a $300,000 funding shortfall in the city public works department, reporters don't typically have the time to independently verify that the layoffs have occurred or to conduct their own audit of the city's books to confirm the shortfall amount; they simply present the information as factual and attribute it to the mayor. Instead of fully gathering and presenting the kind of direct and rigorous empirical evidence needed to support the factual claim, the reporter allows the mayor's statement to stand alone as sufficient evidence. As the sociologist Mark Fishman wrote several decades ago, the mayor's claim is bureaucratically verified—the source is in a position to know, so she's assumed to know what she asserts—which means the claim doesn't have to be meticulously verified.[20]

This kind of evidence may not be rigorously verified, but the reporting process, such as it is, revolves around gathering it. At bottom, the evidence that reporters use to constitute their information and justify their knowledge claims comes down to three basic forms, which C. W. Anderson refers to as "the holy trinity of news objects": *observation*, *interviews*, and *documents*.[21] Each object plays a complementary role in establishing the factuality of news reports, and together they form the raw material that constitutes the knowledge produced by reporting. Observation is often positioned at the top of reporters' hierarchy of evidence, regarded as the most reliable and authentic. It is validated by the journalist's physical proximity to the events she recounts, as well as her firsthand testimony without having to rely on intermediaries. Journalists' veneration for observation is evident in their use of phrases like "shoe-leather reporting" and "boots-on-the-ground reporting" to emphasize the primacy of observation and presence in their self-conception of reporting work.[22] Observation may be more revered, but interviews are much more common: Anderson refers to the interview as "the key evidentiary form in modern news."[23] In the absence in many cases of firsthand observation, interviews take on much greater evidentiary weight. As much as journalists enjoy reciting the old newsroom saw that "If your mother tells you she loves you, check it out," the fundamental practical principle of reporting often ends up being, in Mark Fishman's words, "Something is so because somebody says it."[24] Interviews, and the quotes that often result from them, allow journalists to authoritatively pass on sources' assertions in the source's own words while maintaining distance and autonomy.[25] Documents hold a special evidentiary validity for journalists because of their materiality and their bureaucratic verification—they're "official records" often produced by powerful organizations.[26] Documents have taken on a greater importance in recent years with the rise of data journalism as a form of newsgathering built primarily on official digital records.

Reporters produce news by gathering these three forms of evidence—observation, interviews, and documents—and weighing them through the process of *verification*. Verification is highly esteemed among journalists. Bill Kovach and Tom Rosenstiel have famously called it the central and distinguishing discipline of journalism, and other scholars have described it as the core process that validates journalism as a profession and supports journalists' contention that they are able to authoritatively parse reality.[27] Of course, given the time constraints described earlier, many facts asserted in journalism go unverified, and bureaucratically produced information is often taken at face value.[28] But to the extent that it is practiced as a coherent method, verification is built on corroboration, that is, weighing and fitting together the evidence and reliability of various accounts. While in some cases verification is a distinct process—the long-held practice of prepublication fact-checking at many magazines is a prominent example—it is often folded into the reporting process itself, as reporters, for example, track down documents to support a source's statement in an interview.[29] Reporters' goal in gathering and verifying all of this evidence is to produce news *facts*—claims that are accepted as verified statements about reality, generally beyond dispute or subjective opinion.[30] Reporters then assemble these facts into narratives, giving them meaning and coherence. Put this all together—gathering evidence through observation, interviews, and documents; verifying it through corroboration (or bureaucratic validity); and assembling it into news facts that are authoritatively presented to the public—and you have the process of reporting, of turning information into the news.

That process faces a number of challenges in today's news environment that threaten to corrode its reliability and authority as a newsgathering method. Journalists used to have largely exclusive access to each of the three objects of evidence, but now observation, interviews, and documents are all moving into the realm of the public. Virtually anyone with a smartphone can witness a news event, record a report, and distribute it to a public audience, making proximity and immediacy—rather than professionally based skill or access—the only real qualifications for journalistic observation.[31] More public figures and official sources—led by President Donald Trump—have used social media and other public relations techniques to directly reach their desired audiences, circumventing interviews where potentially unfavorable questions might be posed. And even as they have helped elevate documents' importance, data journalism and open government movements have focused on opening access to official documents and the power to interpret them to the public, eroding journalists' claim to the exclusive expertise to obtain and understand them. In all of these changes, journalists are losing the primary jurisdiction and authority over their fundamental evidence-gathering practices.[32]

There have been other challenges beyond the public's encroachment onto journalism's epistemological turf. Immediacy—which has been a significant constraint on reporting's ability to produce reliable and complete accounts for more than a century—has accelerated in pace and importance over the past two decades. As journalism scholar Nikki Usher puts it, immediacy has become "an overarching, defining feature of online journalism." Immediacy short-circuits many of reporting's traditional (and already time-limited) evidence-gathering and verification methods, often leaving digital journalists without time to interview sources, resolve uncertain pieces of evidence, or corroborate accounts.[33] These difficulties are exacerbated when information is being gathered online, because online information presents several new challenges for verification. The prevalence of anonymity and pseudonymity online makes it more difficult to discern the origin of online information, and the vast amount of information available online can make it more difficult to determine any definitive truth, particularly when so many of those accounts contradict one another.[34] It's easier than ever to create and easily distribute information that appears to be factual, but it is more difficult for journalists to trace and verify that information. And even if a reporter is able to properly practice this process, her factual claims are more likely to be met with skepticism from a public that is more distrustful of journalists than ever. Early in the Trump administration, the term "fake news" was popularized as longstanding criticism of the media expanded to include not only bias but also news reports' basic coherence with reality—something that had rarely been questioned by anyone other than conspiracy theorists. The reporting process is still the main way journalists gather information and present it to the public. But it is beset with difficulties in several dimensions, from its relevance in an immediacy-driven information environment to the exclusivity of its methods to its public validity as knowledge.

News aggregation is especially vulnerable to each of these challenges. Immediacy has repeatedly been described as a defining quality of aggregation work, even more so than traditional reporting. In his study of online journalists in Argentina, Pablo Boczkowski notes that the extreme pace of work leaves little time for conventional information-gathering processes, leaving aggregation as a primary news production method. The journalists simply don't have time to gather new information beyond confirming what others have published or to do any writing beyond stitching together others' materials and coming up with a headline.[35] In this example, aggregation is itself a product of the constraints of speed, a sort of bastardization of the reporting process whose main reason for existence is as a response to the immense demands of immediacy. As we'll see in chapter 2, I find that speed isn't quite this fundamental to the existence of the aggregation organizations I studied, but it is nonetheless a deeply ingrained part of aggregators' work and a nearly ever-present constraint on their verification process. Aggregators also gather information almost entirely online, leaving them vulnerable to the kind of uncertainty and difficulty in verification that is endemic to much of the information in an online, social media–oriented information environment. Aggregators are often following trails of hyperlinks through news sources and social media posts to determine the origin of information online, before they can begin to evaluate the credibility of those sources. More than virtually any other form of newswork, aggregation embodies the struggle that journalism faces with discerning the certainty of claims amid the increasing volume of online information and speed of publishing.

But most fundamentally, aggregation differs from reporting in its relationship to the objects of evidence on which reporting relies. Aggregators can't claim a privileged or firsthand relationship to that evidence as reporters can. They can't rely on their own direct observation of news events; they're not at the scene but at a desk, and all of their eyewitness information is mediated by published accounts or videos.[36] As we'll discuss in chapter 2, they generally do not interview sources, except in some relatively rare cases, and then only very briefly. They rarely generate their own quotes but instead use those drawn from interviews done by others. They have approximately the same access to documents that many members of the public have—in the example at the beginning of this chapter, a document in the form of an online copy of the study played a key evidentiary role for Samantha—but they're limited to what's accessible online. In many cases, what's online has been published by other news organizations, so the work of accessing and interpreting documents is only secondhand, built on the access and interpretations of other journalists. Aggregators are a step further removed from each of the three major forms of evidence on which reporters rely, a structure that leaves them especially vulnerable as they attempt to gather evidence and turn it into reliable news accounts for the public.

Despite these constraints and the fundamental distance from the objects of journalistic evidence, aggregators still manage to produce knowledge. They find ways to assemble evidence and verify it even when so many of the classic evidence-gathering techniques of reporting are practically unavailable to them. But those methods are inevitably a knockoff of those of reporting. Aggregation is built on the same objects of evidence and information-gathering processes that reporting is, but it's defined at every point by its secondhand relationship to those processes. Most of aggregators' work is oriented around finding that evidence—or evidence of that evidence—getting closer to it, and managing their uncertainty about their distance from it. What emerges is a more unstable form of newsgathering than reporting, but one that has developed distinct techniques to attempt to find and present valid information nonetheless.

EVALUATING SOURCES

Since aggregators don't typically use observation, interviews, or documents (at least directly), their primary object of evidence is the published news report. That news report is not an elemental, indivisible object in the same way that the other three are. Instead, it's a hybrid, second-level object that is built out of those three objects, but only as they are filtered through the conventions of corroboration and news narrative. Aggregators use those objects in conjunction with other nontraditional objects—the website and the hyperlink, as C. W. Anderson has identified—but also the social media post.[37] In this section, we'll examine how aggregators evaluate those sources and what role they play in helping build news accounts.

In many cases, aggregators' beliefs about which news sources are most credible closely match the hierarchy that professional journalists as a whole map onto their field: wire services and major national/international news organizations like the *New York Times*, *Wall Street Journal*, and the BBC are at the top, with venerable regional newspapers slotting in just below them.[38] While most aggregators asserted that they approach every story with skepticism, in practice, these organizations' reputations earn them a reprieve from the closest scrutiny. The approach of a breaking news reporter at a national news organization was fairly typical: "Places like the *Dallas Morning News*, the *LA Times*, *Chicago Tribune*, *New York Times*, *Boston Globe*, these are newspapers that have been around forever. They are generally trustworthy on the first pass."[39]

This trust is based on several factors: the news organizations' institutional history and weight built up over time, a mental index of the organizations' recent track record for accuracy, as well as an organization's reporting staff and resources. Most aggregators' criteria for evaluating sources' credibility were heavily borrowed from traditional professional journalism, just as the sources they cited also came overwhelmingly from that realm. Some aggregators described their criteria as simply the same as what any journalist would use: "It's not really too complicated. It's just what you would expect," said one. Another described his preferred sources as, "mostly, it's the ones that anybody would consider reputable, right? So large, long-established news organizations."[40]

Nontraditional news sources, such as blogs or partisan organizations, were viewed much more skeptically by many aggregators, just as they have historically been by professional journalists more broadly.[41] Some dismissed them out of hand as the type of source they would never rely on, though others were more careful not to rule out the possibility. They ticked off situations in which they had used or would be willing to use a blog, as a news director at VidNews explained:

> We want a blog to be able to stand on the same platform as the BBC, you know. Just because it doesn't have millions of dollars of funding, if someone has gone and done this reporting and figured it out, we want to be able to put it out there. So we don't dismiss something just because it's a junky-looking web design, or something we haven't ever heard of immediately. Now, do we enter into that skeptically? Absolutely.[42]

As a practical matter, however, nontraditional sources such as blogs seemed to be rarely cited. With the significant exception of social media posts (which will be addressed below), I saw no sources outside professional media or official governmental, business, or education websites cited in any stories at any of the field sites I observed.

But more so than any division between traditional and nontraditional sources, aggregators evaluated sources based on how close they were to the news itself. This is, of course, a primary consideration for virtually every journalist; they're taught from the first day in journalism school (or the first day on the job) to find firsthand sources, the people who are involved in the events themselves. This principle takes on a slightly different tint for aggregators. Because they're virtually always relying on the reporting work of others, the task of finding primary sources becomes both more urgent and more difficult. In many routine stories, the reporter's task of finding a primary source is so naturalized that it's barely seen as a decision. If the city is closing down a few blocks of Main Street to install a water main, you call the public works director. If the star forward scored the winning goal, you talk to her after the match. But when an aggregator encounters a news story, it's often not immediately clear who the primary source is, or how reachable that source is, particularly if the sourcing in the original story is unclear.[43] Aggregators talk about using sources closest to the situation in two senses: one is the news source or organization that originally published the story and the other is the actual newsmakers and eyewitnesses involved in the story itself. The former group is not actually composed of primary sources—those are secondary sources, relaying information through the news reporting and writing process.

Gaining access to the actual group of primary sources—the newsmakers and eyewitnesses involved in news events—is much more widely discussed by aggregators but much more difficult in practice. Circa, in particular, emphasized including these sources. "Our goal is to try to get to the primary source as much as possible," Circa's editor-in-chief, Anthony De Rosa, told me as I observed him. He said a primary source was not a published news report but rather a witness, official document, or an official source that Circa contacted directly.[44] (Note the correspondence of this definition to observation, interviews, and documents as news' objects of evidence, though even in this ideal, observation could only be accessed secondhand.) Several other Circa staffers talked about this emphasis and gave examples of times they had accessed primary sources, but I didn't see Circa use any of these during my time observing. De Rosa came across one primary source—a document shared on Twitter purported to be an agreement between Houthi rebels and the Yemeni government during the rebels' 2015 military takeover. But despite a journalist friend vouching for the reliability of the document's source, De Rosa didn't include it because he was never convinced of its authenticity, and the president's resignation moved the story beyond that point anyway. "We don't need to have it, so why take a chance?" he said afterward.[45] Contacting those primary sources is much of what makes up the work of reporting, which helped explain why aggregators were so keen to emphasize it as part of their work; they considered reporting's methods the gold standard for newsgathering and the basis for their own, and they hoped to emulate them as much as possible. But incorporating those primary sources in practice was much more difficult for aggregators to do.

To the extent that aggregators did strive to include primary sources, it also led them to a group of sources they considered even more reliable and authoritative than their fellow journalists: officials. Researchers have found for decades that journalists are heavily reliant on official sources because they're convenient, they have access to information that journalists lack, and their statements have the power to enact realities rather than simply reflect them.[46] These were all reasons aggregators treated official sources as the most reliable. But beyond that, official sources eliminate the need for another journalist to serve as a go-between. When an aggregator cites an official source through a medium the aggregator accessed directly, such as a released statement, a social media post, or a recorded press conference, the aggregator is accessing the source in the same way that a reporter might. This practice brings her one degree closer to the information she's communicating and eliminates the need to invest her own credibility in the report of another journalist. For this reason, some aggregators treated primary sources and official sources as virtually interchangeable. This close tie between primary and official sources is evident in De Rosa's definition above. His deputy editor at Circa, Evan Buxbaum, captured well the advantage that access to official sources gives his organization:

> Sometimes you're beholden to official press releases and press conferences or statements from organizations, law enforcement, you know. And that's the ultimate gatekeeper of that information, so you have to rely on official sources. And nowadays, we have the same access through various screening options to watch press conferences as they happen, like anyone else. That obviously is from the mouth of the guy. That's as primary of a source as you can get.[47]

Buxbaum's statement also captures the ambivalence of many aggregators' attitudes about this arrangement: he is not enthusiastic about being "beholden" to official sources whose messages he would rather not relay uncritically, but their ability to allow him to bypass other journalists as gatekeepers of information outweighs his concern about excessive reliance on those officials' accounts. In the hierarchy of sources among the aggregators I spoke with, traditional media sources rank as more reliable than nontraditional ones, but aggregators would prefer to not have to rely on a media report at all. For them, the way to achieve that is to cite an official source.

It was because of this desire to bypass other media sources and cite primary sources directly that aggregators often gave social media more credibility as an information source than many other journalists do. Social media was in many ways the opposite of other primary sources: aggregators tended to talk about it in skeptical terms, but in practice they ended up citing social media posts quite often. "Don't believe rumors you see floating around on social media" has become a truism not only for journalists, but for much of the public as well.[48] The aggregators in this study articulated those ideas, too, and they were generally quite skeptical in practice regarding spurious social media reports and rumors. But social media was also the best way to get information directly from officials and other newsmakers as primary sources. I never saw any aggregator attempt to confirm that something posted on a verified Twitter account (indicated by an official blue checkmark) was actually posted by the person in question. And aggregators never expressed in interviews any doubt about the veracity of information from those accounts, either. In one case, a SportsPop writer articulated these two dramatically different modes of social media credibility in a single sentence: "We pretty much never run with anything based on just a tweet—unless it was, like, Kobe Bryant's blue-checkmark, he tweeted it, we know it's him."[49] SportsPop used a lot of those social media posts by athletes and celebrities as the grist for their stories, and it made sense given their granular focus on sports and celebrity culture. Most of the time, an athlete's social media post wasn't simply a primary source talking about a news event; for SportsPop, the social media post itself *was* the news event. The post substantiated itself not only as a credible source but as virtually an entire story on its own, with only some context needed to fill out its contours. When those were absent—when the poster wasn't an official or newsmaker preverified by the social media platform itself—then social media's credibility as a source plummeted, and aggregators' verification efforts went into overdrive. But most often, social media was a valued and relatively unquestioned avenue to directly access the announcements and quips of officials and newsmakers.

In general, then, the aggregators in this study evaluated sources through a remarkably consistent set of criteria, some of which would be familiar to most journalists working over the past quarter-century. Ideally, aggregators were looking for primary sources that allowed them to bypass relying on other news sources entirely, though these sources often proved difficult to access directly. The simplest and most common way to get information directly from primary sources was often through social media posts, which for that reason enjoyed more prominence and credibility than reporters have typically given them. When looking at the published work of other journalists—which constituted the large majority of sources they encountered and used—aggregators favored sources with a legacy brand, a long track record of quality work, and the original account of the news story they were aggregating. But more deeply than any of those three, what aggregators were examining their published news sources for—both implicitly, through these factors, and explicitly, as they scoured news stories for pieces of information and attribution—was evidence of the work of reporting. An example from VidNews helps explain what this looked like in practice.

SEARCHING FOR CREDIBLE SOURCES: AN EXAMPLE FROM VIDNEWS

Sean[50] gets a story assignment from his editor and immediately jots it down in a Google Doc. He's being asked to produce a story on reports that Jordan has launched airstrikes against the Islamic State, or ISIS, in retaliation for its execution of a Jordanian pilot days earlier in February 2015. This story is "pretty simple," he says. Sean's been working full-time at VidNews only since he graduated from college less than a year ago, but he's become something of a go-to guy for stories on the Middle East. He developed a knowledge of the background of the tangled Middle East conflicts after writing video scripts about them for several months, and he has a much more detailed mental map of the range of news sources in the region and their relative reliability. Reports of the airstrikes have first been spotted on Twitter by a VidNews social media editor working in a glassed-in area in the back of VidNews' small newsroom, one of the vestiges of its former life as a medical office. Sean's editor gets word from the social media editor via Gchat. Both he and Sean dress casually in a short-sleeve button-down shirt and jeans, and the editor also wears a baseball cap. He is sitting in a desk across from Sean but assigns him the story via Gchat at about 7:45 a.m. with a link to a brief *USA Today* article on the airstrikes.

Starting a story with a reliable professional media source like *USA Today* is a promising beginning for Sean, but the work of verifying the report becomes more complex when he reads the story and realizes it's based on a report in the English-language newspaper the *Jordan Times*. He clicks on the link, scans the *Times'* story, and sees that it, in turn, cites only Jordanian state TV as its source for news of the airstrikes. Sean has no way to access Jordanian state TV to assess its report for himself, so he's hit a dead end in his search for the original source of this report. He starts over with a search on Google News, clicking "See real-time coverage" to make sure he doesn't get confused by any older news stories.

The Google News search results point up a problem that will become increasingly cumbersome for Sean as he looks for a reliable source to cite in his story: VidNews does not subscribe to any wire services, so he cannot cite any reporting by the Associated Press, Reuters, or Agence France-Presse in his piece. This is not necessarily a legal restriction; wire services have been litigious in the past about restricting aggregators from reproducing their content in their stories, but that has not extended to merely citing and linking to wire service reports.[51] But VidNews tended to be more conservative than other aggregators about such legal issues and did not cite wire services as a matter of newsroom policy. He and VidNews' senior editor explained later that the organization did not cite wire services' quotes or exclusive facts because those organizations charge for their text and their reporting, and VidNews did not pay for access to those services, even if they were publicly posted by other subscribers.[52]

As he clicks on the results from his Google News search, they each become an increasingly exasperating parade of road blocks as soon as he scrolls down to see the byline on the article. *Los Angeles Times*? It's an AP article. "I can't use any of it," he sighs. The *New York Times*? AP. *Haaretz*? Reuters. *Christian Science Monitor*? AP. Sean mouses over the

Kansas City Star link, but doesn't even bother clicking on it: "You look at the *Kansas City Star*, and it's like, 'Nooooooo.' I mean, it could be, but—nooooooo." CNN has its own story, but it, like the *Jordan Times*, is citing Jordanian state TV. Frustrated, Sean tries other sources that have been useful in the past: Radio Free Europe, an alternative Jordanian TV network named Jordan Days, a network of freelance correspondents called Middle East Eye. None of them have anything on the airstrikes. Jordanian state TV has a YouTube channel, but it's quiet, too. CNN is airing overhead on a newsroom TV and reporting on the airstrikes, but Sean dismisses that as well. "Clearly, CNN's not getting any of this themselves." He points to the attribution in the corner of the screen on the photos it's running—these are old photos, some of which Sean has used himself in the past.

Finally, Sean stumbles onto a bylined article on the English-language website of the pan-Arab TV network Al Arabiya. This story is longer, cites a Jordanian government spokesman on the strikes, and has a death count—fifty-five. It's very little information, but finally, it's something he can use. He shifts to look for a quote he can superimpose as text over an image to lead off his video. *USA Today* has a quote from Jordan's King Abdullah II, but it's from the state's official news agency, Petra, and Petra's website is down. As he continues to refresh the site, Sean concludes that Al Arabiya will be his main source, so he shifts back to that article to give it a closer read. When he does, he's dismayed: Al Arabiya's information from the government spokesman is actually attributed to an AFP article, which is off-limits to him, and its death count is attributed only to "Iraqi media." "Ugh, that's annoying," says Sean. "I just want a nice source that says, 'Hey, this is exactly what happened.'"

Sean heads back to Google News for a second time, and the procession of wire copy continues. A Voice of America article is Reuters copy. The *Wall Street Journal*'s is from the AP. *USA Today* has an updated article with some video footage, but it's from Reuters. He now has thirty-two browser tabs open on his computer and has been searching for a usable source for nearly an hour, and all he has that's not wire-based is the *Jordan Times* story. He tries to write a couple of paragraphs based on that article, but stops when he starts a sentence, "The *Jordan Times* cites media reports which say . . ." He laughs and shakes his head. "You're going through two sources right there." After each dead-end he encounters, Sean pivots to a parallel search he's conducting for video and photo images he can use in the story or to his Google Doc to fiddle with the story's organization. At this point, he has the story's outline completed: he will lead with the basics of the airstrikes and the death toll, follow with King Abdullah's statements threatening action, then move to the background of Jordan's recent shift from ambivalence about airstrikes against ISIS and the increase in U.S. aid to Jordan, and possibly include some analysis of whether executing Jordan's pilot was a tactical blunder for ISIS. Most of the pieces of Sean's story are in place; he just has no usable source to confirm the events that serve as the foundation for the story itself.

Frustrated and running out of options, Sean checks a Twitter list of Middle East reporters, bloggers, and experts that he has open on the Twitter application TweetDeck. He sees people talking about the airstrikes but nothing he can cite. "Unless they're actually there or something, I think the likelihood that I'm going to be able to use it is pretty low. I mean, unless they're like, 'Hey, I'm reporting from Raqqa,'" he says, referring to ISIS' de facto capital in Syria.

While he looks through Twitter, we notice on the newsroom's overhead TV that CNN is talking to one of its reporters in Jordan via satellite, with Jordan's airstrikes on the chyron crawling across the bottom of the screen. Sean pulls up a feed on his computer and plugs in his headphones. After a few seconds, he exclaims, "There you go. She just said Raqqa." Now, he says, he can attribute both the occurrence of the strikes and their location to CNN, rather than the *Jordan Times*' secondhand reports. He goes back to his draft of the story, replacing the *Times* article with attributions and links to CNN. "It's just 'media reports,'" he says of the *Times* article. "They don't have any reportage." With that information finally secured—at 9:15 a.m., an hour and a half after he was assigned the story—he begins to pull together the rest of the piece, using a story from the BBC to attribute a statement by King Abdullah, articles from the *Washington Post* and *National Journal* to add commentary, and finding video through file footage collected from Jordanian state TV, ISIS, the BBC, and the U.S. Air Force and Navy. (It turns out the United States has also aided Jordan with its own airstrikes in Raqqa.) His search for footage takes even longer than his search for a source on the airstrikes, largely because he insists on going to local sources for it, even though CNN and BBC are rebroadcasting the same footage. If you use CNN's broadcast of ISIS or Jordanian state TV footage, he says, your video is plastered with CNN's chyrons and watermarks. But if you get it directly from those groups' YouTube channels, they're clean, straight from the source.

Sean finally finishes writing his script and pulling together footage sources at 11:30 a.m., more than three and a half hours after he was given the assignment. It's an abnormally long time to take writing a story, and when Sean realizes what time it is, he runs his hands through his hair and sighs, "Oy." Sean hands off his script to another editor, who reviews it and passes it on to a producer who assembles the visual elements. The final video, just under two minutes long, opens with ten-second clips of fighter jets from the U.S. Air Force and Jordanian state TV, with words like "EARTH-SHATTERING" and "RAQQA, SYRIA" superimposed in large letters for emphasis as the anchor reads them in voiceover. It quickly shifts to other sources of file footage: ISIS tanks rolling down a street, grainy video of airstrikes from U.S. Central Command, more fighter jets taking off in U.S. Navy video, protesting Jordanians via French television. As the anchor quotes from King Abdullah, Jordanian state TV footage of his recent public address is shown. The video's anchor, who first appears about fifty seconds in, is a female VidNews editor based in another city, with camera-ready wardrobe and makeup typical of most local TV news. (In VidNews' newsroom, anchors like Samantha, both male and female, are instantly distinguishable from off-camera staff like Sean due to their fastidious dress, hair, and makeup.) The video's audio consists entirely of the anchor's narration with the exception of one BBC clip of a translator's voice quoting the father of the deceased pilot. The video is a hybrid of traditional TV news forms (B-roll from international TV networks and government video sources, a script written and delivered in the relatively formal style of TV news) and web video conventions (large text superimposed on screen for emphasis, studio-recorded audio in lieu of natural sound), brought together in a mostly sterile, straightforward product.

The scramble for even the smallest drops of information from Jordan and Syria was a bit worse than usual for Sean on this story—the story did not turn out to be "pretty simple," as Sean had expected. But it was fairly typical of what he faces while producing stories from that part of the world. As one of VidNews' specialists in news from the Middle East, much of Sean's time at work consists of those desperate searches for any nonwire sources that he can put some trust in. In this case, his search could only have ended in one of two sources he would have felt comfortable citing: a statement by the Jordanian government (or report by Jordanian state TV) acknowledging the airstrikes or a statement from a reporter in Raqqa that Jordan had carried out the airstrikes. The former typifies aggregators' reliance on official sources as the best way to get direct information about a news event. The latter exemplifies the importance of proximity in Sean's evaluation of sources—and that proximity hints at the primacy of reporting.

Sean acknowledged that it's possible to simply cite a generally reputable source that gives a secondhand report of the news he's covering, like the *Jordan Times* in this case. But with that source simply citing another one, he said he's not actually doing any of the work of uncovering the roots of this story for his viewers. "There's news everywhere. So just because CNN has it doesn't mean you stop there. You can continue searching for the original source," he said after he turned his story in. He compared a news story to series of layers. A lot of attention and attribution often builds up around one layer—often a prominent traditional news organization like CNN, in international news—but when he starts picking at that layer, he finds it's simply building on the work of another layer, another source to the story. "You have to dig beneath that layer and get to the bottom," he said. "And at the very bottom is the original reporting."

Sean's layer analogy helps illuminate the nature of the work he did in researching and aggregating the reports of the airstrikes. In evaluating the sources he encountered, evidence of reporting was essentially his sole criteria. In reading the sources' accounts, he was looking for indications that they had interviewed the officials involved, or that they had observed some aspect of the events in question—the airstrikes themselves, the aftermath in Raqqa, the planes returning to Jordan. Other than the wire services that he was unable to use, what he found instead of evidence of reporting were sources that were doing the same thing he was doing—aggregating information from other published or broadcast sources. And regardless of how good those sources were, if they were aggregated, they were insufficient to document and verify those events. Sean's statement midway through his ordeal that he simply wanted a source that said, "Hey, this is exactly what happened," is telling. He had several sources at that point that essentially told him exactly what happened, but they didn't have a satisfying account for how they knew what happened—at least not satisfying enough for him to be able to credibly pass it on to viewers. That account needed to include some evidence of reporting, and if that evidence wasn't there, it was as if the sources weren't telling him what happened at all.

AGGREGATION AS SECONDHAND
EVIDENCE-GATHERING

Many of the aggregators I observed and interviewed viewed their work in similar terms, even if they did not articulate it in the same way as Sean. They characterized their work around a belief that every story is built on a base layer of some original reporting work by someone, and the aggregator's job is to bring their audience as close as they possibly can to that reporting. "You can tell when people are doing original reporting," Sean said at one point during his search for sources. "You have to boil it down to who got there first." That work of determining "who got there first" and boiling an account down to what those journalists gathered through their reporting work is a crucial skill in aggregation work, and one that positions it firmly as a secondary form built on reporting.

For all the discussion of accuracy over time, this is the root of the reason aggregators prefer traditional professional news sources—because they are the organizations with resources to provide the reporting aggregators seek so ardently. As the news editor at a social news site said when asked about why he preferred traditional media sources: "I think it is because they're more likely to have reporters on the ground. But at the same time, if I see a story reported by somewhere else, and I can tell clearly from the story the way it's written, the way it's reported, that it is a firsthand report and a firsthand account, I am more likely to trust it."[53] Even outside of traditional journalism, what aggregators are looking for is evidence of reporting. Recall the VidNews news director's explanation earlier in this chapter of why he is open to nontraditional sources: "We want a blog to be able to stand on the same platform as the BBC, you know. Just because it doesn't have millions of dollars of funding, *if someone has gone and done this reporting and figured it out,* we want to be able to put it out there."[54] Those outside the mainstream of professional journalism are considered valuable and reliable by aggregators to the extent that they engage in journalism's central professional activity—reporting.

In news reports, aggregators look for evidence of reporting through language that indicates information was obtained through an interview—phrases like, "the mayor told the *Herald*"—or sometimes simply quotes from sources that aren't attributed to another news organization (though this could simply be improper attribution). Proximity and observation can be detected through datelines or language physically describing an event. Many aggregators also keep a mental index of which organizations have done reporting in which geographical and topical areas in the past. In foreign news, this can mean developing a mental map of which organizations have correspondents in various parts of the world; in tech or sports news, it can entail taking note of which organizations have well-placed sources in particular tech companies or sports teams. Sean explained how he uses this process in evaluating foreign news:

> You start going to some sources and you see that they're just reporting from somebody else a lot of the time. Or you go to a source and you see that it's pretty much always an AP article. . . . I mean, you can tell they're not doing—they don't have, like, a correspondent out there or something. . . . So you can kind of find the guys that either they publish a story, then everybody publishes a story after them, or they publish a story and they're able to add to it because they have a correspondent there. And then once you get an idea of those in your head, you kind of just start gravitating toward those each time you start a story in that area.[55]

Sean's articulation of how he determines which news sources are most accurate and worthwhile is strikingly similar to how many reporters would talk through their sense of how they know which sources on their beat are most credible and useful (if they were asked by a researcher to make their rationale explicit).[56] The difference is that Sean's "beat" is monitoring media coverage by other organizations, and his sources are other journalists.

It's here that aggregation's nature as second-order newswork becomes especially clear. If reporting is at its core a process of gathering evidence on current events of public interest, aggregation is a process of gathering evidence of that evidence. It's the process of determining whether the evidence-gathering techniques of journalism have taken place. Aggregation doesn't disavow reporting's methods; it doubles down on them. Reporting tells its audience, "I was there, I talked to the people involved, I saw the documents, so my account is credible." Aggregation says, "Someone else was there, talked to the people involved, and saw the documents. I don't have any direct knowledge of what exactly they did, but that process is reliable enough that I'll stake the credibility of my own account on it, too." If anything, the latter approach reflects an even deeper faith in the validity of reporting than the former. Aggregation is a sort of scaffold on top of reporting methods, borrowing the certitude that reporting generates. Aggregators attempt to build on reporting's assurance by gauging its presence in their sources, getting closer to it, and augmenting it by setting it against other reported accounts.

The difference between aggregation and reporting is not, then, one of kind but one quite literally of degree. They're both relying on the same objects of evidence to build their news accounts, but aggregation is one degree further removed from those objects. Aggregators seek the same forms of evidence that reporters do, but they do it by examining the texts those reporters produce. The only time aggregators escape this difference in degree and pull close to even with reporting is when they get to examine those objects of evidence directly, through statements by official sources and newsmakers. Getting access to those statements, however perfunctory, is a significant part of aggregators' work.

The process of looking for evidence of reporting in fellow journalists' work is not a new one. Journalists of all types are skilled at examining and inferring other news organizations' sourcing based on their published stories. Journalism scholars Yigal Godler and Zvi Reich call these indirect traces of information "evidence of evidence" and suggest they both complement and replace more thorough verification processes.[57] Gathering evidence of evidence is how journalists evaluate their competitors' scoops and build a sense of their peers' reputations. The difference for aggregators is that these aren't simply competitors' scoops; they are aggregators' news sources, the ones out of which they're building their stories. Aggregators aren't just evaluating these accounts; they're relying on them and building their own credibility on them. And the aggregators I observed weren't always examining news stories for evidence of the reporting that went into them, either. Sometimes they were short-circuiting that evaluation process and simply glancing at the name of the organization or taking the truth of the account for granted. Aggregation, then, isn't a strict process of evaluating sources by searching for evidence of reporting. But one of aggregators' main ways of gauging sources' credibility is by deciphering the reporting that went into those sources—and that method sets them firmly in a secondhand position.

This secondhand position, built on another form of newsgathering, leaves aggregation poorly equipped to accrue authority for its news accounts, as well as professional status for its work. Whatever authority it does attain is ultimately built not on its own methods but on those of the reporting it's relying on. Aggregation is nearly unable to distinctly derive authority from its own knowledge production processes. That makes it very difficult for aggregators to say, as Sean put it, "This is exactly what happened." This weakened authority is likely more visible to other journalists—who are far more likely to be aware that a story has been aggregated—than the public, which means that aggregation's professional status is especially enervated. Professionalism is about controlling a realm of knowledge production, and aggregation doesn't have much of its own to control. Its realm of knowledge production mostly just belongs to reporting.

But most immediately, the upshot of this secondhand nature is that it leaves aggregators more uncertain about the work they're producing. Uncertainty has long been inherent in the newsgathering process, with its relentless pace and reliance on often hostile or mendacious sources for information. It has been exacerbated in a political culture in which news' most basic claims to veracity are widely challenged by politicians, alternative media, and large swaths of the public. Aggregators' uncertainty is acute, even beyond this already heightened sense across contemporary journalism, because of their distance from their sources. That uncertainty shapes each stage of the news aggregation process in small and large ways; we'll examine that process up close in the following chapter.

CHAPTER TWO

Making News by Managing Uncertainty

Morgan[1] knows the ingredients to include in an ideal controversial story: a viral video that incites a range of strong emotions, a narrative approach to explaining the video that ends in a direct "what do you think?" appeal to the audience, and—in this case, at least—angry Facebook comments.

Morgan works on Social Post's Controversy team, a group of about eight full- and part-time writers who produce stories on the latest online controversies. These are the contentious political issues like abortion, gun control, and immigration but also the outrageous viral videos of moms behaving badly or people making hateful comments to strangers. They're the type of stories that fly around social media, incite Twitter rants and Facebook arguments, and are typically forgotten within a couple of days. For Social Post's culturally conservative audience that consumes and shares its stories primarily on Facebook, they're catnip. "The best way to describe my beat is never a gray area," Morgan says. "It's either black or white."[2]

This story, though, is a bit more gray than usual. It's based on smartphone video of a Louisiana state trooper patrolling Bourbon Street in New Orleans who encountered a drunk man refusing to leave a bar. The video begins with the officer talking to the man and his brother on a sidewalk when the officer shoves the brother into a row of trash bins and body-slams the man through the open doorway of a snack shop and onto the floor. It's a sudden and jarring use of force in what seems to be a routine situation, and amid the United States' ongoing conversation about violent policing methods, it's natural fodder for online argument.

Morgan is soaking up that online argument, wading through hundreds of comments at the massive pro-police Facebook page Blue Lives Matter to find opinions she can drop into her story. She sits at her "desk," a section of a long white table separated by low, translucent dividers to provide a sense of personal workspace. Social Post's newsroom sits on the third floor of a downtown office space on the East Coast, with a casual, urban vibe set by the stone walls of converted industrial space and the varied clusters of work areas around the room. Some writers work on couches in the corner. Editors' dogs periodically wander through the office. Virtually everyone there is like Morgan: young, white, and casually dressed.

Morgan was assigned the story this morning by her editor—a relative rarity, as she usually finds her own controversies to cover. But her team is short-staffed today, so she'll have written six stories by the end of the day. Morgan—like Samantha of VidNews in chapter 1—came to Social Post from local TV news. She didn't enjoy going to crime scenes and interviewing people in the wake of tragedies; it made her feel queasy. When the newsroom turned toxic, she left and took a job at Social Post. Here she's covering much of the same emotionally driven, sensational news that she did on local TV, but she enjoys not being so close to it. "Here you can sit from a distance and still cover the news, but have a more delicate way of doing it," she says.[3]

Still, when she got the assignment, one of the first things she did was make a phone call. She wanted a comment from the Louisiana State Police on the officer's conduct, and even though other stories she read had a police statement asserting that the officer's behavior was appropriate, she wanted to get the information herself. The police spokeswoman gave Morgan the same statement she had read in the other story, as Morgan expected. But Morgan also wanted her own quote for the story, so she asked about the officer's training. The spokeswoman said she couldn't comment on the officer's specific training but gave some general information on scenario exercises in the department's annual training refreshers. Morgan quoted the spokeswoman's description in the story, highlighting it with a transition that began, "[Social Post] spoke with . . ." She didn't ask for the name of the man who was arrested, even though the spokeswoman had given it to ABC News for a story she had read. But Morgan spoke proudly of the training information she had received.

Morgan has the basic description of the incident from the ABC News story and the video itself, but she's still looking for other unique pieces of information she can add. She searches Google News, trying to find a local source, which she sees as most likely to have something distinct. "We're not just going to take something from random sources," she asserts. She finds an article in the *Advocate*, a newspaper based in nearby Baton Rouge that has launched a daily New Orleans edition. It includes a quote from the man who filmed the incident, one that expresses some ambivalence about the officer's behavior. It's a perfect piece of information for her: a local news source, information from someone on the scene, and an opinion that tempers the full support of the officer from the state police department. But she still needs some sort of critical perspective that allows her to articulate why the story is controversial, and the simplest way to do that is through Facebook comments.

So Morgan is trawling the pro-police Blue Lives Matter page for antipolice comments, which isn't as roundabout a strategy as it might seem. You'd be surprised, Morgan says, at how many people go to Facebook pages whose premise they totally disagree with to spout off in the comments. Besides, she feels an obligation to draw her quotes from Blue Lives Matter: "I'm using their video in the story, and I guess I feel bad if I don't use their comments, because it's really their story." She finds a couple of usable comments—they have the sloppy grammar and overheated tone typical of Facebook comments, but they make a point in a couple of sentences, so they'll do. One commenter who appears to be a black man notes that the officer is black and the victim is white, and says he hopes white people watching the video will understand "what we go through" when we complain of unjust arrests. Morgan reads the comment to me, then adds, "So, clearly not the best perspective, but it's a good perspective to include. Even if you don't agree with the commenters, you have to include the other side." Morgan's "side" in this story is the police officer's, but as so many journalists have articulated over the years, she feels an obligation to "quote both sides" and let her readers decide. She does this literally, following up this Facebook comment with the state police statements and concluding by addressing the readers directly and asking them to weigh in via the story's comments on whether the officer's actions were appropriate.

With all the pieces of the story assembled, Morgan tries to piece them together with a creative narrative structure. She leads off not with an inverted pyramid-style summary of the incident, but by noting that the officer had just finished up his twelve-hour shift. She generally tries to avoid inverted pyramid-style stories because they bury the emotion in stories. "I feel like everyone else is kind of just giving it all away in the beginning because they're leading with the facts rather than emotion," she says. In this case, she wants to highlight that the officer had had a long day and was still working even though his shift had just ended. "To me, that's more shareable, more powerful. As a reader, I'd rather share that." She uses two screenshots from the video to introduce the fight, and when it comes time to identify the victim, she attributes his name and age to ABC News. She copies some background information from a police news site, pastes it into her story, and rewrites it. She hammers out a headline and teaser, crops a screenshot from the video as the story's lead image, and sends it off to her editor and a copy editor, both working remotely. It's late morning, and her second story of the day is finished.

Those who have done reporting work will recognize many of the routines and practices in Morgan's newsgathering process, but they're compressed and somewhat distorted—sort of a funhouse mirror version of reporting routines. Morgan was sure to get information directly from a key source in her phone call with the police spokeswoman, but she did so in a conversation that only involved a couple of questions and mainly in an attempt to obtain a prepared statement many other news sources already had. She used multiple sources (the *Advocate* and ABC News) to corroborate each other and flesh out details, but she didn't think to confirm many of those key details with her one nonpublished source. She observed objectivity's ritual of quoting both sides, but her "other side" came not from observers or experts but from semicoherent Facebook comments. She focused on weaving the story together as an engaging narrative, but she did so with only the barest of details.

The twin constraints of immediacy—in the form of the six stories she had to write that day—and distance from sources condensed Morgan's newsgathering and verification routines and combined to limit the quality and detail of the story she produced.

That's a common concern for aggregators, and it is one that infuses uncertainty into each stage of the newsgathering process. Still, aggregators have developed ways of working within those constraints by adapting reporting practices to produce news that can support its own claims with some reliability and to hedge when that uncertainty peaks. In this chapter we will walk through that process, from developing news stories and determining newsworthiness to gathering and verifying information to using phone calls and other technologically embedded techniques to directly reach sources. Throughout that process, we'll see the secondhand nature of aggregation come to the foreground through various practices meant to manage uncertainty and produce reliable news accounts at a distance and in a hurry. These practices are the means by which aggregators seek to salvage their journalistic authority. They constitute an intermittently effective hodgepodge of techniques to manage aggregators' uncertainty and render their news accounts a viable knowledge base for authority and professional status.

THE ROUTINES OF NEWS DISCOVERY

Journalism researchers have often described the process of originating news stories with terms like story *suggestion, ideation,* or *generation* to emphasize the fact that stories are not simply externally existing things found "out there" but are constructions created by journalists.[4] That remains the case within journalism more broadly, but in news aggregation, story ideas aren't typically generated or originated; they're found in other news coverage, borrowed, and adapted for the aggregator's particular purpose. Often the main task for aggregators is not to come up with an idea but to determine which of the myriad pre-existing news stories out there makes the most sense for their particular organization to condense, expand, spin off of, or combine. The process of looking at other news organizations as a possible source for story ideas is a long-practiced journalistic routine, one documented well by researchers.[5] But like other news routines, this goes from one (often secondary) routine of many in story ideation to becoming the central part of news aggregation's process of developing story ideas. It's not the only way aggregators find stories, but the story process in aggregation almost always starts with finding something someone else has published.

The aggregators I spoke with often described their routines for discovering stories as idiosyncratic and personal, but those routines tended to be fairly similar. They largely searched for news by regularly checking a set of top news sites such as the *New York Times*, CNN, the BBC, and Google News—another aggregator. For most aggregators, these go-to sources came from the ranks of traditional news outlets, but there were exceptions based on the aggregator's orientation. At SportsPop, these sites were top sports sites rather than general news sites, and at Billy Penn, they were Philadelphia sites. Some Social Post writers checked in regularly at culture sites like the fraternity-life site BroBible or the country music site CMT, which many journalists wouldn't consider news sites at all. Many aggregators also used the Twitter application TweetDeck extensively.[6] Some aggregators trawled particular Reddit communities or incorporated RSS feeds or Google alerts, but the general contours of the news search process were largely uniform.

I was able to see many of these story-searching techniques in rapid succession when one Social Post writer, Alicia, was stuck looking for a story idea for a few hours one day.[7] Late in the day, she calls it the slowest news day she has experienced in fifteen months at Social Post, so the lengths she goes to in order to find a story aren't typical. But the difficulties she encounters are a magnification of several aspects of the story discovery process I had seen repeatedly at Social Post and elsewhere. Alicia works on a team that covers life and culture stories, ostensibly with the theme of inspirational and uplifting news, though it tends to veer a little darker in practice. Alicia has spent much of the previous week breathlessly covering each new development in the story of a Texas mother who shot and killed her two daughters as her husband watched, before she was killed by police. With that story beginning to wind down, Alicia—a cheerful young journalist in her first news job out of journalism school, who spends most of the week I'm there on top of Social Post's wall-mounted traffic leaderboard—is looking for something new to write about. She plugs in "mothers" and "babies" into a Google News search box, finding only stories of a toddler run over in a driveway and a six-year-old shooting his brother with his mother's gun—pretty routine news stories as domestic tragedies go, ones that wouldn't be newsworthy for Social Post without "some crazy, off-the-wall turn of events," as Alicia puts it. She pulls up NewsWhip's social listening tool Spike[8] and searches for "marriage," finding a story on a reality show star comparing her husband to Hitler and then a column with the headline "No divorce is worse than a bad marriage." She briefly tries to brainstorm a way to connect to two, but she concludes it would be force-fit.

After another Spike search for "faith," she heads to her personal Facebook feed, which is filled with local TV news stations and news organizations covering viral stories. She finds a story about a Texas mom starting up her own organic cotton candy company, which might fit with the health kick her audience seems to be on, judging from the traffic they've given previous stories on organic food. She pitches it to her editor, Christy, with a link and a prospective headline in the office-messaging system Slack—"Mom Quits Job In Order To Find A Way To Help Her Son Live A Little Healthier"—but she's not optimistic. She wanders to the website of the lifestyle magazine *Good Housekeeping* and find a story on Britain's Prince William and Princess Kate moving into Diana's old apartment. She tries another Slack pitch: "Prince William And His Wife Will Continue Keeping The Memory of Diana Alive." Christy replies, addressing both pitches: "do you have an orig take on what's going on? im seeing a lot of sheer aggregation."

Christy, Alicia says, is really good at finding stories, but Alicia believes she's starting to get the hang of things. The secret? "I hate everything. I've learned to hate everything," she says. "You have to be really cynical." Now she's toggling back and forth between Google, Facebook, and Twitter, plugging in searches like "mothers and tattoos," "toddler," and "Amber Alert"[9] and scrolling repeatedly through her Facebook feed and Twitter's Trending Topics. Her Facebook feed, she complains, "is constantly overrun by, like, three stories." She finds a local TV story on teenage steroid use and turns it into an unsuccessful pitch of "X Number of Horror Stories Reminding You Why Steroids Are Never A Good Idea." She tries a bit more research on organic cotton candy in an effort to find a fresh angle. Why not call up the mom, I ask, to get that new angle? "If it's worth it, then we'll take the time. But often it just takes too much time, because you have to do so many stories in a day," she says.

Alicia has no formal backup list of evergreen stories for days like these. She tries coming up with them, but they're usually shot down, too. She describes days like today, when she can't find stories she feels good about, as the most frustrating part of her work. "Is that because you feel the clock ticking?" I ask. "Yeah," she responds. "You also feel like you're not doing your job." Alicia eventually finds and writes a quick story on beach advisories because of rare flesh-eating bacteria, but by the end of the day she's back on Facebook looking for another story. She plans to keep looking this evening rather than face the prospect of coming to work tomorrow morning without a story. "I'm always looking," she says. "Even when I go home, up until I go to sleep."[10]

Alicia's search is a good picture of what a story discovery process looks like when it's wholly dependent on the published work of others—at least on a slow news day. She has almost no way to independently come up with a story, and even substantially expanding on one (by, say, calling the cotton candy mother) is considered too great a time investment without a sure payoff. And yet hewing too closely to others' work gets her pitches rejected and her work labeled "sheer aggregation." She's caught between being forced to rely on the news judgment and newsgathering of others and being urged to assert her originality. The cognitive base for her work, and its claim to distinctiveness, are being constricted before she even chooses a topic.

NEWSWORTHINESS AND NEWS JUDGMENT

So what are Alicia and other news aggregators looking for in a news story? It depends greatly on the goals of the organization. (Circa's no-nonsense summaries of global market developments and SportsPop's animated GIFs of the latest athletic mishaps are good examples of how different those goals can be.)[11] But within the structure of those goals, some common elements emerge across organizations. Journalism scholars have identified and repeatedly found overarching themes among journalists defining what constitutes "news." The most commonly cited criteria were developed in 1965 by the Norwegian sociologists Johan Galtung and Mari Holmboe Ruge, who found that events were more likely to be covered as news if they occurred conveniently within a news organization's production cycle, were unambiguous, culturally proximate, unexpected, or involved conflict or elite people or nations, among other factors. Other values have been added and changed over the years, but researchers have found a relatively stable set of criteria that journalists use to evaluate the newsworthiness of events.[12] Aggregators rely on some of those classic factors just as other journalists do, particularly ones like timeliness, with their emphasis on speed, or competition, with their constant monitoring of other news organizations. Like many other journalists, they also have some difficulty articulating the reasons that stories are newsworthy, often seeing their news value as a given, or describing their own assessment of newsworthiness as a "gut feeling."

But there are a few elements that aggregators give special weight when determining what to cover (and how to cover it). The most prominent is the criterion that *news is something that will generate conversation on social media*. Journalists have always gotten excited about "talkers"— stories that get people saying to their friends, "Did you hear the story about . . . ?" But those conversations are now taking place publicly on social media, in ways that journalists can observe more clearly and, more importantly, quantify and tie directly to the traffic the article gets. This value is embedded deep in aggregators' routines of news discovery. When they spend their days scrolling through TweetDeck or searching social listening tools, what they're trying to do, as one sports aggregator put it, is "find out what people are talking about."[13] If people are talking about it, it's news. Even if it fails some of the traditional criteria of newsworthiness, it can be made into news by creatively tying it into a pertinent social issue. The 2015 phenomenon of "The Dress"—a viral internet picture of a dress that had millions of people debating whether it was white and gold or black and blue—is a famous (and extreme) example of this.[14] The Dress failed almost all of the traditional news criteria; it was closer to a twenty-first-century parlor game than a news story. But it generated unprecedented amounts of conversation and traffic, so it was treated as a news story, especially by aggregators and other digital publishers. News organizations around the world worked to "baptize" it as a news story by building in science or fashion angles.[15] BuzzFeed, the organization that first brought the story to the world, devoted two editorial teams to the task of finding new news angles to the story.[16] The Dress was driving enough conversation that its status as a news story was set. The only question was how it could be spun to justify treating it as news under more traditional standards.

The criterion of "what people are talking about" is at its core an economically driven one: it's about tapping into that social media conversation to generate shares and clicks. But it's distinct from "what generates traffic" as a criterion because traffic is a lagging indicator. Journalists don't know what kind of traffic a story will get until after it has been published, and they can only guess based on the performance of prior stories. Determining what stories are generating conversation, then, is a particular way of predicting what might generate traffic but justifying it in a way that expresses the importance that the story has already taken on to (online) audiences. But even the factor of what's generating conversation has some lag as well. Issues that people are talking about widely on social media are stories on which someone else has already begun reaping the benefits of an emerging tide of online attention. To respond to that indicator would be to merely pile on along with everyone else acting on the same information, clamoring with numerous others for smaller and smaller waves of interest as the tide begins to ebb. The goal, then, as one VidNews editor puts it, is to "get ahead of that curve to see what people aren't talking about yet"—a task for which even the most sophisticated quantitative data becomes much less valuable.[17] The criterion of what's generating social media conversation is one that's built around metrics and the desire for clicks, but it also leads aggregators back toward more of a "gut feeling" of what might impact and interest people most broadly.[18]

One of those senses that can be articulated as a news value is aggregators' criterion that *news elicits strong emotions in people.* This, too, is directly tied to generating shares and clicks on social media, thanks in large part to research that has shown that emotions are crucial in how people consume and share news on social media.[19] The aggregators who rely heavily on social media distribution—Social Post, SportsPop, and others like BuzzFeed—are keenly aware of the outsized role that emotion plays in how widely their stories are shared, and that feeds back into their conception of what makes a story newsworthy. Emotional reactions were important enough at Social Post that in some ways, entire beats were organized around them. Morgan's Controversy team was tasked with producing stories that would elicit strong feelings of outrage, disgust, or defensiveness, and Alicia and Christy's Life and Culture team was (in theory, at least) meant to produce stories that elicited wonder, inspiration, and delight. At a daily team meeting in the midst of Alicia's lengthy search for a story, Christy led a brainstorming session where the emotions evoked by the story were the primary orientation. After one writer observed that "Everything we've been covering in all these pieces we've been publishing is sad stories of moms and kids and death," Christy declared, "We need to do something more uplifting. . . . We need some stuff that breaks up this horrible news cycle." She acknowledged that cheerful stories weren't read as widely on social media as they used to be, but she still urged her writers to come up with stories that would put their readers (and themselves) in better moods. Another writer at a social news site referred to his main criterion for newsworthiness as "shareability," which he defined as "something that kind of has a high arousing emotion, whether that's anger or excitement."[20] Arousing emotion has a long history as a part of news judgment—witness the genres of "what-a-story" and "holy shit stories" classified by journalism scholars in the 1970s and 1980s[21]—but it takes on a more central role than ever when the viability of news is built on how widely it's shared on social media.

Beyond these distinct characteristics, though, the sense of newsworthiness of the aggregators in this study mirrored that of traditional journalists. The reason for that is a heavy overlap, both incidentally and intentionally, with those journalists' news judgment. News judgment is central to journalists' identity and their work, often asserted as a primary element setting their form of knowledge apart from that of the general public.[22] But it is also often very opaque. The sociologist Gaye Tuchman once described news judgment as "the sacred knowledge, the secret ability of the newsman which differentiates him from other people" but also as a sort of common-sense knowledge that is so simple that it cannot be explained.[23] Because of this, news judgment has a sort of Swiss-Army-knife versatility in its application: It's how abstract news values become manifest in the decisions of what stories to cover. It's how journalists order facts and choose among them. It's how they predict what audiences will find appealing and important. It's how they make sense of events and determine when something doesn't seem right.[24]

As we've seen—and as we'll explore further in chapter 4—aggregators' news judgment is deeply shaped by their sense of who the audience is and what it might be likely to share.[25] But it's also influenced by the secondhand nature of their work. The aggregators I observed often browsed the websites of leading professional news organizations not only as fodder for potential stories but as a touchstone against which to measure their own news judgment. At Circa, editor-in-chief Anthony De Rosa said he tried to periodically step away from moment-to-moment editing duties to check the app's list of the major stories of the day against the top stories on major news sites. "I usually feel like we've done a good job if I can look at the front page of the newspaper the next day or watch the national newscast, and I look at what they're reporting, and we've covered all their stories," De Rosa said.[26] The practice of checking your news mix against the competition is not a new one, of course, but Circa and other aggregators are also reliant on these organizations for their material, which makes them more fundamentally dependent on their news judgment as well. When aggregators incorporate the content of other news organizations, they also borrow the news judgment those organizations used to recognize an event as news and produce a story on it. That borrowing allows aggregators to extend their news judgment into more subjects and stories than it might naturally go, but it also serves as a constraint. Consider Alicia's search for stories at Social Post described earlier: Her heavy reliance on other sources stunted her news judgment and limited her to consider only news events that had already been filtered through the judgment of other organizations.

As aggregators draft their news judgment off other journalists, the result is often a convergence of news subjects between aggregators and the top traditional news organizations, and among aggregators themselves, thanks to similar criteria for what will interest audiences. At times, this uniformity irked aggregators—recall Alicia's annoyance at the repetitiveness of the aggregators on her Facebook feed, a sentiment also expressed by one SportsPop writer:

> It's this weird echo chamber. Everybody's got the same stories. If I see something first, and then I write about it, then I'll notice, whether it's because I put it out there or it's because of these people

all seeing the same thing, everybody else has it soon. And [when] everybody else has something, I say, "Ah, I should probably get on that."[27]

Aggregators aren't bound to the news judgment of others; they try to develop some distinction within these constraints by presenting their stories as creatively as possible, incorporating context, social media, multimedia, humor, or opinions. Indeed, in many cases, the opportunity to add this kind of creative value was an important part of aggregators' consideration of a story's newsworthiness itself. But as Alicia was, many aggregators are held back by their limited ability to develop a new story and introduce it to the news agenda; Alicia had neither the time nor the mandate to report her own original stories. The reactive nature of her work meant that she had less autonomy to exercise her own news judgment and determine what news was.

SPEED AND THE VERIFICATION PROCESS

Once aggregators determine that a story is newsworthy enough to cover, they have to determine which sources to use for that story and how to verify the information in them. More precisely, their decision is first *whether* to verify, and second, how. The decision about whether to verify isn't as automatic as you might think—or as many journalists might hope. There are two main reasons for that: one is the relentless pace at which some aggregators work, and the other is the trust aggregators place in some of their sources. Immediacy is both the backdrop against which the work of verification takes place and its primary constraint. It's a basic condition of most aggregation work, a constant factor driving aggregators forward and defining what they can and can't do to gather and evaluate information, but often in an implicit, accepted way. There are times when speed comes to the forefront and presses more urgently on aggregators—when big news breaks or during major events with many angles that need to be covered. During the Super Bowl, SportsPop's biggest traffic day of the year, its team of eight journalists produced thirty-nine articles in a five-hour-long whirlwind of activity. But most of the time, it's part of the background, quietly setting the limits of what's feasible.

Every aggregator who addressed the subject asserted emphatically that ensuring that their information was accurate trumped speed. "The pressure to move quickly is nothing compared to the terror of being really wrong," said one aggregator at a national news organization.[28] But it was also clear from their descriptions, and in some cases my observation, of their work that the relationship between speed and accuracy was not quite so simple. The response of one aggregator within a traditional news organization illustrates the ambivalence with which aggregators view the speed of their work in light of their professional obligation to present accurate information:

> Speed is everything. Well, accuracy is everything, so, fuck—don't quote me on that so I get fired. I mean, when they bring new editors in, they say, "Well, what's more important, speed or accuracy?" It's that whole thing. And then you say accuracy, and they nod, and they say, "That's right." And then they say, "But speed is 1B in this scenario."[29]

Still, while aggregators (and their editors) are hesitant to let speed obviate verification, the need to publish quickly compresses the verification process. Some aggregators said they fairly commonly posted stories while waiting for phone calls or emails to sources confirming the information in them to be returned, and at SportsPop and another national sports site, posts were often edited shortly after they were published. An editor at that site said the reason editing had been moved after publication in their workflow was "pretty much 100 percent speed."[30] Other organizations such as Circa and VidNews prided themselves, however, on thorough editing processes in which two editors examined all stories before they were published, and Circa in particular often held off on publishing even highly newsworthy stories when its editors weren't confident in their accuracy. Even at Circa, though, speed introduced limitations to the verification process. Despite Circa's safeguards, one editor, Abraham Hyatt, expressed concern that its speed introduced more problems than it solved. Hyatt, who became an EMT after Circa shut down, compared trying to be the first source on a story to putting the lights and sirens on in an ambulance:

There's a lot of adrenaline. It feels like you're doing something. It feels like you're accomplishing something, but in fact it's counter-productive a lot of times. Driving with lights and sirens, obviously that's an important thing for ambulances to do, but it creates accidents all the time. You flip it on, and people crash—literally, will crash right in front of you, because they're surprised. And trying to be first is the same thing. You feel like you're accomplishing something. You're proving yourself in the media landscape, and you're not—your readers don't give a shit, you know?[31]

In aggregation, Hyatt said, the great danger is that "we're going to put our readers' trust on that thing that we can't necessarily 100 percent verify. And we're doing it to be first." Still, I found a level of carefulness and skepticism at Circa (and VidNews) that tends to characterize many reporting-based news organizations. Speed represents an ever-present constraint on aggregators' verification practices and standards, but not a supreme one. As Nikki Usher found in her study of the *New York Times*, immediacy is continually countered, and sometimes superseded, by aggregators' sense of professional duty to ensure the accuracy of their information as much as they are capable.[32]

VERIFICATION STRATEGIES AND SHORTCUTS

Even when speed is not the determining factor, aggregators may not always verify the information they use in their stories, at least not in any substantial way. The other significant factor in determining whether to verify something is based on the source evaluation criteria outlined in chapter 1: if an aggregator trusts the news organization (and the evidence of reporting in the story) enough, he or she will often forgo any further steps to verify the information, not even cross-checking the story's sources with other published reports. The source will get a link and attribution, and the information will be imported into the aggregator's story. Many aggregators initially asserted that they took steps to verify or confirm the majority of what they published, but when I asked more detailed questions about their verification processes (or observed them), I found they often allowed their sources' verification processes to stand in for their own. They essentially outsourced verification to the news organizations they cited, provided they held enough trust in those organizations' willingness to verify their own stories.

A few journalists acknowledged this dependence directly. "If the *Philadelphia Inquirer* wrote a story about a fire, I trust that that fire happens," said Billy Penn reporter/curator Anna Orso. "Sure, I could also call the police and verify that the fire happened, but if I'm calling the police to verify it happened I already trust it enough. When you have a staff this small, I don't have time to call the police every time a fire happens. I'm going to trust the *Inquirer*'s correct and if it's not, we'll correct it. It's not the end of the world."[33] Jonathan Kalan, editor-in-chief of the now-defunct history-centric news app Timeline, was even more explicit about allowing other organizations' verification processes stand in for his own:

> We're looking to [news organizations] that we think are respected enough and have a rigorous enough process so that if they published it, it's something that has been fact-checked and sourced. And so we're putting the onus essentially on them, but making it clear to readers that that's what we're doing by saying, "This is our source for this."[34]

For many complex or difficult-to-access news stories, this is a practical and efficient approach to verification. For Orso, the *Inquirer* is trustworthy enough and Billy Penn's resources scarce enough that forgoing verification on its stories is a minimal, sensible risk on a daily basis. And in practice, this system makes sense. Orso and Billy Penn's other two reporter/curators were spending most of their days doing reporting on their own enterprise news and feature stories. It would have been incredibly inefficient to be constantly making routine phone calls in addition to that reporting work to confirm basic stories by other news organizations so that Billy Penn could tweet about the story and link to it on its website. Just as it does in traditional reporting, the practical possibility of verification also plays a role in deciding whether and how to verify. If a story could be confirmed with a simple phone call, the aggregators in this study were much more likely to try to verify it than one that would require at least a day's worth of reporting.

Given this practical limitation, verification and source evaluation were often virtually synonymous for the aggregators I spoke with and observed. In these cases, the verification of information is not so much the process of independently confirming information but simply critically evaluating the published source and making a judgment regarding its truthfulness. Several aggregators described their typical verification practices as a process of quickly googling unknown sources to determine their background, funding, ideological perspective, and professional provenance. They also made use of collaborative discussions, sharing a link among coworkers on a group chat and asking critical questions evaluating the report in a common-sense way—questions such as "Does this seem likely? Does this fit into what we already know of the situation?" as BuzzFeed's Jim Dalrymple II described it.[35] In general, this type of process is essentially evaluating the validity of other organizations' verification processes—or sometimes on a more basic level, simply their reputation for verifying information—rather than engaging in an original, independent verification process themselves.

Beyond verification as source evaluation, the other most common form of verification among aggregators was the process of using multiple sources to crosscheck stories. Though no organization I observed or talked with had an ironclad rule of multiple sources on every story, most aggregators said they virtually always try to find multiple sources reporting a story, and I typically found that in practice as well. Part of that desire for multiple sources was an attempt to guard against producing work that was too derivative of a single story, lacking in context and borrowing too heavily from an original source.[36] But part of it was because aggregators often didn't trust single sources, especially on breaking news or "bombshell" stories.[37] Conversely, the sight of several major news organizations reporting the same thing is a very reassuring one for aggregators—one that alleviates any doubts about whether the events have actually taken place and shifts their inquiry toward more secondary questions about details and explanatory factors. I rarely saw aggregators do any independent confirmatory work on a story that multiple mainstream news sources had reported, as Social Post's Morgan did at the beginning of this chapter. And several aggregators described their primary verification process as essentially looking across major traditional news sites to see if they had all reported on a story and if their details were aligned. If so, that was considered enough to confidently publish a story without any further verification.

Corroboration is at the core of verification for aggregators, just as researchers James Ettema and Theodore Glasser found with investigative journalists during the 1990s.[38] But for aggregators, the corroboration process is much simpler and more abbreviated because they deal largely with polished, edited, publicly disseminated accounts that all have the same general purpose of shedding light on complex events. Most of the more difficult work of comparing and corroborating potentially disparate accounts has already gone into producing the news stories they're working with, and the resulting product is fairly homogenous and easy to evaluate. When a major news organization reports that a government official resigned under pressure because of an ethical scandal and other news organizations quickly match the initial report, the first organization has had to do the difficult work of gathering and corroborating reports on this previously unknown event. But the corroboration work of the other organizations—and especially the aggregator comparing all of their accounts—is made much easier because of the earlier corroboration work of the original news source to produce the initial report.[39]

THE CONFIRMATORY PHONE CALL

The most widely professed—if not the most widely practiced—form of verification among aggregators was the practice of calling or emailing an official source involved with the situation to seek confirmation of the central facts involved. When I asked about verification procedures, virtually all of the aggregators asserted that they made these confirmatory calls. But as they racked their brains when I followed up with questions about specific examples, it often became clear that this was an exception rather than the rule—something that was done once every few weeks or months, rather than a part of their regular routine.

There were some exceptions. SportsPop's writers called or emailed officials and spokespeople for clarification or confirmation several times during my week of observation there, and the breaking news aggregation teams at BuzzFeed and another national news organization appeared to contact sources regularly.[40] The *New York Times'* Express Team virtually always contacts sources directly—something asserted in our interview by its editor, Patrick LaForge, but also evident from the original information in each one of the team's articles. (That was the main reason LaForge said he wouldn't describe much of the team's work as aggregation.)[41] On the whole, however, confirmatory contacts to sources were a curiously venerated form of verification, especially for how relatively rarely they were practiced. Among an aggregator's work, this method was characterized as the pinnacle of reliability. Every other form of information gathering or source of information was questioned by at least a couple of aggregators, but no one questioned the reliability of information gathered via phone call.

In many cases, these phone calls are probably not best characterized as interviews. They are often meant simply to confirm the veracity of a published report and perhaps ask an additional question or two. Follow-up or probing questions are generally necessary only if the source cannot cleanly confirm the story on the first pass. Billy Penn editor Chris Krewson described the typical calls in his previous aggregation work at the *Hollywood Reporter* this way: "The phone call lasts five seconds, and it's, 'Hey, we heard this story. Can you confirm that this happened? Yes, no, or no comment?' And sometimes a no wouldn't even stop the post from going up."[42]

Like other verification methods, confirmatory phone calls and emails tend to be used when aggregators are uncertain about a story's veracity or when the story is particularly significant. One national sports site that almost never contacted sources directly nonetheless had a policy of always calling before publishing a report of an arrest or death. Likewise, Circa's Abraham Hyatt said he tried to verify a piece of news over the phone "maybe once" during his time there, but that "really big news stories had—always there was a discussion going on in Slack of, who could we get to confirm this? Usually we had some source or some contact or some phone number, so one of the other guys would jump on and grab that and try to call to try to nail down something. But those were big, big breaking stories. Those were, you know, like Ebola in the U.S. kind of thing."[43]

Despite their perceived value, these phone calls are rarely the first option attempted. Source evaluation and corroboration take place first, and phone calls are generally reserved for cases where only a single source is reporting something or where there are discrepancies or missing information between sources. As a breaking news reporter for a national news organization described, she seeks to corroborate information through aggregation first before shifting toward direct contact with sources.

> A lot of times, aggregation is sort of the thing that we do in the first few minutes that something is happening, but then as you go farther along, you're making calls on your own and trying to hammer out some of the details. And so those two things are happening simultaneously.[44]

Other times, though, the confirmatory phone call isn't really meant to verify uncertain information. Take the example of Morgan's phone call at Social Post from the beginning of this chapter: she didn't actually doubt that the police statement she had seen in several articles was legitimate. Instead, her phone call to the police was more about two other goals: getting some additional information beyond the statement and being able to show her readers she got the information herself. These were common motivations for phone calls. Aggregators sometimes made calls if there was a key piece of information that was missing from the stories they were aggregating—one they felt they could easily get by calling someone. But beyond that, aggregators liked to be able to show that they had done the work of contacting the source directly. Not only did it lend them the credibility that came with getting their information firsthand, but it gave them legitimacy as journalists and news organizations—it differentiated them from other aggregators and showed that they were part of serious news organizations that did the true journalistic work of reporting, even if that reporting was a two-minute phone call largely confirming the work of others. Given the greater claim to epistemological validity and authority that reporting has, it's not hard to see why these aggregators attempt to cloak themselves in its practices.

I saw this in the conspicuous way many aggregators would frame this information in their stories (like Morgan's attribution as "[Social Post] spoke with . . ." rather than a simple "Jones said . . .") and in the eagerness with which aggregators sought to assure me in interviews that they routinely made these phone calls. Even if a source is unavailable and the aggregators get nothing from the call, they seem to feel more comfortable running stories after making the call, simply because they can indicate in the story that they went through the effort of trying to contact the source. For such a perfunctory practice, confirmatory phone calls and emails play a substantial role in establishing both the veracity of aggregators' information and their own legitimacy as journalists. They are efficient ways to validate the credibility of information before republishing it, but they constitute quite an atrophied form of information gathering, especially given their venerated place within aggregators' conception of their own work.

GATHERING INFORMATION THROUGH
TECHNOLOGICAL PRESENCE

Aggregators do have other ways to gather and verify information without relying on others' published work, though. Specifically, they are becoming more capable of gathering their own evidence directly from newsmakers, improving their certainty about the veracity of their information through technologically enabled forms of presence. Several aggregators described making use of live video feeds of press conferences—either online or on cable news channels—to gather information directly from official sources at the same time as reporters present in the room. Likewise, when law enforcement and political sources post statements and update information on social media, they give aggregators access to official sources at the same time and in the same way as reporters. Several aggregators said this equality in access played a major role in their ability to close the gap between their own work and the firsthand evidence gathered through reporting. "In terms of newsgathering, we're looking at the same sources of information as most desk journalists are," said Circa senior editor Daniel Bentley. "We're seeing the wires, we're seeing press releases, we're seeing statements, we're seeing tweets. So we might not have someone in a press conference, but most press conferences are televised anyway."[45] This is especially the case with widely televised subjects such as major political campaigns and sports. As Social Post's political editor noted regarding the 2016 U.S. presidential campaign: "You really don't need first-person sources to say, 'Person says thing on television.' "[46]

As journalism scholar Barbie Zelizer explains, physical presence holds a remarkable resonance for journalists. Proximity to an event is a crucial source of journalistic authority, an important component of both the credibility of journalists' reports and their view of themselves as legitimate professionals. (Recall the "shoe-leather reporting" discourse we looked at in chapter 1.) The role of presence in the journalistic ethos has grown in recent decades, Zelizer argues, with television's disproportionate emphasis on live events that can be witnessed, but proximity to events is also becoming rarer as the number of reporters shrinks around the world.[47] The access to televised or live-streamed press conferences and speeches is a valuable conduit for proximity for aggregators, giving them ways to tap into the physical presence that is so central to reporting. Circa deputy editor Evan Buxbaum aptly described this sense of remote reportorial presence enabled by video feeds like these:

> I can't tell you how many times I've felt very connected to stories that I'm—I'm in Seattle right now—and I'm 3,000 miles away in my little corner of the country, and I'm watching the same information and getting the same information as if I were feverishly writing on a notepad and trying to make phone calls, or whatever. It's just kind of a different approach to information-gathering, I guess. But I don't think it's any less effective.[48]

SportsPop's writers used live streams to enable this type of presence twice during my observation there, as its writers covered Super Bowl week press conferences by halftime performer Katy Perry and NFL player Marshawn Lynch that aired live on cable TV. In both cases, the live stream allowed SportsPop to post one of the first articles on the press conference, within about fifteen minutes of its conclusion. But in both cases, the presence afforded by the live video was incomplete; the writers had to search Twitter for transcripts or quotes posted by reporters who were present in order to determine the wording of statements they had not caught clearly on the video feed. They couldn't ask questions, nor could they describe the event's surroundings with any substance—not that they seemed to have much desire to do either of those things.[49] The use of video technology to extend the proximity to news events resembles some of the technologically mediated forms of witnessing Zelizer outlines, including citizen eyewitnessing, such as cellphone video of war zones and breaking news events.[50] Notably, though, it inverts the changes brought by citizen eyewitnessing: Zelizer argues that citizen eyewitnessing via mobile technology has eyewitnessing's classic proximity and immediacy, but it lacks the features of role and report that make eyewitnessing journalistically substantial. Aggregators' technological presence, on the other hand, retains much of journalistic role and report, but it lacks proximity, the fundamental constitutive element of eyewitnessing.

Though their presence and reporting power are incomplete, these technological forms of presence allow aggregators to perform one major function of reporting—accessing primary sources—and to do it cheaply and quickly. In some cases, those logistical advantages outweigh the advantages of reporting to the point that despite aggregators' professional esteem for reporting, they'd rather be aggregating, as one of SportsPop's writers articulated:

> Sometimes the problem is that it takes so much longer to write a reported story, to actually go out and report a story, than it would to just sit at my desk and find what other people have done and react to it. . . . If I was focused, if there was a lot happening, I might do eight to twelve posts, if I'm just sitting at my desk. If I'm out there doing something, if I'm reporting, then I've got to find the guy. A ton of baseball writing is just standing around, waiting for guys at their lockers, and sometimes you just stand there for two hours and not get anything, and then you have to go back the next day. And I mean, it's anxiety-inducing, to be honest, if you know that you could've gotten—you know, I might have gotten 300,000 page views if I'd have just sat at home that day.[51]

Media scholar Mats Ekström describes reporting as "producing a considerable body of knowledge in a short span of time," but as this SportsPop writer describes, it is actually quite slow and inefficient—to an anxiety-inducing degree—compared with aggregation.[52] These technologically enabled forms of presence are a significant part of that advantage for aggregation, allowing aggregators to gather evidence synchronously with reporters without leaving their desks. Technological presence might limit the power and range of reporting in ways that physical presence doesn't, but for aggregators, it's still an important means of transcending their secondhand nature.

The most basic conclusion to draw from these aggregators' verification process as a whole, then, is that they do care about getting things right, about making sure the information they provide is accurate. This is a minimal standard, but it's one that aggregators are sometimes thought not to have or one that they occasionally (anonymously) admit not caring about.[53] There is a vast underbelly of viral content production, of puppy slideshows and urban legends shading into false news, where the truth of the content seems to be immaterial or at best outweighed by the number of clicks it gets.[54] But as we move toward *news* aggregation, toward organizations whose goal is to inform audiences (while still getting as many clicks as possible), the accuracy of the information takes on a much greater importance. I encountered no aggregators whom I would characterize as cavalier about their work's accuracy. And by and large, aggregators have developed efficient basic safeguards of that accuracy, from careful source evaluation to corroboration to confirmatory phone calls. Beyond those basic safeguards, though, aggregators' verification methods quickly reach their limits.

The twin constraints of many aggregators' verification process, speed and distance from sources, circumscribe their aggregation efforts in substantial ways, closing off the feasibility of contacting and comparing multiple primary sources. Ultimately, much of their verification process rides on other organizations, and much of the information they use comes prevalidated by the verification routines of other journalists, which stand in quite heavily for their own. Still, aggregators perform verification as a *strategic ritual*, a term popularized by sociologist Gaye Tuchman to describe journalistic objectivity and applied to the verification process by a group of journalism scholars led by Ivor Shapiro.[55] This ritual is ostensibly intended to make sure information is accurate, and that indeed is one of the things it accomplishes. But more than that, the verification ritual is strategic in that its deeper purpose is to perform that confirmation, both for the public and for the aggregator's editors. The performance of that ritual is meant to bolster aggregators' authority—to make an argument that they are serious professional journalists working for trustworthy news organizations.

In order to make the case for their authority, the aggregators in this study tended to want their verification ritual to conform to the traditional journalistic one as much as possible. That's why the confirmatory phone calls and technological presence were such important components to them; they are the elements of the verification process that most closely resemble the work of reporting, the most authoritative form of journalistic information gathering and verification. They may somewhat improve aggregation's epistemological viability, but more centrally, they improve the *appearance* of aggregation's epistemological viability, which is crucial to the justification for aggregation's authority before the public.[56] But these capabilities notwithstanding, aggregators' verification process is pretty thin as a method of confirming the accuracy of knowledge claims. If reporting, as scholars have argued, is a time-constrained mishmash of techniques meant to pass on officially validated claims to the public, then aggregation is an even more constricted and makeshift set of methods that borrows much of its validity from the process of reporting itself.

GRAPPLING WITH UNCERTAINTY

Ultimately, this secondhand verification process isn't enough in some cases to assuage aggregators' concerns that they might be disseminating inaccurate information, leaving them with a sense of uncertainty. When their own information gathering and verification processes are incomplete, they are left to trust the work of others and to ask their readers to trust it, too. Circa's Abraham Hyatt deftly explained the precarity inherent in this situation, looking particularly at the process of relying on a single source:

> You're putting all your chips down on somebody else's reporting. You don't have a chance to go through multiple news stories, say, "Yeah, it looks like these are the common things in all these news stories that appear to be legitimate. We're going to use that as our update." Instead, you're saying, "This is something that's come through. We don't know what kind of unknown sourcing behind the scenes is there that exists or doesn't exist, and we're going to put our entire—brand is not the right word—but we're going to

put our readers' trust on that thing that we can't necessarily 100 percent verify."[57]

This is a risky and frightening situation for aggregators to be in, and they are to some degree in that situation much of the time they are working. The example in chapter 1 of Sean at VidNews scrambling to find a usable source reporting on Jordan's bombing of ISIS is a case of this kind of uncertainty. The lack of reporting in Syria left him extremely alert to his vulnerability in relying on sources far removed from the situation.[58] It's a common situation in international news, where, as Circa editor-in-chief Anthony De Rosa described coverage of a coup in Yemen he was writing about, "There's not that many people who are actually seeing that firsthand. Even the people outside of our newsroom are relying on people that don't work for them, or they don't have direct contact with. It's like second- or third-hand sources."[59] Even in cases of more routine domestic news, the aggregators I spoke with were often aware of the care with which the original story had been put together and the ease with which they could misstate an important point as they repackaged it. "I know what goes into our construction of a story, and it's very easy to not be aware of some nuance, right?" said Patrick LaForge of the *New York Times'* Express Team. "They may not even necessarily attribute a paragraph to somebody, but they may have some understanding that is very precise in the wording and so forth. And so to just take it and sort of summarize something that somebody else is reporting, you might step on a landmine you don't even know about because you didn't report that story out."[60]

This is the day-to-day uncertainty aggregators must manage—sometimes heightened, sometimes minimized, but always somewhere in the background. It's not necessarily unique to them among journalists. As political scientists Leon Sigal and Bartholomew Sparrow have argued, journalists' uncertainty is endemic to the production of journalism—uncertainty about their access to political information, their dual role as both observers and participants in the political process, the economic viability of their organizations, and other factors.[61] This uncertainty is what gives rise to the routines that structure journalists' work. But aggregators' strand of uncertainty is more acute. Thanks to the mythology of reporting, reporters often harbor a great deal of certainty in the ability of the reporting process to confirm and convey the truth about a given situation or event. Some of that certainty may be unfounded—reporting is hardly science—but it at least rests on the evidence that reporting provides direct access to. Without direct access to that evidence, aggregation is a more uncertain enterprise, beset not only with the uncertainties Sigal and Sparrow outlined but a deeper and more fundamental uncertainty about whether the accounts they're producing are actually accurate. Their core uncertainty is not just professional; it is epistemological as well.

We are in an uncertain age. Much of twenty-first-century politics has involved creating and exploiting uncertainty, whether that involves stoking populist fears about immigration and terrorism, disregarding scientific consensus on climate change or vaccines, or casting doubt on virtually every major journalistic operation as irredeemably biased fake news. This is a profound challenge to journalism's authority, which rests on its ability to portray news with enough certainty that it is understood as reality. The drive to authority pushes journalists toward declaring news as certain even when those declarations are covering for uncertainties in the news production process.[62] In his recent book, *Apostles of Certainty: Data Journalism and the Politics of Doubt*, journalism scholar C. W. Anderson argues that deeper uncertainty has led journalists to work harder to display certainty in their work, borrowing from techniques of social science through the spread of data journalism, polling, and similar phenomena.[63] But as journalism pushes in many ways to become more certain, aggregation is nudged in the opposite direction, toward uncertainty. Each of the factors that make it distinct from reporting—its distance from sources, secondhand nature, makeshift verification techniques—also make its claims more uncertain than reporting. The ever-present uncertainty to be managed in their work reflects the uncertainty of the era in which they live, even more so than reporting does.

Aggregators have a variety of techniques to communicate that uncertainty to their audiences. These will be familiar to many journalists, but they play a more central role in how aggregators present their news.[64] Attribution is the simplest and most common of these. Aggregators use simple statements like "according to the *Herald*" not only to give credit to the sources of their information but also to distance themselves from that information and the censure that will come if it turns out to be inaccurate, in a similar way that journalists have used quotes to distance themselves from their sources.[65] Hyperlinks accomplish much the same purpose as a tool for externalizing responsibility for information, though they are less conspicuous as markers of distance than textual attribution to other sources.[66] BuzzFeed's Jim Dalrymple II, for example, laid out two purposes for linking and attributing scrupulously: the first was ethical, and the second was that "It also just covers you, like if for some reason they were wrong, you can go, like, 'Well, you know, we reported what they reported, so . . .' "[67] Of course, the aggregators I spoke with also recognized that this distancing could only do so much and that ultimately they were responsible for the accuracy of the accounts they published. But attribution is a small way to deflect a bit of that responsibility while also fulfilling an ethical obligation. When the information is uncertain enough that mere attribution isn't sufficient, they may express their skepticism more explicitly. "We have a very conversational style when it comes to these sorts of things as far as our writing goes," said Craig Calcaterra of NBC Sports' baseball site Hardball Talk. "So we'll say things like, 'Hey, take it for what it's worth, but this guy's saying,' or 'Nothing official, but the word is . . .' and so that signals to the reader that this is just chatter."[68]

Sometimes when confronted with this degree of uncertainty about the news they're reporting, the aggregators I observed simply changed the angle of their story in order to sidestep the issue of its veracity entirely. That's what SportsPop did when one of its writers asked if she could write a post speculating on the identity of a surprise Super Bowl halftime guest. An editor quickly informed her that the Associated Press had moved an unconfirmed, anonymously sourced report that the guest would be hip-hop artist Missy Elliott. The writer, disappointed, pivoted her pitch to a post on "five people who would be a better guest than Missy Elliott." Another editor approved the idea, describing the angle to her as, "The AP is reporting this. It's not confirmed. Until it is confirmed, let's hope it's one of these people."[69] In this case, the writer and editor responded to the uncertain report (and the abrupt obsolescence of the initial pitch) by making the truth of the report immaterial to the story written about it. When a story occasions even more doubt than this, some aggregators said they would write a post specifically to express that doubt and seek to tamp it down. Of course, one of the other options when a report is this uncertain is—as some readers may be shouting at their book right now—to simply *not run a story about it.* And aggregators do take that option many times. But other times a story has become so popular that—according to the principle of newsworthiness based on generating conversation—it has accrued sufficient news value that ignoring it (and forgoing the traffic it would provide) would seem irresponsible. As one Social Post editor put it, "it's blown up to such a magnitude that you can't not cover it."[70] The mandates to produce news quickly, and on the subjects people are talking about most, push aggregators into greater uncertainty. They can manage this by either bypassing or challenging the truth of the report on which they're basing their work.

This is not to say that aggregators always have a tangible sense of uncertainty. In many cases, especially routine stories that are widely reported, they casually accept the truthfulness of the reports they use and are genuinely untroubled by them. The staff at Billy Penn seemed especially nonchalant about their reliance on other news sources in the day-to-day link-posting they did on Twitter and their website. Part of that was because they were working with a small universe of Philadelphia news sources that they knew well. The certainty they felt was not necessarily because they were doing their jobs particularly well as aggregators (though they were good at it) but because their sources—all the other reporters and editors in Philadelphia—were doing *their* jobs particularly well. They owed their confidence to the consistently strong work of other journalists. At Social Post, too, despite their heavy reliance on sources like local TV news stations and nonjournalists' Facebook posts that other journalists might view as shaky, writers only rarely expressed uncertainty about those sources. Even in his statement earlier about uncertainty at the much more skittish Circa, Abraham Hyatt said that simply corroborating sources would cut down substantially on his concern about presenting their information.

In a sense, the aggregators in this study—and journalists more generally—operate on two levels of certainty. There are things they feel they *know* happened and things they feel they have enough evidence to *show* happened. Virtually all journalists have a mental list of things that they're confident have occurred on their beats that they nonetheless don't have enough evidence to publish—things they have been told off the record or have deduced from circumstantial evidence. Aggregators encounter a similar phenomenon on many of their stories: They're fairly certain that something occurred, but they lack the evidence to present it to an audience. As one VidNews editor told another while working to verify an internationally sourced video: "I don't really have any doubts about the authenticity of that video, but if we can't confirm it, I don't want to run it."[71]

The resolution to these conflicting levels of certainty for many reporters is simply to either not publish the information or work through reporting methods to make it certain enough to publish. But there are times where both of these options are difficult for aggregators: they feel an obligation to cover stories that other news organizations have written about and that people are talking about, and they don't have access to the reporting methods that allow them to become more certain. For some aggregators, like the ones at Social Post, that first level of certainty—simply feeling reasonably sure something happened—is sufficient. If the report is enough to convince them that it's probably accurate, then it's enough to publish—just include a link and attribution. But others, like the ones at Circa and VidNews, operate on the second level of feeling they need to show evidence of news events virtually all the time. They're continually working to alleviate their own uncertainty and that of the reader by moving through the verification processes I've described—even if in some cases they're already reasonably confident that something occurred. Their process of making news is one of managing their uncertainty, of alleviating it around the edges and attempting to present news to audiences without allowing that uncertainty to undermine their own authority.

A SECONDARY NEWS PRODUCTION PROCESS

We can see that at every step the secondary nature of aggregation directs and bounds its newsgathering processes. For the aggregators in this study, news production begins with a story idea that comes from looking at other news organizations' work, often through the lens of how much traffic that story would draw or what sort of value the aggregator might be able to add to it. Aggregators' news judgment drafts off of others, as they determine what's newsworthy based on what others have covered and how audiences have responded to it. Once they've found a newsworthy story, they often verify it in often superficial ways that largely outsource the true work of validating a story to the news organization that has originally produced it. The pinnacle of their verification techniques is a phone call whose purpose isn't fact-finding but confirming the reports of others. When possible, they try to use technology to witness news events directly and overcome this secondary nature, though their reporting presence through it is never complete. Then when presenting their stories, they use several techniques to artfully acknowledge or elide the uncertainty that stems from their secondary nature, including sidestepping or casting doubt on the truth of the report they're relying on.

Most of these practices have analogs in traditional reporting. Reporters find story ideas by monitoring the competition, and they use the decisions of other news organizations to help calibrate their news judgment. Reporters weave information from other published accounts into their stories, both with and without attribution. They make quick phone calls to confirm the reporting of others. And they carefully use language in their stories to distance themselves from uncertain information. None of these practices were born with aggregation, but all of them play a much more substantial part there. In reporting, their role is more tangential, a supplement to the primary work of interviewing people, observing events, and obtaining and examining documents. But in aggregation, they are the entirety of the work. The result is a sort of bastardization of reporting, where all of reporting's marginal activities become central and its central activities are viewed at a distance. These secondary newsgathering methods thus bear a much heavier burden in ensuring the validity of news than they were ever meant to. When those methods can't fully bear that burden, aggregators are left with uncertainty—and the audience is left with skepticism and mistrust.

Yet aggregation rarely collapses under that weight. Errors were scarce among the aggregators I observed, and the net result was that these abbreviated forms of newsgathering allowed aggregators to publish an incredible volume of news that was largely accurate—though generally shallow and simplistic—at an extremely fast pace. Even a bastardized form of reporting routines is enough to ensure mostly accurate news on a daily basis, provided it has other people's reporting to stand on. In this sense, aggregation's techniques are not catastrophic for journalistic authority; they're still capable of producing generally credible news on current events. More precisely, they corrode authority, gradually eating away at it through their diminished ability to produce accounts that justify certainty. Aggregation is often dependent on reporting for its epistemological viability, and even when it has that reporting to rely on, it is sharply constrained in its ability to speak authoritatively and credibly about its claims to knowledge of those events. Thus, it serves as a weak base for journalism's claims to authority, and its weakness is compounded by the fractured relationship between its practices and the professional identity of those who practice it. We turn to that dimension in the following chapter.

CHAPTER THREE

Inferiority and Identity

Aggregators and the Journalistic Profession

Jennifer, VidNews' senior editor, is surprisingly excited to show me what she considers one of her organization's worst stories.[1] Jennifer is a gregarious young woman sitting at a vacant desk in VidNews' small newsroom, explaining the organization's shift in branding and editorial focus from an emphasis on gathering multiple sources to one on context and explanation. The best way to do that, she says, is to show me one of their most-viewed videos of all time—a 2013 video about a baby accidentally flushed down a toilet in China.

She pulls up the video on a desktop computer and breathlessly talks me through it, pausing every few seconds to annotate it disparagingly. An anchor ends the lead-in by intoning, "WJXT has the details," a reference to a Florida television station that was no closer to the story than VidNews. No description or context of our own, Jennifer notes.

WJXT's report consists of secondhand information from Chinese sources. At one point a WJXT photo grabbed from some unnamed source flashes on the screen. "Backdoor way to show someone else's pictures," Jennifer interjects. Later, the video cites another set of call letters—an Iowa television station—for a detail. "I don't even know who that is," Jennifer deadpans.

The VidNews anchor adds more detail, quoting the English-language Chinese newspaper *China Daily*. Jennifer pauses the video. "At that point, there's really no need to ever go to *China Daily*, because we already told you everything."

The story wraps up with a few more details from other second- and thirdhand sources—no original information, no context, no analysis from VidNews. Just a barebones account of an offbeat news event from a haphazard arrangement of sources, backed by a hodgepodge of others' photos and short video clips.

Jennifer turns to me after the video ends. "We would never do anything like that again. Ever," she says sharply. "One, there's no glory or honor in it. But two, it's not a legally viable business strategy." There was nothing specifically illegal about it, but it was skirting the edges of what's considered fair use of copyrighted material, she says. It is the duty of the information borrower to make sure they're not eliminating the need to click through to their sources and to provide some transformative value of their own. "Worse," she adds, "from sources that had no more firsthand knowledge than we did."

For Jennifer, that video exemplifies the difference between professional and unprofessional aggregation. Her critiques of it are a laundry list of the markers that the aggregators in this study employed to distinguish between responsible and irresponsible work, ethical and unethical, high-quality and low-quality. It used sources that hadn't done their own reporting. It cut corners to use photos it didn't have the legal right to. It excerpted heavily from other sources, eliminating the reader's need to click through to those sources themselves. And it didn't provide any value through context or explanation. The result was work that was not only legally dubious but that gave aggregators no professional esteem, no reassurance that they were performing a valuable and meaningful task, no "glory or honor."

We might not think of glory and honor as important elements in understanding news aggregation. It's routine desk work, recycling the material of other journalists to fulfill a company's economic goals that might feel distant and exploitative. But aggregators' struggle for professional identity and worth is central to who they are and how they do their work. That professional value is notable in many cases because it simply isn't there. In other words, glory and honor matter so deeply in aggregation precisely because they're in such short supply. Professional status is important for aggregators, just like it is for other journalists. It is a significant aid in their efforts to have the information they produce be treated as authoritative by the public and other journalists, and it is also an important part of what makes their work feel worthwhile. But aggregators are largely defined by the absence of professional status, not its presence.

The professional identity of the aggregators I interviewed and observed was rooted in a sense of inferiority to traditional journalism that was based largely on the ways their information-gathering practices have imitated and bastardized reporting. Their inferiority has been stoked by journalists' public discourse disparaging aggregation as "piracy," "theft," or at best a cheaper, lower form of journalism.[2] But it went deeper than how they are discussed by the rest of the news industry. Many of these aggregators' sense of inferiority and sometimes even shame was rooted in the work that they do, and it colored every part of how they see themselves as journalists, even flowing back into their work to shape it.

In many cases, however, these aggregators pushed back against that inferiority. They were building a professional identity for themselves based on shared norms and ethical standards as well as a sense of the value of the work they do and how to heighten it. That identity, of course, was partly strategic, aimed at improving image—a way of convincing audiences, advertisers, and colleagues that they're producing serious journalism. But it was also a crucial part of actually building strong journalism practice. The connection between the practices of knowledge work and professional identity is a bidirectional one, with each deeply influencing the other. In one direction, the secondhand nature of aggregation work erodes aggregators' professional identity and, in turn, a weakened identity erodes journalists' desire or ability to make that work more effective. But by investing in and seeking to rebuild that identity, some aggregators have sought to interrupt this destructive cycle by elevating the quality of their work, increasing its viability as knowledge production and as a basis for journalistic authority.

In explaining the roots, effects, and resistance to this professional inferiority in this chapter, I'll start by offering a brief overview of what journalistic professionalism is and how it relates to identity. I'll then look at who aggregators are and what the conditions of their work tend to be like, then explore how aggregators are perceived by their fellow journalists and how they perceive themselves. Finally, I'll examine the ways aggregators are seeking to build a professional identity by articulating the value in their work, using and honing particular skills and developing nascent ethical standards. Throughout, we'll see a set of journalists whose work practices shape their identity, particularly through their secondary relationship to journalism's most valued practice, reporting.

JOURNALISTIC PROFESSIONALISM AND IDENTITY

Professionalism, at its core, is about controlling knowledge and converting it into authority. The aim of the professional project is to maintain a monopoly over a particular kind of knowledge—in journalists' case, this is the ability to disseminate current information about events of public interest.[3] Journalism has often been characterized as something of a quasi-profession, and it lacks many of the classic characteristics of a profession. It has no formal training or certification, no means to keep outsiders from practicing its craft, and it has relatively low public esteem.[4] But within the Weberian framework of professionalism, these particular traits are less important in evaluating journalism's professionalistic qualities than the means by which journalists seek to expand their jurisdiction and elevate their professional status. Journalistic professionalism, then, isn't built so much on a set of objective employment characteristics as it is on journalists' own belief that they are professionals and their attempts to build their work on that.[5]

Professionalism serves a variety of functions for journalists, from establishing a community of people who interpret reality together to controlling the behavior of journalists in lieu of direct discipline by management.[6] It allows journalists to effectively normalize desired forms of behavior, ostracize undesired forms, and quickly socialize new journalists into those norms. Any group of people can articulate standards that they hope to uphold, but the social authority that comes with professionalization allows journalism to impel its practitioners to abide by those standards, even without many formal barriers in place. Perhaps most importantly, though, it establishes journalists' cultural authority to be listened to as producers of trustworthy accounts of current events and thus help define reality.[7]

The glue that holds much of professionalism's force together is identity. Professionalism relies on a group's self-conception as professionals—their own collective idea that they have "a special status that enables them to exercise control over their own work," as the political scientist Timothy Cook put it—and the ability of that self-conception to take hold deeply enough to outweigh competing interests.[8] In turn, professionalism *produces* identity, providing a cohesive purpose and culture from which journalists can derive pride and belonging. The authority of professionalism and its identity thus form a potent mutually reinforcing structure.

On the whole, journalists have readily taken on an identity as members of a profession, continually invoking their professional status as a safeguard of their values and a distinguishing marker between themselves and adjacent fields.[9] In a field where formal mechanisms of standardization and enforcement are rare, identity plays an important role in ensuring the continued coherence of the journalistic profession. Identity is partly drawn from ideological values, which scholars have often characterized as a set of idealized roles of journalism in society.[10] But the primary wellspring of professional identity that we will see in this chapter is the work of journalism itself—the meanings and conditions of the practices journalists engage in—and the ability of those practices to produce knowledge that can serve as a basis for authority.

For aggregators, professional identity takes on particular significance because it's often quite tenuous. Professional identity is not distributed evenly throughout journalism; those at venerated institutions (like the *New York Times*), in valued subareas (like investigative reporting), and with a great deal of time invested in the profession tend to accrue more of it. Professional identity tends to track closely with professional esteem, something of which many of the aggregators in this study had little. Aggregators' work is often denigrated by their peers, and these aggregators tended to have less invested in the profession than many of their predecessors of previous decades. Aggregation, then, offers an acute case of what happens when journalism's professional identity begins to erode—how that influences self-perception and their work itself, and whether anything can be done to resist it. We'll next look at the roots of their marginal professional identity, starting with their backgrounds and work environment.

The first thing that's important to note about aggregators is that it's especially difficult to generalize about them. Many aggregators have reporting backgrounds, but others' experience is in digital media production or opinion writing. Others come from outside journalism entirely. Social Post had several people like this: one aggregator was a former attorney who had been doing legal writing for a nonprofit, another a marketer for a book publisher who had seen Social Post's job ad on Craigslist.[11] Many aggregators have a journalism degree (just over half of the ones I interviewed), but many others have never taken a journalism course. Most of the aggregators I interviewed had some sort of prior experience working full-time in digital media, but others came from more traditional backgrounds like television or newspapers or from outside media entirely. Though many aggregators hadn't worked or been schooled in journalism formally, it was clear that nearly all of them had been socialized into many of the precepts of the profession informally. They talked about journalistic ethical principles, like showing their work and having a duty to inform the audience.

Regardless of their background, most of the aggregators I encountered were quite young. About two-thirds to three-quarters of the aggregators I interviewed were under thirty, and only a couple were over forty.[12] One Social Post editor who was thirty years old described herself as "one of the oldest people in the office."[13] In many places, aggregation was considered entry-level work or close to it; with a few exceptions, most of the nonsenior editors at each of the five organizations I observed had about two years or less of full-time journalism experience when they were hired. "It's really, like, an under-twenty-five kind of game, under twenty-seven," said one breaking news reporter at a national news organization, who was twenty-four.[14]

This youth, combined with the increasingly flexible labor that characterizes the media industry more generally, results in a very transient workforce as well.[15] As of February 2019, two to four years after the principal observation and interviews for this study, about three-quarters of the aggregators I interviewed had moved to new employers. Of those who remained, many were no longer primarily aggregating but had moved into reporting or editing. Many aggregators viewed their job as a stepping stone—a temporary position that could get their foot into a news organization's door but was best used as a transition to slower-paced or more fulfilling work. Gabriel Snyder, who edited the influential aggregation site The Atlantic Wire in the early 2010s, compared aggregation to the graveyard crime reporting shift as one of journalism's new entry-level rites of passage. "I think for the most part, it's a job that people can't do for too long," Snyder said. "It allows people to build some muscles that serve them later. It could just be a way to earn a paycheck until a better gig comes along."[16] Most aggregators, then, are out of aggregation before they can accumulate much personal status through it—if there is any to be gained in the first place. Though some leverage it internally into reporting or editing work, most aggregators start from a marginal professional position, either because of their youth, their lack of journalistic experience and pedigree, or both. The nature of the work itself only exacerbates those professional deficiencies.

FAST, CONSUMING, AND MONOTONOUS: THE WORK OF AGGREGATION

The dominant element of aggregation work is its speed. SportsPop and Circa's writers could produce a story (or, in Circa's case, an update), start to finish, in ten to twenty minutes in breaking-news situations. Even in a newsroom like Social Post where things seemed less urgent, writers were often producing six or seven articles a day. The speed was almost always tacit—I rarely saw deadlines issued—but the pressure to produce quickly was always present. Immediacy was thoroughly naturalized among aggregators. It was almost never questioned or justified; it just *was*. Aggregators often knew without being told when a story needed a quicker turnaround, and they began to get visibly antsy when they felt a story was taking too long to put together, as if an internal timer had gone off. This sort of unspoken, always-on immediacy is hardly unique to aggregation: Several scholars, led by Nikki Usher in her study of the *New York Times*, have identified immediacy as "an overarching, defining feature of online journalism," in Usher's words, and documented its impact on journalistic work.[17] Many aggregators have simply accepted this speed as a condition of working in online journalism today, and some prefer it. "It feels like my normal working speed," said one breaking news reporter.[18] Aggregators would perform tasks at a pace that some-times bordered on bewildering, but they rarely appeared rushed, except during particular breaking-news situations when the urgency of their approach became palpable. The speed at which aggregators worked was rarely a source of explicit stress, but it was a constant constraint on their work and something that contributed to a sense of a grueling, monoto-nous work environment.

Traditional journalists might associate constant speed with the energy and din of a lively newsroom, but the aggregators I observed worked largely in silence. Most communication took place via messag-ing applications like Slack or Google's Gchat, even among journalists sitting next to each other, so the work environment was hushed, even though workers communicated with each other almost constantly. SportsPop's silence was interrupted occasionally by directives or out-bursts that made little sense without knowledge of the ongoing chat app conversation. At VidNews, producing videos required more coor-dination among the editors, producers, and anchors of its staff, giving the newsroom a bit more of an audible buzz. But every organization I observed had at least some staffers who worked primarily or entirely from home, which, when combined with the quiet digital workplace communication, largely resulted in newsrooms that were more sparse and subdued than their predecessors.

This hushed, sped-up environment fed into aggregators' primary mode of work: processing a relentless cascade of information pouring into the aggregator's consciousness through a computer screen. Dom-inic Boyer, in his 2013 study of German digital journalists, described this practice as "screenwork." In screenwork, an immense number of tasks—monitoring the news from a variety of sources, composing and editing text, sending messages to coworkers, interacting with audiences on social media—are filtered through a single screen-based interface.[19] With so much of their work mediated through their desktop monitor, aggregators would often become locked into it, their attention focused on the single screen restlessly flitting between scores of constantly changing stimuli within it. It was not uncommon for them to have as many as twenty to thirty web browser tabs open or to be conducting at least three or four simultaneous chat conversations as they sifted through those tabs. For many aggregators, the constant waterfall of tweets on the Twitter application TweetDeck served as both a home base to which they continually returned and a visual metaphor of the relentlessly moving information flows that they were always process-ing. My questions for them would visibly pull them out of this intense screen-based focus, as they would pull back from their screens, take a couple of seconds to collect themselves, and formulate an answer before leaning forward into their screens once again. One editor described the work as absorbing and mentally consuming: "Like no job I've ever had before in my life, you just walk away like a zombie, because you're just focused, straight-on."[20] As Boyer also found, the ability to maintain this kind of extended focus and master a deluge of information produced its own kind of satisfaction in some cases. Circa deputy editor Evan Bux-baum aptly characterized the simultaneous sense of both exhaustion and exhilaration at this practice:

> It's like a constant, constant flood of information that you're wad-ing through on a daily basis, which is exciting for people in this business, those of us who get a kick out of this stuff. I mean, it's a flood of information, and you just have to dive into it, and at the end of the day, you're mentally exhausted, and you just go, "Where did the time go?" And I dig that. I like knowing things, and I like being informed.[21]

Screenwork, then, is a practice of both continual action and deep iso-lation, something that keeps aggregators constantly engaged but in a limiting and occasionally stultifying way.

The speed of aggregators' work and the all-encompassing isolation of screenwork can combine to produce a feeling of monotony. This tedium was heightened by the fact that aggregators were working with others' material rather than experiencing the creative rush of produc-ing their own. But it went beyond that to the nature of the work itself; as one Social Post editor said, "Even when you're doing all original stuff, it's still a hamster wheel."[22] Billy Penn editor Chris Krewson spoke of his time directing an aggregation team at the *Hollywood Reporter* with similar weariness: "I got really tired of that really fast. . . . Man, that's a treadmill. I've never worked that hard in my life, and I've never felt more burned out at the end of a shift than trying to ride herd on that thing all day."[23] Complaints of this nature aren't new for journalists. Since its modern origins, the relentlessness of journalism's everyday rhythms has been invigorating to some reporters while driving others to burnout. In 2010, the *Columbia Journalism Review*'s Dean Starkman characterized journalism in an era of constant deadlines and staff cuts as the Hamster Wheel, describing it as "motion for motion's sake" and "volume without thought."[24]

Aggregation's elixir of urgency and monotony is especially potent when the object of coverage is whatever people on the internet are talking about. This beat, rather than the bureaucratic institutions (city hall, the public schools) that have traditionally structured news beats, makes for shorter lulls and more round-the-clock information-gathering routines. I saw this vividly in the wearied aftermath of SportsPop's coverage of the 2015 Super Bowl, its biggest traffic day of the year. SportsPop's team of eight—one at the game, a couple at home, and the rest in the newsroom—produced thirty-nine posts in five hours, posting every five to ten minutes continually from the pregame festivities through the final play. The site's flurry of postgame posting finally began to abate shortly before midnight, and SportsPop's editor, Will, and I stopped to catch our breath, gather our things, and leave. I asked Will if he would be back in the office the next morning at 6:30 a.m. as usual, and he said he would. My face registered a look of alarm and I let out a quiet "Wow," but Will breathed a sigh that told me I shouldn't have been surprised. "The internet never sleeps, Mark," he said. "The internet never sleeps."[25]

Editors recognize this potential for monotony, and they see its effects in high turnover and low morale. Many of them adjust for it by building in on-location reporting assignments to function in part as "breaks" from aggregation; or at larger news organizations, by loaning aggregators to other desks as a change of pace. (One aggregator at a national news organization said, "I don't think that anybody [at my organization] is doing it full-time. I think that they recognize that would be very exhausting."[26]) The "reporter/curators" at the local-news startup Billy Penn started out switching off between full-day shifts of aggregation and reporting. But they dropped the aggregation to just four hours at a time because it proved too monotonous, and reporting was too difficult to sustain working only every other day. "I enjoy doing it for a few hours every couple of days, but it's not something I would want to do on a full-time basis," said one Billy Penn reporter. "If that was your full-time job, then I think you'd get real bored, and . . . I'd feel like I wasn't using enough skills, almost."[27] Not all of the aggregators I talked to disliked their aggregation work, but for many of them, reporting was the carrot that their editors used to make aggregation more palatable.

Add all of these characteristics up and it starts to become clear why aggregators change jobs so often and why many of them said the work was more suitable as a short-term option than as something around which a journalistic career could be built. The work of aggregation is defined by a relentless pace and a juxtaposition between the constant activity and immobility of screenwork. It tends to be exhausting but without many of the psychic rewards of reporting—visiting new places, talking to people, observing important events, finding out things that no journalist has found out before. Aggregation does have its own skills to be mastered, opportunities for creativity, and sources of pride, which we'll look at in the final section of this chapter. But in large part, aggregation's grueling monotony feeds a sense of unease and inferiority, something reinforced by the profession and burrowed deep within aggregators' professional identity.

AGGREGATORS' PLACE WITHIN THE NEWSROOM

Professional identity begins with the organization. Marjan de Bruin writes that professional identity may simply be "organizational identity in disguise," and while the two can be distinguished and even set at odds—think of the many newspaper journalists who have seethed at their employers' insufficient commitment to the ideals of journalism through cuts and layoffs during the 2000s and 2010s—they are often closely related.[28] The organization is the site closest to the individual journalist, where professional ideals and values are often filtered and socialized. We might therefore expect that aggregators' sense of marginality would begin with the people closest to them, in their own newsrooms. Aggregators working for startups like Circa or Social Post might be expected to be buoyed by a shared sense of purpose with all the others doing aggregation alongside them. But if professional identity is purely distilled through the organization, we might expect those in more traditional organizations to be seen as second-class citizens within their own newsrooms, superfluous to the true journalistic work going on there. Perhaps surprisingly, then, many aggregators in this study appeared fairly well integrated and valued within their newsrooms, though a perception of inferiority inevitably crept in. Aggregators in traditional news organizations were valued for their potential, and they drew legitimacy from the professional reputations of their organizations, but they were not on equal footing with their colleagues who do mostly reporting.

SportsPop was the only one of the study's five field sites where aggregators were part of a legacy news organization. Its staffers sat at a cluster of desks near the center of its sprawling, wide-open, window-lined newsroom, just a few feet from the managing editor's preferred perch. SportsPop writers and nearby reporters and editors would occasionally lob half-yelled observations and jokes at one another, and the managing editor would frequently dart over to plan with SportsPop's editor. SportsPop ran brief pieces by the organization's traditional reporters about once or twice a day, and they pitched funny anecdotes they encountered during their daily reporting work to SportsPop's editor. SportsPop's writers asked reporters for help on pieces they were writing, too, and occasionally even shared bylines with them. Will, SportsPop's editor, attended the organization's daily planning meetings, and SportsPop's writers produced occasional reported pieces that appeared in the parent organization's main product, though they seemed nonchalant about that exposure.

Several editors in the organization spoke of the importance of tightly integrating SportsPop into the rest of the operation, allowing SportsPop's writers to nudge the newsroom toward a more audience-centric approach and the rest of the newsroom to lend SportsPop some reporting muscle. "It's natural, I think, for those teams to kind of go in different directions," one editor said of the two groups. "But we've benefited from them actually sharing physical office space, being in the same meetings, actually knowing each other, collaborating, and airing it out when there are grievances."[29] That integration appeared to play out quite effectively in practice. SportsPop's writers were a vital part of the organization, and influence in the newsroom ran both ways: traditional reporters were orienting some of their work toward SportsPop, not merely allowing SportsPop to orbit around them.

Others working within traditional newsrooms described a similar symbiosis between aggregation teams and the rest of the newsroom, especially arising from physical proximity. At the *New York Times*, Stacy Cowley said location of the writers for the NYT Now app meant they worked closely with the rest of the *Times'* sizable web team: "We're physically embedded with the homepage, so we're sitting right there, kind of drafting on the news judgment that the news editor on duty and the homepage editor on duty are making. And we tend to agree with them."[30] As much as aggregators operated within a digital realm, their physical presence in newsrooms elevated their organizational status as they became visible to other journalists as a potential collaborator and fellow professional rather than simply an anonymous laborer somewhere within the organization.

The parent news organization provides the aggregator with two key assets in these relationships: legitimacy and opportunity for professional advancement. For aggregators, attachment to a respected legacy news organization is an important source of job satisfaction and professional pride, just as it is for reporters. When I asked an aggregator at a major sports news organization about how he stayed motivated to do his (fairly monotonous) work, his organizational affiliation was central:

I think being at [this news organization], just, like, being able to work at that [organization] in general. Knowing that even if it's a slow news day, you're responsible for something that's on the homepage, or you're responsible for something that maybe somebody cited in a piece [in the organization's primary news product]. I know that drives a lot of people, and I can speak for myself and say that it does for me.[31]

With that organizational legitimacy also comes greater institutional weight for aggregators' own work as well. Several SportsPop writers referred to the reputation and standards of their parent organization when providing a rationalization for their own professional and ethical standards. By attaching an organization's reputation and status to its journalists' work, news organizations have long given journalists professional authority and deepened their burden of responsibility.[32] When those journalists have marginalized professional status and do mundane work, as aggregators often do, that organizational legitimacy becomes particularly important.

The opportunity for professional advancement is an especially valuable incentive as well, given how transient many aggregators are and how many of them would rather be reporting. Several editors recognized this, too, and gave aggregators a chance to do deeper reporting projects not only to break up aggregation's grueling pace but also to give them the chance to impress other editors and move into reporting long-term. At the *New York Times*, movement across beats and desks is common, so it was easier for members of the Express Team—which reports breaking news that's generating conversation online—to see the work as a temporary stint that might lead to advancement within the organization. "We try to encourage people to think in terms of a career," said the team's editor, Patrick LaForge. "So you spend a couple of years doing this, and you've learned some useful skills for finding stories online and some visual presentation skills, and that will make you a better reporter if you head out on the campaign trail or as a foreign correspondent or something. And I expect very much that that would happen."[33] But even in organizations without a history of moving journalists freely across units, aggregators see their jobs as a valuable foot in the door. Impress your editors with sharp writing, good work on deadline, and the occasional strong piece of reporting, and you're *this* close to a coveted reporting job.

But despite these benefits conferred by their news organizations, many aggregators felt they were on lower footing with those organizations—less valued and more expendable. The organization provides general legitimacy to aggregators, but it can sometimes be difficult for those aggregators to accrue additional status within those newsrooms themselves. Some aggregators felt as though their work was seen by their colleagues as lower-skilled, less substantial, and less time- and labor-intensive than reporting or editing. This can make gaining legitimacy an ongoing struggle, because even good aggregation work may not be highly valued within the organization. One journalist who did both aggregation and reporting at a national news organization contrasted the newsroom's attitudes toward the two:

You're going to get kudos for a really well-reported, smart, and well-read story. For a story that does really, really well [in drawing traffic] that you just aggregated, the most you'll maybe get, if it's really getting a lot of attention, is like, "Ha ha, hey, that story is doing really well."[34]

Even good aggregation work doesn't generate much status within the organization. If it does get noticed and appreciated, that appreciation is in the form of potential for success in other work, not for its own value in itself. The editor of an aggregation team at a sports news organization articulated an attitude toward aggregators in the newsroom that seemed to match the relationship I saw elsewhere, comparing aggregators to baseball's minor league system for young, developing players:

> It's a way for us to get a lot of really talented young people in here and the best of them are going to either move into more leadership positions within it or roll off into other positions on the site. . . . I think people have a lot of respect for some of the best people and realize that they're already helping the site tremendously. At the same time, if you think you're the Yankees, maybe you don't have quite the same respect for your minor league team.[35]

Within this newsroom, aggregators were viewed as a talented pool of potentially valuable journalists for the news organization but who were clearly subordinate to and less respected than the "big-league" journalists.

At times, though, the lack of status within the newsroom may be a problem more deeply rooted in aggregators' self-perception than anywhere else. Two managers of aggregation units within traditional newsrooms said they believed other journalists largely regarded the aggregators as full, professional members of the newsroom, but that their greater challenge was getting aggregators to see *themselves* as a fully legitimate part of the newsroom. This challenge speaks to the depth of inferiority that runs through aggregators' professional identity. They have so thoroughly internalized a professionalized hierarchy of the value of newswork—reporting at the top, with aggregation somewhere far below—that they become in some cases more wed to the sense that their work is inferior to that of reporters than the reporters themselves are. Both aggregators and their nonaggregating colleagues considered doing reporting work as the surest route to improved standing within the newsroom, even more so than doing aggregation well.

The organizational context of aggregators' work has some subtle but substantial influence on their professional identity. Traditional news organizations have an important role to play in lending professional status and weight to aggregators' work and in giving them a sense that aggregation is part of a viable career track. But in those newsrooms, their inferior relationship to the rest of the profession becomes more obtrusive. Instead of insulating themselves with an organization full of colleagues doing the same work, they're sharing a newsroom each day with people who are doing the work they want to be doing. In SportsPop's case, this organizationally structured relationship remained generally productive and mutually beneficial, though some feelings of inferiority lingered. But for other aggregators, the organization becomes just one ever-present site for their marginality within the profession to be acted out.

PROFESSIONAL PERCEPTIONS AND INSECURITIES

It isn't hard for news aggregators to determine their professional standing among their peers, as the news industry has not been shy about its feelings toward them. As recently as the late 2000s, broadsides against aggregators in the form of columns, speeches, or quotes in news articles seemed to appear almost weekly. Aggregators were regularly called "parasites," "vampires," "content kleptomaniacs," and "bottom-feeders."[36] Their work was described as "sketchy," "sleazy," "piracy," and "theft."[37] The critics ranged from reporters and columnists to powerful editors and executives like Rupert Murdoch, the *Washington Post*'s Leonard Downie, and the *New York Times*' Bill Keller. Aggregators, wrote one media columnist, were "akin to those lazy-ass and/or dumb kids in the fifth grade who would ask if they could copy off my homework or would 'write' term papers by rephrasing the Encyclopaedia Britannica."[38] The rhetoric has toned down dramatically since then; you're much less likely to see one of those terms used to describe aggregation today. Aggregation has largely been accepted as a part of news production—one that's rarely praised and often simply ignored. When aggregation does get attention, it's typically in tongue-clucking pieces documenting a news organization's disappointing shift from reporting to aggregation or in tell-all accounts of cutting corners and chasing traffic doing aggregation at "viral" news sites.[39] Journalists have come to accept news aggregation as a substantial aspect of today's newswork, but that doesn't mean they have to like it.

Many aggregators are acutely aware of this perception of their work, too. Some, certainly, dismiss it.[40] But others are sensitive to it, and in some cases that public criticism has changed their practices. One aggregator said her site's shift toward more clearly identifying its sources and differentiating its content stemmed in large part from that wave of criticism during the early 2010s:

> Part of it was sort of a crisis of conscience. Part of it was the argument that was going on at the time: "What the hell are you guys doing? You're just stealing our content. What is your purpose?" So we got a few of those grenades lobbed at us—you know, and other sites, obviously, as well—and you start to think, like, well, there's something to that. Like, maybe it's not enough just to parse through the news.[41]

The shift in editorial standards that VidNews' Jennifer illustrated at the outset of this chapter also resulted in part from criticism of their work, both in public and in private.[42] She described one notable exchange, in a meeting with an executive from a traditional news organization she was hoping to partner with. "He said, 'I haven't looked at [VidNews] in a couple of years, but my impression is shallow skimmers, not serious.' And I was just like, oh, ugh!" Jennifer said, pretending to plunge a knife into her chest. "But it's fair. But it really was, it was fair."[43]

Many aggregators are deeply concerned with how they're perceived by their peers, and more than anything else, they want to be seen as one of them—as serious, credible professionals. But unless they're working for respected legacy news organizations like the *New York Times* or the

Washington Post, they largely lack this full professional recognition. So depending on their place within the journalistic field, the aggregators I spoke with developed different complex ways of managing this dissonance, at times seeming to disregard their professional reputations while also revealing how important they were to them. SportsPop's writers would shrug off the criticism they got on social media for the breathlessness of their tone, chalking it up to the way their earnestness clashed with the snark of the rest of the online sports media world. But SportsPop's writers also expressed great concern not to sully the reputation of their parent organization. At Social Post, while several writers were blissfully unaware of the site's reputation for shallow conservative viral news, its top editors seemed preoccupied with it. "We had this perception of being . . . right-wing clickbaiters. And we're like, 'God, we're more than that,'" said Social Post's editor-in-chief. "My mantra has been, we've got to move closer to that world where there is that respect, each and every step of the way."[44] At Billy Penn, almost every staff member pointedly dismissed the site's image among local journalists, which was as a breezy and unserious news source. But they were able to do so in part because they relished the attention they had received from national publications like Poynter and the Nieman Journalism Lab as an innovative startup. In each of these cases, aggregators responded to their marginal professional status with a layer of cool unconcern. That layer wasn't merely a façade; it was a genuine part of their professional identity. But it also interacted with their desire for professional status to produce a deep, defining professional ambivalence.

This ambivalence manifested itself on the organizational level as well. Organizations strove for professional status in several ways, perhaps the most reliably effective of which was to position themselves as a journalistic or technological innovator. This was especially important for Circa, which was regularly the subject of curiosity and analysis in the tech press.[45] Circa's editors derived much professional satisfaction from their sense that they were developing a new form of mobile-centric news. They stood as an exception among the aggregators in the study: the only organization whose journalists were universally proud of their aggregation work—and they were *very* proud of it.[46] They spoke about the satisfaction they took in knowing they were doing something no one else had done, and they saw several other mobile aggregation apps as their direct descendants. Some of this gratification came from within, but much of it also rested on the fawning professional discourse that surrounded Circa. "If Circa hadn't been popular, I'm not sure it would have been quite as fun. We were cool kids, you know? Everybody liked us," said writer Abraham Hyatt a year after Circa's shutdown. "We got written up really well, and it was fun to work there. It was fun to be part of the popular, new journalism startup."[47] For other organizations, too, such as Billy Penn and VidNews, being recognized as an organization taking a novel approach was a central part of its journalists' identity and an important source of professional status—something that allowed newer, more marginal organizations to stand up alongside more established ones. Social Post was less concerned with being perceived as an innovator and more oriented toward gaining professional status by adhering to the traditional norms of journalism—or at least convincing themselves they were doing that. Social Post's staffers had a strange and telling relationship with the concepts of objectivity and bias, which played heavily into their bid for professional status. To all appearances, Social Post was a patently conservative news organization. Its headlines both implicitly and explicitly expressed outrage and disgust at liberal positions and approval of conservative ones. Its choice of stories consistently reinforced a view of a proper social order built around the American conservative pillars of God, family, and country, and unsubtly highlighted deviations from that. Its main Facebook page had *conservative* in its name. Yet I heard a more studious devotion to objectivity and neutrality there than anywhere else. "One of the mottos and mantras we live by here is that we're not supposed to give an opinion," said one Social Post writer. "We're just supposed to write up the facts, put it in black and white, and then let the reader decide."[48] And indeed, the articles were often written in relatively neutral, dispassionate style. But Social Post's writers seemed untroubled by the dissonance between these values and the overall product their organization put out; when I pointed out that their headlines often seemed far from neutral, I invariably got a shrug and an uninterested, dismissive comment.

Social Post's writers experienced its quasi-commitment to journalistic norms as a deeply ingrained (yet not very closely considered) organizational value. But at the top level, it was a strategy explicitly intended to gain professional legitimacy in a long-term bid to expand readership. As Social Post's editor-in-chief described it:

> We knew we had to be seen as legitimate if we were going to make it. So there were certain times—I remember during Mike Brown [the Ferguson police shooting in 2014] where it was like, "We've got to clean this content up a lot. Like, we've got to get a lot more standards. We have to get a lot more open." If you polarize an audience, they're not going to come down. Effectively, you're stopping the amount of people that could respect this article. So that really changed everything from the hires we had, how we had trained them, who we hired, the processes, where the stopgaps were in the editing and approval and pitching processes. . . . I think long-term if you're not getting legitimacy, it's really hard advertising-wise. And you're not bringing anything new to the table that brings that gravity towards you.[49]

The path laid out here is clear: in order to be successful, Social Post needed a larger, longer-term audience that could attract consistent ad dollars. To do that, it needed to be seen as legitimate by audiences, advertisers, and other journalists. And the route to legitimacy was adopting professional standards: more thorough editing, more transparency, and more neutrality. This path precisely mirrors the economically based theory of the origins of objectivity in nineteenth- and early twentieth-century journalism put forward by several scholars.[50] In this case, though, it did not lead to a "he said, she said," hollow procedural objectivity. Instead, it produced a writing style and organizational rhetoric that mimic professional journalism's but are overwhelmed by a subject matter and tone that overtly serve up red meat to conservative audiences.

Overall, aggregators' deficit in professional status is great enough that these attempts to gain legitimacy can't put them on the same footing as many of their fellow journalists. The result is a sense of inferiority that manifests itself in several ways. At times, editors of aggregation teams explicitly discussed their dissatisfaction with being seen as substandard and their strategies for changing that perception, as in the examples of Social Post and others I mentioned earlier. But for ground-level aggregators, it came through in other ways: statements like, "I'm not doing high art here," as one SportsPop writer said, and light-hearted self-deprecation about the relative insignificance of their work.[51] In one instance, a SportsPop writer was asked to watch a live Super Bowl press conference by the halftime show performer, pop star Katy Perry, and write a quick-turnaround list-based article (or "listicle") about it. After the article was published, her editor sent her a quick message on the office messaging system sarcastically thanking her for "your important work." "v[ery] important," the writer shot back.[52]

The inferiority can be more overt as well. One SportsPop writer described his work this way: "I have no illusions about what it is I'm writing. I write about sports, and I make a few obvious cracks, and I put in a picture, and I hit send, and hopefully people like it."[53] The writer, who came from the world of blogging, said this with an air of nonchalance. But the insecurity tended to be more acute for aggregators who had a more professional journalistic background, who had either worked in reporting or received a journalism education. Their professional context is much more fully developed; they're aware of what their friends in the industry are doing and of what journalistic work they had hoped to be doing. "Nobody graduates from journalism school and wants to do aggregation," one aggregator at a national news organization told me.[54]

This insecurity arises both internally and externally from the work they're doing. On one level, it's driven by the ignoble status that's been attached to aggregation through public discourse and continually reinforced to them through jabs on social media and cutting remarks and skeptical looks in private conversations. But on another level, it is rooted intrinsically in the work of aggregation itself. When they do repetitive, sedentary work each day, they're continually being reminded how much they'd rather be doing something else. These external signals and grueling conditions combine to send a clear message to many aggregators: you may be doing a form of journalism, but it isn't pure, *real* journalism—not the kind that will earn you respect from your peers and authority among the public.

And what is at the core of real journalism? The answer, both to many aggregators and to the broader journalistic profession, is reporting. Most aggregators I talked to readily defined themselves as journalists, but when they didn't, or when they were ambivalent about the title, it was because they weren't doing "shoe-leather" reporting. Their own work always seemed smaller in comparison to reporting work, as the editor of a social news site expressed: "You look at people who are reporting from the ground in Syria or are doing really in-depth stories about Detroit or something, and you think, 'Wow, that's real journalism.' "[55] Through such statements, aggregators are echoing the values of the industry that have for decades elevated reporting as its purest and most crucial form of work. Reporting has been central to the identity of journalists, to their myth about themselves. "Good Old Fashioned Shoe Leather Reporting is the one god an American journalist can officially pray to," observed media critic Jay Rosen in 2015. "There can never be enough of it. Only good derives from it. Anything that eclipses it is bad. Anything that eludes it is suspect. Anything that permits more of it is holy."[56] Many of the aggregators in this study seemed to believe this, too—even as it relegated them to the margins of their own profession.

Rosen was articulating one of two primary reasons for reporting's close connection with professional identity. This first factor is cultural: reporting has accrued its own mythological value within journalism's professional culture, and for many of the aggregators in this study, to do that work was to participate in that culture and experience the sense of belonging and meaning that came with it. But the connection also arose from an epistemological basis; to engage in reporting was to earn the privilege of experiencing a superior way of knowing the news. The social news site editor's reverence for people "who are reporting from the ground" hints at both of these elements. It evokes a powerful cultural myth of the intrepid reporter risking his or her safety in far-off locales. But it also expresses a wistfulness for a type of knowledge based on direct observation rather than reading others' reports and the authority that comes with that knowledge. The practice of reporting, in journalists' minds, allows them to know and tell stories that no one has told before—an epistemological claim that is central to both professional identity and authority. As this social news site editor said later in our interview, "I think until you're doing something that really feels like this is a story that I haven't seen a million other times, there's no reason to really call yourself a journalist." Professional identity, then, is rooted in practice, as other journalism scholars have observed.[57] But the tie between practice and identity takes different forms; in this case, both cultural and epistemological.

Of course, the line between aggregation and reporting is blurry, and many aggregators do both, often in the same day. When that happens, aggregators often take on an identity as a reporter, allowing the more desirable identity to subsume the other. I never met anyone with *aggregator* in their job title. They were usually a *reporter, editor, producer,* or *writer*, and that's how they saw themselves. If aggregators did any reporting work, they tended to see it as their main work, with aggregation as the "must-do" work that took place in between the reporting. If they didn't, they sometimes used the reporting-like work processes of aggregation—like quick, confirmatory phone calls—to allow them to claim the presence of reporting in their work. Incorporating reporting into aggregators' everyday work routines was an invaluable boost to their morale and job satisfaction, an important strategy for retaining workers and reinforcing their importance to the organization. SportsPop's editor insightfully described the perception of the two practices with a comparison of aggregation to baseball's sacrifice bunt—a play that epitomizes the use of a mundane, unambitious skill to advance the larger goals of the team.

> I think for most of us, we're writing this quick-hitting stuff, and it's tough to feel rewarded because it's almost like we're bunting every time. I mean, really, that's what it is. It's like each of us is laying down a bunt one right behind the other, and we're just scoring runs by bunting the entire time. But every now and then, one of us gets to take a swing, and when it goes over [the fence], that's super rewarding.[58]

For journalists at SportsPop and elsewhere, aggregating news is scoring runs by bunting; it is ultimately a successful strategy, but one that curtails ambition and forgoes the fundamental activity of journalism—reporting, or in this analogy, swinging the bat in an attempt to get a hit—to achieve those ends. Reporting, on the other hand, offers the opportunity to hit a home run, to create something that is actually meaningful and can establish one's own authority and professional status and generate genuine satisfaction.

The primacy of reporting as a source of professional identity was especially vivid at Billy Penn. The millennial-focused Philadelphia news site employed three "reporter/curators" who interspersed a few shifts of aggregation per week with their reporting duty. Though aggregated content made up a substantial part of Billy Penn's website and Twitter feed, its journalists did more reporting than aggregation, and aggregation barely registered a blip on their professional identity. When I asked one reporter/curator, Anna Orso, whether she preferred reporting or curating, the answer was so obvious to her that she initially had to ask me to repeat the question. "I'm a reporter. I'm a reporter through and through. So I don't think that my boss would be surprised to learn that I like reporting better," she said. "I don't think that that's a secret. We're all reporters."[59] It is no coincidence that Billy Penn was the most contented newsroom I spent time in; they did the least aggregation and placed by far the least emphasis on it. Billy Penn's journalists saw themselves as autonomous reporters at a cutting-edge startup, and aggregation was just something they did in the background to help keep their site flowing with news.

But for others whose reporting work was more minimal, the legitimacy that reporting afforded was a more far-off hope. Many of them longed to do more reporting, either in their current job or in another. The same went for their organizations as a whole. It was common to hear editors talk about their plans for their organizations to shift away from aggregation and toward reporting; alongside journalistic norms and cultivating an innovative image, this was a key organizational strategy for gaining professional status. They were often quite explicit about this. Social Post had two full-time reporters in the organization, covering Congress and the White House, and though they were more expensive and produced less content than its aggregators, Social Post's editors were open about why those reporters were there. "There's a prestige thing, and it does, as you staff up, make [Social Post] into a political player," said the political editor. "It's different. You're different. So . . . you don't write a story that's just 'as reported by,' 'as reported by.' "[60] That editor said his ultimate goal for the site would be to consign aggregation to a subject-specific niche like a campaign blog.[61]

At Circa, too, editor-in-chief Anthony De Rosa spoke of his plans to use money from the company's next round of venture capital funding to expand the staff so that it could engage in longform investigative projects to run on its website.[62] This seemed to me like a poor organizational and logistical fit with the kind of the extremely short, constant breaking news coverage Circa engaged in, but as De Rosa explained it, moving into investigative reporting was not about gathering information per se so much as it was a way to build cachet within the news industry and then use that halo effect to broaden its user base.

Of the organizations in this study, only VidNews seemed to successfully make good on its plans to move away from aggregation and into reporting. VidNews had already undertaken the shift in aggregational style that Jennifer described in this chapter's introduction during my visit in early 2015, but later that year, it began a second transformation, moving into originally reported videos and opening a Washington bureau. As Jennifer described, the change in approach was radical. "We've been joking a lot lately about whether we should characterize ourselves as an eight-year-old company or an eight-month-old company. And most days it really feels like eight-month-old," Jennifer said in mid-2016.[63] Nevertheless, I noted that VidNews' website still contained aggregated videos, and when I asked about aggregation's role in VidNews' plans, she hedged quite a bit before giving a carefully articulated vague answer about procuring permission for third-party material and transforming that material. Jennifer was clearly eager to move the perception of her organization away from aggregation. Though VidNews was still doing some aggregation of the news, as she described it, aggregation had virtually no place in its big-picture plans. It was a reporting organization now.

It's not uncommon for aggregation-based news organizations to shift toward reporting in this way. The Huffington Post and Buzz-Feed have done it most prominently, beginning with aggregation but eventually hiring prominent reporters and landing major scoops and building out substantial reporting staffs that have helped burnish the professional prestige of an organization whose business model remains largely predicated on social media-friendly aggregation. The shift has been a crucial source of organizational legitimacy, as the organizations use traditionally esteemed forms of newswork to indicate that they have similar degrees of authority as other organizations that have engaged in that work.[64] Circa's De Rosa called this transition "the natural order of things." Most every serious organization doing aggregation wants to eventually get into reporting; they just don't have the resources. "It's difficult to start with an organization reporting right away and be able to have a sizable audience and be able to cover as much as you need to without some aggregation," De Rosa said.[65] It creates a life cycle for organizations: start with a small staff and use aggregation to stretch it further both by garnering more pageviews and giving an impression of breadth of content. Then as funding increases, build out a fuller staff and move into more "grown-up" reported material, leaving another upstart to aggregate it and start the cycle again. Whether that life cycle is completed or not, the plans to complete it are almost as important to young news aggregators as the reality itself. It was important to Circa and Social Post to be continually *aspiring* to report (and to broadcast those aspirations), since that was the marker of a "serious," professionally oriented organization on the path to accruing authority. It meant they understood that reporting was the key to true professional status, that they didn't have that status yet, and that they felt it was important to get. Those were crucial signals, both to the profession and to its own journalists, of a news organization moving toward legitimacy.

Throughout the fixation on moving into reporting, both by organizations and individuals, the underlying value among aggregators is evident: reporting is where the authority is, where the status is, where true journalists want to end up. Aggregation is a stepping stone, a temporary practice, something to be grown out of. The inferiority of their work runs deep in aggregators' identity, and it comes from what other journalists say, from the monotony of the work itself, and from an ingrained sense of the centrality of reporting to journalism. Still, it's not dominant, nor complete. Some aggregators love their work, and many of them take great care to do it the best they can. There is room amid this deep-seated sense of inferiority for aggregation to develop as a source of professional pride and a practice worth building professional standards for. In this chapter's final section, we'll look at how aggregators are building the foundation for that kind of value.

A PROFESSIONAL IDENTITY FOR AGGREGATION

Aggregators may have a sense of inferiority regarding their work drilled into them, but that doesn't always mean they accept it. Many aggregators are quick to appreciate and articulate the value in their work. In many cases, that starts with pushing back against the popular dichotomy between aggregation and reporting. Several of the aggregators I talked to were resistant to the idea of my studying aggregation as a distinct phenomenon. "I think people talk about aggregating like it's this new thing," said one SportsPop editor. "People have been reporting on people's reports also since the beginning of journalism time."[66] Aggregation, they said, was a fundamental part of journalism, something that virtually everyone did, even (or especially) reporters. "All media organizations are aggregators," said Gabriel Snyder, former editor of Gawker and The Atlantic Wire. "There [are] different ways of doing it, some of it overt, some of it not so overt. But it is just fundamentally part of being a journalistic operation, is [that] you have to be good at passing on information reliably."[67] These arguments— and I have made similar ones elsewhere in this book—are an effective way for aggregators to reduce the professional distance between their own work and the journalists and news organizations they hope to be aligned with.

Many aggregators also argued that their work provides substantial value in the current information environment, especially in its ability to organize and make sense of information. They described it as a service to audiences, a way of providing them the information they need and are interested in without being parochial about whether it originated with a journalist's own organization. Beyond that ability to pull together a breadth of information, aggregators touted their ability to make sense of it for the audience, to step back and synthesize information across sources for a more holistic look at an issue than a single reported article.

VidNews' news editor articulated this value in a way that put aggregators' work on equal footing with reporting:

> There are two types of journalism. There's one type where people go out and discover new things, they report new information. And there's a type of journalism in which people explain or package ideas in a new way that engages viewers or readers in a better way than they had been before. And you can do both very well, and you can do both quite poorly. So I'd like to think that we do the second. We present information in a way that hopefully reaches somebody who maybe hasn't quite understood it before, or hasn't seen it before at all, or maybe hasn't seen this perspective on a news story before, or maybe hasn't seen it in this visual a way before.[68]

This is a remarkably perceptive characterization of the second-order journalism of aggregation: it's built around repackaging information that has been gathered by other journalists, but at its best it does so in a way that amplifies that information and creates new understanding. A couple of aggregators tied this ability to their willingness to incorporate opinion and analysis into their work, as opposed to objective reporting's traditional focus on presenting only the "facts." Gabriel Snyder, the former Gawker and Atlantic Wire editor, argued that aggregators could bring a broader, more analytical perspective that fit well with a real-time news environment in which being able to outline the state of play across the media environment took on particular value. As news becomes faster-paced, with a cacophony of competing voices rising from social media and around the web, several aggregators said aggregation is uniquely suited to help audiences avoid feeling overwhelmed by information overload.

That articulation of value was an important part of establishing a sense of professional identity. The ability to point to some social good that resulted from the knowledge they produced allowed them to identify their own work, rather than reporting, as a basis for a modicum of authority and professional status. And for some, the work practices themselves could serve as a basis for identity and satisfaction as well. Though many aggregators described their work earlier in this chapter as being monotonous, even those who disparaged their work conditions generally found moments of joy in it. Given how routine and relentless their work seemed to me, I was surprised at how many Social Post writers said they loved it. They appreciated the freedom of being able to hunt for their own stories and the creative challenge of framing them engagingly. They enjoyed seeing that their stories were being shared and talked about by thousands of people on social media, and they especially loved finding ordinary people with fascinating stories (usually told on Facebook or local TV news) and being one of the first to share those stories with a broader audience. "Finding really good stories or really cool things that nobody has talked about or really given a platform to before, and being able to be a voice for somebody that way, I think, can be really rewarding," said one Social Post editor.[69] That joy of discovery was echoed by numerous aggregators as one of the most satisfying parts of the job. There were other little things in which aggregators took great pride: funny or cleverly written stories, insightful interpretation, making connections that others had failed to see. "When I've put up a good piece and I've sucked the marrow out of that story, and I've slapped a great headline on it and just done a good job of aggregating, it's just really satisfying," said one aggregator for a general news site.[70]

Aggregation may generally be perceived by others in the news industry as a poor basis for professional status—journalism's equivalent of unskilled labor. But aggregators exhibited and articulated several skills that make someone great at their work. Some of these matched the skills required for every other form of journalism: curiosity, skepticism, concise writing, the ability to quickly learn about various subjects. Others took on distinctive importance—skills that might be nice to have for other journalists but became essential in aggregation. A few of these grew out of the immediacy and screenwork that is prevalent in their jobs. The ability to work quickly is paramount for aggregators. But not simply to write quickly: to process information quickly and be prepared to publish it almost immediately. Editors had different terms for these dimensions of speed as a skill. Snyder of Gawker and The Atlantic Wire referred to it as "keyboard presence, which is the ability to use the keyboard as a live instrument."[71] That is, he said, a comfort with publishing quickly rather than only releasing something after extensive review. Another editor of an aggregation team spoke of hiring people with "a high metabolism": the ability to digest information extremely quickly but as one's natural, comfortable pace.[72] This is imperative to a screenwork-based job, the kind of skill I saw aggregators exhibiting constantly as a basic condition of their work. Many of the aggregators I witnessed were masters at navigating the deluge of online information on their "beats," darting endlessly from screen to screen, but always with purpose and without distraction, making near-instant judgments on the type and reliability of the information they were encountering. This high-speed, high-level information processing is the distinctive skill required by screenwork and, by extension, aggregation.

At a few organizations—Circa, as well as some legacy outfits like the *New York Times*—editors saw reporting as the best way to pick up these skills, and they preferred for their aggregators to have reporting experience. This could be viewed as simply another way of reinforcing the centrality of reporting to journalism, of insisting that reporting is the only legitimate journalistic experience. It does do that in a way, but it also helps legitimize aggregation as well. It inverts the standard career path of aggregation as a warmup to reporting, and it inverts the importance of the tasks by suggesting that reporting could act as a prologue to aggregation work. It imbues aggregation with professional seriousness, and it's a strong statement that the skills of aggregation are significant and hard-won. Aggregators recognized these skills, worked hard to hone them, and took pride in them. They drew sharp distinctions between the people who excelled at their work and the ones who didn't. These aggregators showed signs of developing a base of technical and cognitive skill that they used to assign professional status, though there wasn't much evidence that legitimacy drawn from that skill extended much beyond their fellow aggregators. A similar dynamic was at work in aggregators' adherence to professional and ethical standards, which are beginning to emerge as an important tool in aggregators' quest for authority.

Developing Ethical Norms and Values

For a practice with a reputation as cheap and corner-cutting, practicing and articulating ethical values is a critical way to establish journalistic bona fides. Ethical standards do this across professions more generally: they play a key role in asserting an industry's autonomy and justifying its cultural authority.[73] If a profession can declare ethical standards, practice them consistently, and publicly castigate bad actors who don't, it appears trustworthy and authoritative. In aggregators' case, forming ethical norms is a way to align themselves with the professional journalists they see as desirable and distance themselves from other aggregators they don't, drafting off of the authority of the journalists who have set the foundation for their own ethical values.

The values that aggregators articulated to me were partly drawn from long-held journalistic norms, but they had been adapted for the particular work conditions and professional challenges of aggregation. Some of the ethical principles aggregators cited as most important to their work have long been considered basic standards of journalism: accuracy, political independence, keeping news coverage and business interests separate. But others took on particular importance within aggregation. These values have not been formally codified or universally articulated among aggregators, so they do not rise to the level of fully realized professional norms. But they have aspirational value as aggregators seek to distinguish good work from poor work and invest the former with authority.

The most fundamental ethical principle in aggregation is that of *attribution*. It was largely the first principle cited when I asked interviewees about ethical attributes of their work, and it was often stated in a common-sense, taken-for-granted way, as if the principle was so obvious that it only needed to be articulated as a formality more than anything. One breaking news aggregator's description was typical in its tone: "I mean, you have to be respectful, and you have to cite people. And so I mean, that's the obvious part. Like, citing people's work is everything."[74] In some forms of aggregation that almost solely consist of linking to others' work, like Billy Penn's stream of links on its website or some email newsletters, the standard almost vanishes into the background because attribution is built into the structure of the work.[75] Attribution was usually simple in practice: clearly name the sources for the information you used and prominently link to those sources. Linking performs several functions for aggregators. It's an adaptation of the journalistic norm of crediting sources so as to demonstrate transparency and independence from the information being provided, both of which can bolster journalists' credibility and authority.[76] But as it was understood by aggregators themselves, much of the norm's meaning was submerged beneath its routinized nature. Likewise, plagiarism didn't seem to be significant concern; it almost never came up in interviews or observation unless I specifically prompted it. It wasn't as though it didn't matter but rather that it had been so unthinkable for so long that it wasn't worth articulating as a distinctive ethical standard.

Curiously, though, many aggregators were quick to make snide remarks about times their own work had been aggregated by others without attribution. This was perplexing, given how impeccably I saw this norm practiced. It's quite possible that my experience was skewed because I wasn't able to gain access to a more disreputable class of aggregators who have little regard for attributing their work. But I think that more centrally, aggregators used these impressions of other aggregators' violations to isolate them as deviant and reinforce their own propriety—especially to a visitor like me. Attribution was so taken-for-granted that it didn't have much power to elevate aggregators' professional status—unless they could paint others as violators of it.

A second major ethical principle regarded the *excerpting* of content: aggregators should keep their excerpts of others' works to a minimum in order to keep from stealing others' content and to preserve the originality of one's own. Several aggregators said they avoided long block quotes of other articles or tried to keep from giving away the heart of a long story. The general rule was that excerpts should be short enough that the reader should still have reason to click through to the original story. But this principle was much more ambiguous than that of attribution because aggregation inherently relies on others' accounts, and most forms of it inevitably involve quotes or close paraphrases of other sources. On many basic news stories (such as an offbeat crime story), it was virtually impossible to sufficiently describe the events and still give readers a reason to click through to the original source. But despite the ambiguity of standards around excerpting, they seem to have settled into a generally uncontroversial acceptance, at least in assent if not practice. Like the attribution standard, the standard for excerpting mattered to aggregators, but it wasn't strong enough to form a professional identity around. The two standards are too basic and don't get to the heart of the core value of aggregation—that of filtering a flood of information and making sense of it for audiences.

An emerging third ethical standard—*adding value*—is built on that core value, is more distinct to aggregation, and has served as a more robust part of aggregators' professional identity. "Adding value" is vague, though, and it has the whiff of a buzzword. It refers to the obligation to add value for the audience to the material one is aggregating. In his widely cited 2012 blog post outlining guidelines for aggregation, the late editor and journalism trainer Steve Buttry listed "adding value" as one of those core guidelines and defined it with a variety of examples like data analysis, commentary, related stories, or reporting.[77] Aggregators talked about it in similar terms. Adding value can consist of bringing in a new piece of context, comparing sources to each other, verifying (or disproving) a rumor, or explaining a news story's significance. But the key element is a broader question: Is this story adding something significant to the sources from which it draws and the overarching narrative it is a part of more generally?[78] As several aggregators described it, adding value is a broader, overarching principle that the parts of the story constitute an ethical whole. As the editor of a social news site noted, one could attribute information assiduously and still end up producing a story that is ethically and professionally substandard:

> If your entire story is, you know, the first sentence is, "according to the *New York Times*," the second sentence, "according to CNN," third sentence, "according to MSNBC," then also, I mean, you're citing correctly, but you're not really adding anything. And so then you take a step back and you think, well, why I am writing a story? What am I kind of adding to the conversation? . . . When we're not thinking critically about adding to the conversation, it's easy to kind of recycle stuff, and recycling is not that far away from plagiarism.[79]

Adding value is what these aggregators used to separate themselves from each other and distinguish their work from the material they aggregate. The standard itself is largely distinct within journalism to aggregation—though it is a sibling of the business-school buzzword *value-add*—and asserts the value of aggregation in its basic articulation. It thus serves an important professional purpose beyond its ethical one in helping aggregators carve out a distinct realm of expertise.

Additionally, the notion of adding value serves as a means for journalists to assert authority over texts and sources, as journalism scholar Scott Eldridge argues, by reinforcing the idea that journalists apply interpretive skills to bring greater meaning and value to the information that others produce.[80] This function becomes particularly important for aggregators because it allows them to make a bid for that authority not over traditional news sources who come from outside of journalism but over other journalistic texts. If they can successfully add value, aggregators are demonstrating that there was something incomplete in another journalist's work that they could apply their particular skills of contextual understanding to improve.

But the idea of adding value has stark limits in its ability to serve as a foundation for authority and professional status. It's quite nebulous and exceedingly pliable in its application and, in practice, the value that aggregators add is often rather minimal compared with the value produced in the journalistic texts they draw from. And while aggregators might be keen to perceive the value they add in their own work, it can be less visible to others in the field. The case of VidNews is instructive. Adding value was the supreme ethical principle when I visited VidNews, echoed in various terms by most of the people I observed there. Looking back at Jennifer's example of VidNews' flushed-baby story from this chapter's introduction, its primary sin in her mind was that it added no value. From the audience's perspective, it had no reason to exist. Adding value remained a core part of Jennifer's ethical framework when I talked to her a year and a half later, but ultimately, it wasn't enough to serve as a foundation for the professional status VidNews sought. The route they chose to become a full-fledged, legitimate news organization was to report. If it's manifested in tangible, practicable ways, adding value could prove to be a source of professional distinction for aggregators, though its professional authority is far outweighed by that of reporting.

LINKING IDENTITY AND PRACTICE

I spent the previous two chapters examining aggregation's flawed epistemological foundation for its claims to authority—the ways aggregation's derivative relationship to reporting's knowledge and the uncertainty that relationship generates combine to undermine its authority as a form of news knowledge. But as we have seen in this chapter, it's not just a weakened epistemological base that erodes aggregation's authority: it's also a lack of professional identity and a sense of inferiority. In other words, aggregators' authority is weakened not simply because they're not able to know things and assert them as confidently as reporters but because they're not able to participate in the professional identity- and status-making that reporting work provides. David Ryfe argues that journalism's professional culture is embedded, more than anything else, in practice—in the everyday routines and habits of newswork.[81] This connection between practice and identity is a consequential one for many aggregators who have rarely, if ever, been able to participate in many of the reporting practices that engender a sense of professional identity and value.[82] Instead, their sense of inferiority tends to be rooted in their work practices—often a fast-paced, repetitive blur of screenwork that requires intense attention and allows little time outside the newsroom. Their practices bear many of the hallmarks of deprofessionalized work, including lower autonomy, fewer specialized skills, and a knowledge base dependent on others within the profession for information.[83] That deprofessionalization inevitably undermines identity.

The connection between practice and professional identity also comes through their organizational context, with aggregators' youth, replaceability, precarity, and limited opportunities for advancement through their work also constraining identity. The practice–identity link can also be both cultural and epistemological, as in the role of aggregation's inferior relationship to reporting in its difficulty establishing identity. Aggregators who don't report miss out on participating in professional journalism's cultural mythology surrounding reporting as well as its privileged ways of knowing, both important factors in fully identifying as a professional journalist. The confluence of these factors creates a potentially bleak picture for many of the aggregators in this study—that they're clinging to edges of the profession they long to be part of, and the way to secure their status in it is not necessarily to do their job as well as they can, but to do different work entirely. With that kind of marginal status, it's difficult for aggregators to build acceptance among their peers that the information they produce is authoritative, let alone the public.

This connection doesn't only run from practice to identity, though; it also operates in the opposite direction. A strong sense of professional identity encourages elevated journalistic practice. This is a significant part of the way professional identity and professionalism support authority: professional standards are articulated and subscribed to based upon a common sense of identity, those norms are validated when they are enacted in practice, and they become authoritative when they are accepted as legitimate by other fields and the public.[84] This is what aggregators (and other journalists) are attempting to do with their articulation of ethical standards. On one level, the articulation of standards is meant to reinforce authority discursively, performing professionalism rhetorically without any necessary connection to practice. But standards are also inherently tied to practice, meant to improve the work itself. Especially in the standard to "add value," the aggregators in this study intended to build on the distinct value that they believed they provided in their contextualized knowledge and to move more aggregation work closer to that ideal. Other scholars have identified contextualization and reinterpretation as key parts of aggregators' and other digital journalists' potential claims to professional distinctiveness and even authority.[85] The ethical principle of adding value highlights and prioritizes these epistemological functions, pushing aggregators to fulfill them more robustly. This principle is only able to do so in limited ways because it has only vaguely been articulated but also because the well of professional identity it is drawing from for its buy-in from journalists is not very deep. But in this standard we see a glimpse of the role of professional identity in reinforcing both the viability of aggregation as knowledge work as well as aggregators' authority—even simply the authority to articulate standards that can influence practice in a professional field.

Clickbait, Analytics, and Gut Feelings

How Aggregators Understand Their Audiences

Most days, all SportsPop's writers were doing was summarizing the latest conversation-starting sports news in quick posts with attention-getting headlines. But watching them work sometimes felt like I was seeing magic.

Their stories would be published on the website and, within minutes, the count of the number of times the story had been shared on social media—prominently displayed on the homepage and each individual story—would begin soaring. Hundreds. Thousands. Tens of thousands. A thousand shares was the basic benchmark for a successful piece, with stories routinely topping 10,000 shares across social networks. Some stories took a while to gain momentum, but most of the time, SportsPop's writers knew whether they had a hit or flop within a half-hour.

But the writers rarely saw any of those shares themselves. Dozens of times a day, SportsPop's staff would publish an article, quickly share it on Twitter (and on Facebook, though I never directly saw this occur), move on to the next story, and by the time they checked back on it an hour or two later, a thousand people would have shared the article. The numbers were so large and accumulated so quickly that I was left wondering, "Who *are* these people? How did the story get to them so quickly?" My questions along these lines were met with shrugs. SportsPop's aggregators didn't seem to know or care; they were content to write for an ethereal audience that appeared to them largely through aggregated numbers. Except for the occasional Twitter mention of their personal accounts—SportsPop's official social media accounts were the domain of the social media editor—there was almost no connection between the astronomical numbers on their stories and any material audience. SportsPop's staff sat at a row of desks at the center of a bright, expansive newsroom several floors up in a suburban office building, churning out stories to please an audience they'd almost never seen in person and only occasionally interacted with online. Yet they prided themselves on knowing what intrigued and bored that audience, what it loved and hated, all based on those numbers appearing and climbing on their stories.[1]

SportsPop's algorithmic aloofness toward the audience captures the paradox of the relationship with audiences among news aggregators—and among much of digital journalism more generally. Aggregation is an extremely audience-centric form of news, one where journalists' perceptions of their audience's desires largely dictate what they write about and how they frame it. Yet that view of the audience is anemic. It consists of numbers of social shares and page views, and it's convened around social media platforms and algorithms. It's stripped of the tangibility and three-dimensionality that comes with actual people making news part of their everyday lives. The measurements for the audience in many ways *become* the audience itself.

This chapter foregrounds two important components in the relationship between journalistic authority, knowledge work, and professionalism: the audience and economics. The audience plays an indispensable role in sustaining each of these phenomena. Journalistic authority is inherently relational; it must be continually recognized by a party other than the one exerting it. Journalism's authority is perpetually negotiated among a variety of actors, including critics, sources, and the state, but none is more central than the audience journalists claim to speak to and for.[2] The knowledge that journalists work to produce does not exist in isolation, either. It's knowledge for a particular audience, an inherently social product that does not fulfill any journalistic purpose until it is shared and accepted within a broader social sphere. And a core part of journalists' claim to professionalism is their aim to serve the greater good of their collective audiences, envisioned as "the public." This normative aim of public service is a primary justification for the status of many professionals, but it's particularly important within the professional identity of journalists.[3] To the extent that journalists possess authority, epistemic viability, and professional status, it's all underwritten in some way by their audiences.

But that relationship is dependent in part on a particular vision of the audience—as rational, democratically oriented actors who desire knowledge from the news, are invested in determining the reliability of that knowledge, and will assign credibility and authority based on that assessment of reliability. This public has long existed in the journalistic mind, but the fragmentation of news audiences in the digital age has made journalists' vision of that public less tenable.[4] Economic forces bearing on journalists have also pushed them away from this vision of the audience toward a mass of aggregate consumptive behavior as represented in the online metrics that are crucial to their financial health.[5] This is the environment in which many aggregators work, where each piece of content must stand on its own to accrue this mass consumptive audience in order to justify its own existence on economic terms. It helps explain the great paradox driving this chapter—many of the aggregators in this study were singularly, relentlessly audience-centered in their practice, yet their audiences were largely missing from their role in helping justify journalists' authority, epistemological practices, and professional status. The absence of the audience helps weaken each of those elements. This paradox hinges on the vision constituting these aggregators' audience: a thin, consumptive, algorithmically driven audience with much power to shape their behavior but little ability to reinforce the authority upholding it.

This tension between building journalism's orientation toward the audience on high-minded ideals and building it on commercial motivations has long been an animating one for the profession. Journalists' professional identity is built in part on their independence from commercial interests, even as those interests have always influenced and constrained their work.[6] The type of sensationalistic, potentially pandering work that some of the aggregators in this chapter do has analogs in the gossip columns, tabloid headlines, and breathlessly teased, lurid TV news segments that have been around for decades. But this tension between visions of the audience tends to be more acute in digitally native journalism because the audience has become more visible there.

It can't be treated as a distant, unobtrusive, and abstract phenomenon; it must be perceived in a more present and direct way, and the question of how it will be perceived becomes a more pressing one. In addition, for aggregators and other digital journalists whose authority and professional status are especially marginal compared to the journalists of the previous century, the audience's role in upholding those attributes is particularly tenuous. If aggregators' approach to the audience becomes overtaken by commercial forces and thus weakens the audience's already shaky ability to undergird their authority, the bottom could fall out of that authority especially quickly.

This chapter examines this tension in the work of aggregators, with particular attention to SportsPop and Social Post. Those two organizations hew closely to an economic model that brought modern aggregation to prominence in the late 2000s and early 2010s. In that model, aggregation is used as a means of quickly and inexpensively producing a high volume of content that is intended to attract as large of an audience as possible, primarily via search traffic and clicks and shares from social media. It is built on advertising as the overwhelming or even sole source of revenue, and the massive scale of audience required to make this model viable is a function of extremely low digital advertising rates, thanks in part to a glut of online content driving ad demand down in an ugly economic cycle for digital publishers.[7] This pushes publishers and journalists toward a preoccupation with online metrics that track user behavior and can serve to translate each piece of content into economic terms. Of the organizations I observed, the journalists at SportsPop and Social Post were most pressed by these economic constraints and oriented toward this consumptive, algorithmic view of the audience. SportsPop, one of its cofounders told me, was built and sustained on "a very simple goal: . . . we want to attract as many users to [the parent organization] as possible."[8] That meant trying to draw a younger audience than the organization's primary one by producing content that's socially oriented and as widely shareable as possible. Social Post was a relatively new startup that had begun to attract a sizable, devoted audience, especially on Facebook and among conservatives. "I think to some extent we will always be driven by the fact that we're a publication that is read by a lot of people," said Social Post's political editor. "That's part of what we are branded as, advertised as."[9] At both organizations, that economically driven emphasis on scale and social media sharing drove aggregators to define their audiences through the metrics they saw on their articles. These economic constraints are far from unique to those two organizations, and I'll include data from the other aggregators in this study as I explain the dynamics at work. These sites were simply the ones where the economically driven, quantified vision of the audience clashed most with aggregators' drive for authority and professional status.

We'll start by examining how aggregators viewed their audiences and where those views came from. Then we'll look specifically at the role metrics played in many aggregators' work—how they influenced their news judgment, presentation style, and even their psyches. Finally, we'll explore at the ways aggregators articulated and wrestled over norms around the idea of clickbait and aggressively courting clicks through sensational stories and boundary-pushing headlines. Through it, we'll see a continual conflict between aggregators' economic master and their professional aims, one that leaves the audience both ubiquitous and unknown, everywhere and nowhere.

PERCEIVING AUDIENCES BETWEEN THE SELF AND QUANTIFICATION

As journalists, aggregators inherit a long history of ambivalence regarding their audiences. Ever since the emergence of modern professionalized journalism in the late 1800s and early 1900s in the United States and much of Western Europe (and more recently elsewhere), journalists have identified their highest purpose as service to the public. Their raison d'être, journalists say, is not making money for furthering political causes but providing vital information to a democratically engaged public.[10] But when it comes to what that public actually desires, journalists have an equally long history of ignoring and dismissing it. Their vision of the audience has generally been a vague one—an amorphous, incomprehensible mass that, to the extent that it can be known, is uninformed, unappreciative, and irrational.[11] At the same time, their bosses have tended to view audiences as consumers, constructing them as a "market" that exists around their consumption of the organization's own product.[12] The *New York Times*, in other words, doesn't exactly speak to "the public"; it speaks to the *New York Times'* audience, which is a group of people created by the *Times* based only on their consumption of the *Times*. It's in this way that journalists' (and executives') perceptions of their audiences are more than just hermetic images within their own heads; they have the power to constitute those audiences themselves. News organizations mobilize their audiences' interests and desires based on their visions of those audiences, which influence the product they provide for those audiences and how they measure audience preferences. The vision of the audience, in many cases instantiated through measurement of the audience, constructs the audience itself.[13] For decades, media companies have gathered information about audiences constructed as consumers through survey and marketing data, and some of that has been made available to the journalists working for them.[14] But journalists have typically ignored that information for several reasons: disdain for such a commercial view of their audiences, skepticism of generalized characterizations of those audiences, and concern about weakening their autonomy by relying too heavily on audience desires.[15]

But journalists have always had *some* picture in their minds of who their audiences are and what they care about. Historically, it has been based on the people in their own immediate social worlds—family, friends, colleagues, and ultimately themselves. If you asked a twentieth-century Western journalist about whom they were writing for and how they knew what those people wanted, you'd likely hear about people they had run into recently, or conversations with family members, or notions about just knowing in their guts or by common sense what people are interested in.[16] There are some notable exceptions to this, of course. Letters to the editor and phone calls to the newsroom have also played an important role in forming journalists' impressions of their audiences.[17] And in TV news in particular, journalists have readily accepted an economic frame for their audiences, widely referring to them as "markets" and deeply incorporating survey and marketing research into their audience perceptions.[18] But on the whole, for a profession ostensibly oriented around its audiences as its primary calling and reason for existence, journalists have historically displayed remarkably little interest or initiative in determining precisely who those audiences are.

That's changed substantially in the past couple of decades. The public journalism movement of the 1990s sought to bring the public's concerns to the forefront and to use journalism as a means to press the public's agenda on the powerful. It wasn't widely adopted, but it did bring fresh attention to the importance of the public to the work of journalism.[19] During the 2000s, new participatory technologies like blogs, wikis, and social media allowed some of public journalism's ideas to be realized more fully, as nonjournalists—"the people formerly known as the audience," in media critic Jay Rosen's famous formulation—began to participate directly in reporting, disseminating, and commenting on the news.[20] As a practical result for journalists, audiences are now more obtrusive than ever, filling up email inboxes, Twitter mentions, and Facebook comment queues with streams of opinions and insults.

But neither of those two developments have shaped the contemporary journalist's view of the audience more indelibly than the dominance of digital journalism in the 2010s by increasingly sophisticated metrics measuring audiences' most minute behaviors with individual pieces of content at the most massive scale. As journalism's traditional print-based business model collapsed and news organizations felt a growing need to attract ever-larger audiences online, these more precise, real-time metrics of audience behavior took on a greater urgency.[21] Metrics began to structure journalists' workflow, as they were pressured to produce more stories that would draw more clicks. They began to influence journalists' emotions, becoming a minute-by-minute roller coaster of euphoria and anxiety for journalists whose worth to their employers was defined by their ability to draw traffic.[22] And metrics began to shape journalists' view of the audience itself, turning the audience into a quantified, rationalized commodity whose purpose is to consume rather than actively participate.[23] Media companies have been measuring audiences with increasing rationalization, and seeking to incorporate that rationalized feedback into their media products, for nearly a century. But that feedback has become much more voluminous, instantaneous, quantified, and salient within journalists' working world.[24] The audience is finally at the front of the journalistic mind but not in a robust, democratically rich way.

It's not surprising, then, that many aggregators described understanding their audiences as a key skill in their work. The manager of one aggregation team said he looks for "a really natural sense for what a reader would want to see" as one of the key qualities he looks for in hiring.[25] It was not hard to see the economic underpinnings of this skill, such as when a SportsPop journalist explained why it was necessary:

> You think [your story] is great, and it probably is. But it's like, who is this great for? And I think that it's always important to write for yourself, but it's also a business, and to not recognize that it's a business is a little silly.[26]

As the aggregators I spoke with described it, the skill of understanding the audience involved an intuitive sense of what interests large audiences and how to select news and frame it to attract their attention. One editor at a social news site described it in terms of "a baseline understanding of human emotions . . . being able to recognize the point of view that most people align themselves to while they're reading the story and then being able to clearly but intricately weave that into their story."[27] In other words, understanding the audience in his case meant knowing what specific emotions were most conducive to social sharing and how to identify and elicit those emotions in a story.

Aggregators' visions of their audiences were informed by many of the same sources that their predecessors have used—family, friends, and themselves—along with close attention to online metrics. Parents and grandparents were a popular proxy for uninitiated audiences, and several writers used themselves as stand-ins for their audiences as well. One aggregator for a national news organization explained how she saw her own "common-sense" interests as a representative of the audience as distinct from (and potentially more valuable than) her journalistic news judgment:

> There are some things that I will read about as a person, just if I were just a regular human being, I'll read about it. And so I don't

think I'm that much different from most of the people who read our website, and I think if journalists divorce themselves from thinking, "Oh, is this what [my organization] would write?" they would probably come to the conclusion that they would read this in their own free time.[28]

Interaction with audiences on social media played a remarkably small role in most aggregators' perceptions. Several said they had sworn off reading comments on Facebook or underneath the article, and during my observation, I never saw an aggregator interact with anyone on social media who wasn't a source or fellow journalist. Two interviewees who wrote email newsletters said they took great enjoyment in the connection with readers they felt through the email responses they got, and Billy Penn was quite closely connected to its audience of Philadelphia millennials through the events it hosted and the reporting work it did. But on the whole, aggregators had no real relationship with their audiences. They cared a great deal about what those audiences liked, but they didn't interact with them, and they had little means of knowing about them beyond metrics and guesswork based on projections of their own families and personal interests.

At Social Post, that attitude toward audiences wasn't characterized by disconnect so much as disdain. Social Post's writers and editors had an extremely well-honed sense of what its largely conservative audience was interested in: military, guns, inspirational stories of Christian faith, country music, small-town living, "marital values," former football star and outspoken Christian Tim Tebow, bad parents. That sense came almost exclusively from two sources: traffic to their stories and comments on Facebook, where all of their stories were immediately shared and drew an overwhelming share of their traffic. Social Post's social media editors were especially attuned to its audience's interests. They sat together at a desk on the far end of the newsroom and spent their days posting stories to one of Social Post's several massive Facebook pages with vague statements like "Whoa!" and "Incredible," and wading through its hundreds of Facebook comments. They had the front-row view of the tastes and splenetic outbursts of Social Post's audience, and they were blunt about they saw. During my week there, Social Post writers, and especially its social media editors, described their audience using these terms:

> "I think a lot of our audience is kind of fueled by disgust and outrage."
>
> "They don't have a great sense of humor, either."
>
> " 'Who cares' is their favorite thing to say."
>
> "Our audience loves to hate on people who do things unconventionally, particularly on parenting. Everyone thinks they're a perfect parent."
>
> "[They hate when we post] anything that has to do with a celebrity that millennials like. . . . People want to know, they want to click, but they don't want to admit to themselves that they clicked."
>
> "They're fearful about where their country is headed."
>
> "[They're like] my grandma. She watches Fox News a lot. She just doesn't understand the world we're living in. She's kind of our target audience. She's very sweet, though."[29]

Most of these comments were made matter-of-factly, without malice. They were treated simply as necessary knowledge to do their job and understand what to write about. But when I asked if their own values lined up with those of their audience, writers were fairly eager to tell me where they didn't, and somewhat sheepish to tell me where they did. I suspect that some of this was because they anticipated that I, as a presumably liberal academic, would look down on them if I sensed they were all conservatives serving up partisan red-meat bait for other conservatives. Instead, they said that carrying a neutral, fact-based style became especially important when they disagreed with their audiences on an issue. In effect, having views that differed from their audiences allowed them to practice what they saw as objective journalism and thus enhance their professional identity. If they hadn't disagreed with their audiences, they might have viewed themselves as partisan opportunists. But since they did disagree, they got a chance to act as neutral, dispassionate journalists, reporting just the facts, no matter how emotionally charged their audience.

But their divergence from their audience's values also carries a strong scent of cynicism. They were writing stories that reinforced values they didn't believe in not ultimately because they felt the truth needed to be told but because those stories would be clicked on and shared. They were feeding a suggestible audience the "disgust and outrage" that fueled it, not necessarily because they shared that outrage but because they wanted to reap the traffic it produced. They knew their audience well, and they were using that knowledge to manipulate it for commercial gain with startling efficiency.[30]

SportsPop had a similar disconnect—not from its audience's core values but from its interests. It focused on the kind of sports stories that tended to interest people who didn't care much about sports. Its Super Bowl coverage centered on the halftime show, commercials, and quirky happenings on the broadcast rather than analysis of the game itself. After an interview in a newsroom office, SportsPop's editor, Will—a twenty-something former college athlete himself—asked me what I thought of the site. I told him that his staff was very good at writing things people wanted to share, but that quite honestly, as a sports fan, almost nothing I'd seen them write that week would interest me. Will's response surprised me. "Funny you should say that," he said. "If I wasn't working for [SportsPop], I wouldn't be reading [SportsPop], either."[31] This might seem an appalling admission of apathy and cynicism, but it was actually a valued trait at SportsPop. Its editors wanted their writers to put aside their personal interests and objectively gauge a story's value to the site's readers, as measured by social shares and page views. Framed this way, it took on a selfless, almost noble cast: *You're not writing for yourself, your friends in the media bubble, or the news junkies. You're writing for average people, and you're putting their interests above your own.* This attitude reinforces a sense of professionalism widely invoked across disciplines: the ability to do a job regardless of personal feelings.[32] It also might seem in some ways like a remedy to journalists' longstanding apathy toward its audiences, but the people's interests weren't ultimately paramount to SportsPop, of course. They were writing what the people wanted so that they could turn their clicks and shares into revenue for their company and recognition for themselves. The audience was central to SportsPop's project—more significant than it has been throughout much of journalism's history. But like so much of that journalism of the past, SportsPop's work still wasn't *for* the audience. The audience was transparently a means to economic ends, rather than an end to be served in itself.

Audiences also appeared to SportsPop and Social Post's aggregators as distant and disconnected because they were measured that way. This was an odd juxtaposition, since online metrics made audiences a constant presence in those organizations. They were in the numbers at the top of every article on SportsPop's website. They were on the video board on the wall at Social Post showing the site's top traffic-drawing writers. They were instantly accessible through dashboard programs like Chartbeat. Their feedback was immediate and relentless. Within seconds of each Facebook post that Social Post's social media editors made, they could see the shares and likes tick up. They knew whether a story would be a hit or a flop within a minute. But metrics also served as a buffer against the audience. It took those real, flesh-and-blood people and filtered all of their opinions and desires for that story into a few clean, sterile, aggregated numbers. It kept them at arm's length, even as it brought them into almost every newsroom decision.

The audience has always loomed in the background of news production, especially when it comes to determining what's newsworthy and why. The media sociologists Pamela Shoemaker and Stephen Reese describe news judgment, journalists' process of understanding what news is and how it fits together, as an audience-oriented routine. What journalists are essentially doing when they decide what's news, they say, is trying to predict what audiences will find appealing and important.[33] That process has become even more explicitly audience-oriented during the 2010s, as metrics have taken some of the guesswork out of that prediction and tied it directly to journalism's economic goals. In his study of late 2000s Philadelphia news, C.W. Anderson noted that "It is not an exaggeration to say that website traffic often appeared to be the *primary ingredient* in *Philly.com* news judgment."[34] Researchers are mixed on just how much journalists' reliance on metrics influences the content they produce. Some scholars, like Anderson, have illustrated the ways in which a preoccupation with metrics pushes journalists toward quicker, simpler stories on more sensational topics.[35] Various quantitative studies have found a link between web traffic (or attention to web traffic) and decisions about story coverage or website placement, but that influence has been bound by journalists' resistance to having their judgment dictated by audiences and by organizational constraints such as perceived competition with other news organizations.[36] A reliance on metrics does seem to be influencing journalists' decisions, though perhaps not as much as the popular image of the journalist as click-chasing rumormonger might have it.

There was some shading in the picture of influence of metrics among aggregators, too. Some aggregators proudly declared their indifference to metrics or its lack of influence on their work. At Circa, editors covered eat-your-vegetables news stories without seeming to give much attention to metrics on a day-to-day basis. They would primarily consider metrics simply as a way to prioritize their work: if there were two stories that needed to be updated, they would usually work on the one with more followers first. At VidNews, metrics were virtually invisible. I never saw anyone looking at them, and they were only mentioned if I brought them up. Because VidNews' videos ended up spread out across the web, it was difficult to gather accurate, centralized metrics for them or to characterize their audience as any cohesive whole. Most of VidNews' journalists had no firm idea of who they were producing news for, something its top editors were rather sheepish about. "Right now, our only metric is, 'Did *we* think that was interesting? Did *we* think that was good? Do *I* want to watch that?' " said VidNews' senior editor, Jessica. "And in that way, we've got our heads down too much. But that hopefully will change."[37]

But for other aggregators, metrics were so central to news judgment that the question of newsworthiness could almost have been condensed into "Will people click on this?" In some cases, it was exercised bluntly, such as when Will, the SportsPop editor, assigned a story on pro golfer Tiger Woods being in last place in a tournament. I asked him if Woods was one of those athletes who will draw traffic no matter how inconsequential the news about him. "Every time. Every time," Will responded. "You don't even have to think [about whether to do a story]. It's just, 'Tiger? Yup.' "[38] Other times, though, the influence of metrics was on a higher order. Some editors exercised news judgment by standing in for the audience themselves. They would make a declaration of a story's newsworthiness not by asserting their own news judgment as professionals but by talking as a hypothetical audience member—one they knew through metrics. This happened several times in an editorial meeting of a Social Post team covering inspirational stories as they sat at a large conference-room table brainstorming story ideas for a slow news day. One writer—Alicia, whom we met searching for story ideas in chapter 2—pitched a story about the 1980s rock singer Bon Jovi surprising a fan battling cancer, which prompted this exchange with her editor, Christy:

CHRISTY: There's got to be something more to it than, "Bon Jovi surprises fan battling cancer."
ALICIA: It's Bon Jovi. Do you need more?
CHRISTY: The audience's answer would be yes.[39]

Christy didn't tell Alicia that *she* thought the story wasn't significant enough; she didn't have to. She told her that the audience thought that. And the audience's judgment of that story's newsworthiness—as understood through Christy's years of closely tracking metrics on Social Post's stories—*was* her judgment. It didn't just form the foundation for her judgment; it supplanted her judgment. Not only that, but the audience had more authority regarding questions of news judgment than even the editor herself. At Social Post and other social media-oriented aggregators, this tactic of filtering questions of newsworthiness through an explicit representation of the audience formed by metrics was embedded in the news selection process. One editor at a social news site said one of the basic questions of its story conception process is, "Who's sharing this, and why are they sharing it?"[40] The goal in this case is to generate "shares" of a story on social media so the news judgment process involves taking on a hypothetical reader's identity to understand exactly how those metrics will be produced.

Metrics also influence aggregators in other, less sweeping ways. Even if they don't stand in for news judgment, metrics help form a picture of what topics and ongoing stories audiences are especially interested in. Aggregators might decide to find another angle to continue writing about a popular story (this was a particularly favored strategy of SportsPop), or they might simply file the information away to use in future judgments about a topic's news value. More immediately, aggregators used metrics on other organizations' stories, employing social listening tools like Dataminr, CrowdTangle, and Newswhip that use data from social media to determine which stories were being shared most widely and quickly. They did this to get an in-the-moment glimpse of what people were talking about. As one aggregator for a national news organization put it:

> I like seeing what my colleagues are doing that people are clicking on and reading, because it kind of gives me a sense of where the wind is blowing. Like, where are people interested? What are people interested in reading about today? What kinds of stories are really compelling people at this moment?[41]

As this aggregator hints, using metrics this way is especially valuable for finding stories to write about, particularly since news that will generate conversation on social media is a key criterion of newsworthiness for many of them.[42] The metrics and data from social listening tools also help mitigate one of the primary shortcomings of relying on metrics to shape news judgment—it's a backward-looking indicator, something that can only tell you what kind of interest there is in a story that's already been done. As the same aggregator added a minute later regarding traffic, "It's not a helpful thing, because it's reactionary. It gives you what's happening after you've already made a decision about whether or not you're going to invest time into it. And so the usefulness of that is, I think, pretty limited."[43] Real-time social media metrics cut down that lag time by telling journalists what people are talking about *right now*.

But even with real-time data, that lag still exists. Aggregators can't be first on a story if they use social listening tools to find it, and they're not likely to have the most popular article on it unless they can come up with a dramatically original angle. Every aggregator wants to be the one writing the story that others see on their social listening tools and try to follow up on, not the ones doing the following. And the quest to be the trend-setter pulls aggregators away from metrics and toward the undiscovered—toward reporting. "You can't chase the trending. It's already trending. It's hit its moment. It's only going to go down, in most cases," said the senior editor supervising SportsPop (though SportsPop did plenty of chasing the trending). And that, she said, means getting out and talking to people.

> That's what we need to do, is hitting that wave before it crashes. . . . We have to be able to recognize in the various sports, within society, etc., the things that are resonating, what's interesting and what's not quite broken through, and capitalize on that, and do that first. That's where we have impact, not being the seventh person to write about [professional football star] Marshawn Lynch not talking [to the media].[44]

Here we have the source of significant tension between two attitudes toward metrics. On one hand, many aggregators spend so much time immersed in metrics that they're inclined to operate with immense confidence in their ability to know their audiences' preferences through metrics. They even do this to the point that they use those metrics to stand in for their own news judgment, as Social Post's Christy did in the editorial meeting. But on the other hand, they're also keenly aware of metrics' limitations in guiding them toward long-term resonance or even in enabling them to predict which stories will generate the best metrics. This tension is not only about the efficacy of metrics but also about how well they can know their audiences at all. And it mostly hangs there unresolved. It's visible when aggregators use metrics throughout their day but steadfastly assert that they have no real influence on their news judgment and when aggregators talk about their audiences' desires with complete self-assurance but simply shrug when stories they had thought would gain a lot of traffic instead go nowhere. The specificity of their knowledge of their audiences' interests exceeds that of almost every journalist in the profession's modern history. Yet it's not enough to guarantee that their efforts to cater to those interests will be successful.[45]

This reality gives a distinct tint of capriciousness and incomprehensibility to their pictures of the audience. At the socially driven aggregators in particular, virtually every story is produced because someone there thought it would find a substantial audience. But most of them don't. At SportsPop, about fifteen of the site's stories per day (less than half of its daily output) account for the significant majority of its traffic, according to Will, the editor. "The other twenty or thirty didn't necessarily need to be written," Will said—except that its staff didn't know which of the articles would be the ones to hit. Throw forty stories a day up against a wall, and see which fifteen stick. "This has been a part of my job that I never really anticipated, to be honest," one of SportsPop's writers told me as he scanned SportsPop's numbers on Chartbeat at his desk. "The longer I do it, the more confused I am." There are days, he said, when "the internet just doesn't care"—no matter what he and his colleagues write, it doesn't get much traffic.[46] None of them really understands why; they just have to convince their bosses that it's not a meaningful indicator of the site's direction. They've run up against the limitations of metrics as a way of understanding their audience, but it's almost all they have. So all they can do is continue to rely on that metrics-based sense of what the audience wants and wait for the audience to respond like it has in the past.

This is the root of aggregators' (and digital journalists' as a whole, as other scholars have documented)[47] frustration with metrics: as much as they might try, the audience can't be formulated. What most aggravates aggregators is not just that their stories don't get much traffic, but that they can't understand why. They've used the most precise knowledge they have about what interests their audience and added their own professional judgment to tailor their story to it, all for the goal of getting people to click on it and share it with others—and it doesn't happen. Their knowledge of their audience is perhaps the most crucial piece of expertise they have to their success, and it isn't enough. Will, SportsPop's editor, wrapped up one interview by wearily illustrating how deeply that frustration eats at him:

> A big part of my night, when the baby's asleep, when my wife's asleep, when I'm trying to sort out a Red Bull addiction, is going over everything I've written that day and figuring out why the hell this thing didn't share well, and why this only got 2,000 page views and this got 200,000. So it's enjoyable in that ultimately I think it makes me better, but I think at the same time, it's stressful. It's constantly just like, "Oh God, we've got to hit this benchmark. I want to hit a million page views again today. I want to hit a million uniques today." So you hit it, and it's like, "Yes!" and then immediately after

that, you're like, "Fuck. Tomorrow, we've got to do the same thing over again." It's just this constant, seven days a week, twenty-four hours a day, just constantly trying to beat yourself. And yeah, I don't see that changing anytime soon, because I'm a freaking crazy person.[48]

Will took pains to note that his obsessive following of metrics was a personal choice, not something imposed on him by his managers at SportsPop. Still, the amount of stress caused by his obsession is unsettling. The uncertainty that metrics provided in their information about the audience left him trying to decipher them as if they were a code which, if cracked, could reveal secrets about the audience and the untold treasure of page views that lay within. And his organization's own singular dedication to bringing in as many readers as possible added to that stress as well, even though he emphasized that his evaluation wasn't tied to traffic. SportsPop needed him to bring in traffic, and he needed to extract all the knowledge he could from metrics in order to do that.

Metrics were processed as a source of pride and fulfillment as well. Even at organizations that didn't emphasize traffic, seeing an article be read and shared widely was among the most satisfying experiences aggregators had in their work. "It's always fun when you can send a big news alert, and you suddenly see a flood of 5,000 people come in to read the article," said Stacy Cowley of her work on the *New York Times'* NYT Now app. "You can be bringing the news to people right where they are. They're probably waiting in line somewhere or whatever, and yet they're so excited about this that they're jumping in to read it."[49] Getting substantial traffic didn't just mean winning bragging rights; it symbolized a connection. It allowed them to envision a bond with their audiences, and since their audience interaction was so thin, that might be the most substantial bond they had—represented through soaring numbers on a screen and brought to life with their mind's eye.

Through metrics, aggregators' audience is continually obtrusive, a constant but largely naturalized constraint on their news judgment and decision-making. Yet the incompleteness of metrics means that the audience is also largely invisible. It's conjured up almost instantly around their content but ultimately unknowable and frustratingly fickle.

Metrics are the source of some of aggregators' greatest pride and fiercest ambition, yet the satisfaction and connection they provide is fleeting. Metrics have made the audience impossible for these digital journalists to dismiss, as their predecessors did. But the gap between journalists and their audience remains as large as ever.

The uncertainty fostered by a metrics-based conception of the audience is potentially damaging to the authority of journalists who hold it as well. Given the relational nature of journalistic authority and the role of audiences in sustaining it, metrics simply don't provide enough knowledge about the audience to enable journalists to claim authoritative standing regarding that audience. For most journalists, metrics are only part of a fuller understanding of the audience, which includes interactions with sources or discourse on social media. Both of those means of knowing the audience could help form a basis for authority as well. A reliance on metrics, then, certainly does not preclude this sort of claim to authority. But for journalists whose view of their audience is dominated by metrics, as those at SportsPop and Social Post were, their knowledge is so thin and one-dimensional, despite its ubiquity and precision, that any claims to authority rooted in their audiences would ring hollow. An audience constructed through metrics is not robust enough to grant journalistic authority.

DEFINING A NEW NORM AROUND CLICKBAIT

Professional journalism has norms and standards surrounding treatment of the audience—serving the public is journalists' foremost aim; journalists should be honest and (more recently) transparent with audiences[50]—but it's not clear how those apply in an environment ruled by metrics. What does it mean to serve the public when you're writing stories about sports and celebrities in order to attract the largest possible audience to your publication? Is writing a clever but unrevealing headline sophisticated or merely dishonest? Journalism as an institution hasn't given its practitioners much guidance on questions like these. But as budding professionals who have a deep desire to justify their own work as authoritative, it's inevitable that aggregators and other digital journalists would fill that void with standards that take shape through the way they critique others' work and rationalize their own.

Enter *clickbait*. It's a term that began in the small sphere of media workers' professional discourse but quickly spread into the broader public lexicon.[51] Virtually anyone who's familiar with getting news online has a sense of what the term refers to: attention-grabbing headlines plastered atop disappointing stories, articles that seem perfectly engineered to get us to share them on social media without imparting much actual information, or stories that make us click through to tell us what could have been summarized in a tweet. Yet clickbait has tended to take on an "I know it when I see it" air, because firmer definitions have proved elusive. Oxford's English Living Dictionaries refers to clickbait as "content whose main purpose is to attract attention and encourage visitors to click on a link to a particular web page," which could also apply to virtually every tweet ever posted by a news organization.[52] The official *Oxford English Dictionary* tightens the definition a bit, adding, "esp. where that web page is considered to be of low quality or value."[53] In a widely doubted 2014 piece called "Why BuzzFeed Doesn't Do Clickbait," the organization's editor-in-chief, Ben Smith, defined clickbait much more narrowly, in terms of "curiosity gap" headlines like "This Woman Won't Go To The Beach Again For One Terrifying Reason" that garishly obscure key information in order to sucker users into clicking.[54] His definition was echoed in the most practically influential definition issued to date—the one given by Facebook in its 2016 announcement of a crackdown of clickbait in its News Feed. Facebook defined clickbait strictly in terms of headlines, specifically those that "intentionally leave out crucial information, or mislead people, forcing people to click to find out the answer."[55]

As Smith, Facebook, and many others have indicated, the definition of clickbait does center on the headline, and specifically whether it seems to misrepresent, oversell, or obscure what's in the story in order to attract more clicks. But there's also something more—something nebulous that makes Smith's narrow definition unsatisfactory, something that makes a "What State Do You Really Belong In?" quiz *feel* like clickbait, even though its headline is perfectly direct and honest. Some of this element also ties back to the "low quality or value" characteristic that the *Oxford English Dictionary* identifies; no one ever complains that an excellent piece they just read was clickbait. Clickbait, then, isn't a practice that has been cleanly defined by professionals or academics. But we might offer a preliminary framework for a definition: it is content (especially headlines) whose fundamental purpose is to draw clicks to a web page when *either* that content oversells or obscures the material on the page, *or* that content is of low quality or value.

Across the various definitions, *clickbait* exists as a term of disapprobation for one primary reason: to allow people to denounce others' work as substandard and manipulative and thereby bolster their own social status. This goes for both audiences and professional journalists. Media observers have complained that the term has become overused,[56] and Tim Marchman of the iconoclastic sports website Deadspin has (correctly, I think) argued that it's become a way for news consumers to rather lazily assert their superiority over the producer of a piece of content and their savviness regarding the commercial structure of the web: *"I'm too smart for that to work on me."*[57] For journalists, especially the ones in this study, it has become an important way to draw boundaries, distance themselves from irresponsible actors, and thus assert themselves as professionals, just as aggregators did in chapter 3.

Clickbait is a particularly potent term of professional demarcation for aggregators because it represents a practice that hits especially close to home for them. It's a product of the same economic model that drives much of their work: a need to attract mass audiences to each piece of content in order to bring enough revenue from low-dollar online ads to make the organization profitable.[58] Like aggregation, clickbait has a long history within news: it has pre-internet analogs in the screaming headlines of yellow journalism and tabloids and other modern-day equivalents like the teasers peppering local TV news.[59] There's little that is particularly novel about the digital incarnation of this phenomenon other than the complex role that discourse around it has played in setting standards and establishing professional status for digital journalists and publishers. Clickbait's forerunners received much more professional disapproval from their contemporaries than aggregation's predecessors did, but both have arrived at a similar place in the internet age—ascendant together, driven by the same commercial forces, objects of the same professional derision. It's important, then, for aggregators who aspire to professional status to understand clickbait and have a ready explanation of why it doesn't apply to them.

The aggregators in this study overwhelmingly tended toward Ben Smith's narrow definition of clickbait that tied clickbait to misleading audiences with headlines and then disappointing them with content. "Clickbait," said Social Post's editor-in-chief, "is where you're setting an expectation for the viewer that isn't necessarily met."[60] Though he didn't use the term *clickbait*, Circa contributing editor Ted Trautman described this practice well:

> People oversell in the headline, and then the deck, and certainly the text of the article, kind of scale back the claim sort of implied in the headline. And so it's all about getting people to click. You know, "Is Putin about to launch nuclear missiles," question mark, and then the answer is no, he's not about to do that. But there's a truck that moved, or something much smaller.[61]

Aggregators, just like other journalists, look on these practices with disdain. One referred to curiosity-piquing headlines and social media posts as "the black arts," and another described many of the pitches his editor gave him as "shitty clickbait kind of news."[62] One SportsPop writer described writing overheated, disingenuous opinion articles as "trolling for attention or clicks," referring to the longtime online practice of making antagonistic statements one doesn't believe in order to anger other users.[63]

Journalists' distinction between people who practice good journalism and those who simply chase cheap attention is embedded in the professional hierarchies of the field and—if the aggregator is in a traditional news organization—their newsrooms. One aggregator in a national news organization talked about how grateful he was that aggregators' ability to draw traffic had little bearing on their value to his organization. "I don't think people give that much credit to the people who are doing clickbait stuff and who are always on the top of the page views, because anybody can kind of do that," he said.[64] This, of course, meant that much of his own work was not highly valued by his organization. But he was expressing his gratefulness at that because he, too, thought his traffic-oriented aggregated work was antithetical to producing good journalism. He preferred to gain professional status through his reporting.

By reinforcing this boundary between clickbait and good journalism, then, aggregators allow themselves to affirm professional journalistic values and place themselves on the right side of the divide. This is one of the primary purposes of ethical norms more broadly—to distinguish between insiders and outsiders regarding a profession, especially in times of instability.[65] Even in an operation like SportsPop, where gaining traffic was clearly valued both individually and institutionally, its editors were eager to emphasize that it wasn't *that* kind of aggregator, the one that cynically posted material just to get clicks. Instead, they proudly recounted the site's reported work and noted that there was little organizational pressure to get heavy traffic. The managing editor overseeing SportsPop's parent division emphasized the importance SportsPop places on its craft with an illustration involving a controversial National Football League running back, Marshawn Lynch:

> Look, I could put the words Marshawn Lynch in a headline right now, in the URL, and I could have five poorly constructed sentences, and we could probably get 100,000 page views. So that's just reality. But—and maybe I'm naïve—but I think that if you have five really great paragraphs with really good, strong information, you'd get 500,000 page views. Content does matter.[66]

Even if SportsPop's aggregators' work involved writing just a few paragraphs on the latest utterance on a popular player who was sure to draw clicks, she was reinforcing a boundary between them and other aggregators who were doing largely the same thing. To do that, she had to create a distinction—people who aggregate these stories with a few poorly constructed sentences versus people who do it with several meaty paragraphs. Aggregators' definitions of clickbait were strategic in that sense. They tended to be narrow because a broader definition—especially for the more traffic- and social media-based aggregators—might have included their own work. Instead, they needed to make sure the realm of professional journalism was just large enough to include themselves, yet not so large that they couldn't exclude others somewhat like them.

Clickbait ultimately lacked the disciplinary power of other ethical norms, such as avoiding plagiarism. A significant part of that disciplinary weakness stemmed from its unclear boundaries; it was easy for a potentially offending aggregator to gerrymander the boundaries to include her own behavior because there was no agreed-upon definition to measure those boundaries against. Several aggregators who have been accused of producing clickbait disputed that the term had any real meaning as a way of distinguishing irresponsible journalists. The attempt to package a story as attractively as possible to gain a broad audience, they argued, is something all news organizations do online, not just those who are "clickbaiting." "I think everyone's trying to write clickbait, right? Everyone's trying to get people to click on their stuff," said SportsPop's editor, Will. "That's why everybody's here—getting people to click."[67]

This argument drives at a deeper problem with enforcing clickbait as a norm: boundaries can't be coherently drawn and violators of a norm can't be excluded when there are no widely shared values behind the norm.[68] In this case, the ambiguity surrounds the normative value of understanding and reaching audiences. This is arguably a more valued skill now than at any time in professional journalism's history, but it is also the core skill of creating clickbait. This convergence makes clickbait a practice that is nearly as beguiling as it is loathsome to many aggregators. It also introduces a moral indeterminacy that isn't present in, say, the norm of attribution: journalists aren't publishing articles in trade magazines and attending training sessions on giving as little credit as possible without veering into plagiarism, but that's essentially what they're doing regarding attracting audiences and avoiding clickbait. The norm is difficult to enforce because the boundaries are unclear, but those boundaries are unclear because there is little difference between the values underlying proper and improper behavior.

Social Post provides a good illustration of how clickbait and its attendant norms work in practice. Its writers and editors defined clickbait in terms of ensuring that expectations for the story are met—writing headlines that don't overpromise, and stories that don't underdeliver. Anything beyond that was generally fair game. When I observed Social Post writers putting together stories, though, the final headline was invariably more sensational and breathless—hotter, in Social Post parlance—than the one initially suggested by the writer. In several cases, this final, overheated headline was applied without the writer's input.

In one case, Elizabeth, a serious and skeptical Social Post writer in her late twenties, was writing a story about Scotty McCreery, a former "American Idol" winner turned B-list country music star who was robbed at gunpoint in 2014.[69] One of the three men alleged to have robbed him had been convicted, and one local TV station's story said he wouldn't give up the names of the other two because he was worried he'd be killed. After writing the story, Elizabeth plugged her original headline into the content management system: "Country Star Was Robbed At Gunpoint In His Own Home. Now The Verdict Is In For the Criminals." She dropped a few other potential headlines into a channel on the office messaging system Slack dedicated to headline help. After a couple of suggestions from editors around the newsroom on how to refer to McCreery, she pitched two headlines to her editor, Oscar, in Slack. Her preferred headline was "American Idol Winner Scotty McCreery Was Robbed At Gunpoint. Now the Verdict Is In." It was less sensational than another she had suggested earlier, and I asked why. "There's a way that we could make this very sexy and make people click, but we have to be fair to what the content is," she said. But she submitted another, "hotter" headline to Oscar, too: "Criminal Who Robbed American Idol Winner Scotty McCreery At Gunpoint Says He's Sorry, But Refuses to Answer 1 Big Question."

Oscar, not surprisingly to Elizabeth, preferred the hotter version. But he suggested amping it up just a bit more by referring to a "disturbing reason" the man wouldn't reveal his accomplices. Elizabeth was hesitant—she thought the reason was pretty ordinary. "I don't want to oversell it," she told me. "But I guess it is disturbing." She sent Oscar two messages back: "yeah I like that idea" "we just always do disturbing." As she fiddled with the headline, I asked her if she thought it was clickbait. No, she said, because clickbait is not meeting expectations in the story. As a reader, "I'm going to get into it and I'm going to find that thing he refuses to do, and it's going to be clear—'Oh, he won't tell on his friends.' " I noticed Elizabeth was now giving a heavy sigh every minute or two, and I told her it seemed like the process of writing a headline was more stressful than the rest of the article. Elizabeth agreed. "It's the part that's going make or break the article. It could be a great article, but if it doesn't have a good headline, no one's going to click on it." In the end, the headline took on a more breathless tone than any version she had pitched to Oscar, sounding almost like a movie trailer voiceover: "He Robbed A Country Music Star At Gunpoint. He Won't Say Who Did It With Him For a Dark Reason."[70]

Under its final headline, Elizabeth's story was clickbait by the rough definition I laid out earlier, as it ostentatiously withheld key information about the story. Most readers (as well as most aggregators in this study) would say it would meet their common-sense definition of clickbait. But it wasn't clickbait by Elizabeth's definition, because the story fulfilled the promise of the headline. Social Post's loose standards around clickbait allowed Elizabeth to publish a story she could feel good about—albeit grudgingly—while giving plenty of leeway to use manipulative methods to draw in an audience. This is what makes the norm of avoiding clickbait such a weak one, since its standards and definitions can be changed so easily to suit an organization's purpose. The clickbait norm had two functions in this case: Its secondary function was to establish some minimal boundaries for Social Post's journalists to work within when crafting headlines. But its primary job was to give writers like Elizabeth a sense of professional identity and satisfaction in their work even as they lacked the autonomy to avoid doing things they might have been inclined to see as dubious. The norm, in other words, was more about aiding identity than guiding behavior. More broadly, the malleability of both the clickbait term and the normative standards around it reinforce just how thin and one-dimensional aggregators' conception of their audiences is despite the audience-centric nature of their work. Even in a profession that has traditionally dismissed its audiences, their view of the audience is so enervated that it edges toward professionally proscribed territory.

A NEW TWIST ON AN OLD PROBLEM

Reporters and editors in newsrooms everywhere are wrestling with the increasing institutional power given to the online metrics that push the audience to the forefront of journalistic work but reduce that audience to a skeletal quantification. After decades of assuming that good work would find an audience, journalists are uneasy about doing more than they've ever done to attract the audience's attention, but they are also captivated by the ability to glimpse how their work is reaching that audience in real time. These tensions have been especially acute in the social media-dominated, click-chasing world in which many of the aggregators in this study work, but they reveal some of the fissures in journalists' perception of their audiences more broadly.

Normative values regarding not abusing audiences' attention for the sake of economic gain had some influence among the aggregators I observed; nearly all of them were at least a little queasy about overplaying stories for clicks. But those values were often submerged beneath the organizational imperative to attract a larger audience, which dovetailed neatly with personal ambition. The result for the more traffic-driven aggregators was work that dabbled in manipulative tactics regarding its readers. Social Post churned out dozens of stories a day feeding the partisan worldview of its audiences, using overheated headlines atop relatively dispassionate stories to inflame its readers' disgust or reinforce their identity. At SportsPop, the editor, Will, at one point assigned a column to one of his writers expressing the opposite view of a developing social media firestorm, prompting objections from coworkers over whether this writer believed the opinion he was writing. (He insisted he did.)[71]

Aggregation, especially the traffic- and social media-driven version, veers closer to this kind of cynical pandering to clicks than its practitioners would like to admit. That's where the norm of avoiding clickbait is meant to step in as a tool for reconciling professionalism with an overbearing click-based economic structure by allowing aggregators to cater to audiences' consumptive desires without treating them callously or cruelly. But the norm is remarkably weak—only the minimum application of professional standards to a form of work that's dominated by economic interest. It lacks the coherence necessary to meaningfully govern practice, because its underlying values are perpendicular to the core values that drive the work as a whole. The logic that drives clickbait— that the audience is a collection of consumers best known through online metrics and best encountered en masse—is also the logic driving much of aggregation. And journalism is relatively impotent to police against that logic because its own conception of the audience has been so anemic. The soil from which journalists might grow robust standards for treating audiences holistically and respectfully is dry and rocky from decades of neglect. The audience might seem to have moved toward the center of this era of digital journalism, but the current approach is largely just a quantified veneer on the same aloofness journalists have long had toward their audiences.

The vision these traffic-driven aggregators hold of their audience as a narrow band of consumptive interests makes it difficult for them not only to justify norms regarding that audience but also to lay claim to authority with that audience. An audience that is constituted and reconstituted from story to story based on the whims of whoever happens to be on social media at the time is not likely to recognize any meaningful authority or professional status for the people producing those stories. But this vision of the audience is also a product of journalistic authority and professional status that have already eroded. Media scholar Anthony Nadler argues that journalism's view of the audience is "postprofessional," having undergone a paradigm shift in the 1970s and 1980s marked by declining faith in journalists' editorial discretion and the ideal of autonomy, along with an embrace of market-driven consumer preference as a chief value.[72] The decoupling of the audience from journalism's professional and authoritative functions within this particular form of aggregation is only the most evident fallout of a much broader and older shift. There's evidence that journalists have been pushing back against the most extreme iterations of this trend, as the advertising-based, traffic-driven, mass-audience model began to give way as the dominant model of news publishing in the mid- to late 2010s. News organizations have shifted toward subscriptions, memberships, and efforts to connect more substantially with a smaller core of loyal audiences.[73] Even this change, though, is likely at root not a normative but a strategic one, spurred by the insufficiency of online ad revenue and the de-emphasis of publishers in the algorithms governing Facebook users' feeds.

With audiences, as with epistemological practices, aggregation holds up a funhouse mirror to the values of traditional journalism, a form of knockoff knowledge both reflecting and distorting the audience perceptions held by the form it's mimicking. The approach to the audience taken by some of the aggregators in this study is out on the margins of journalistic practice, but the tensions that approach reflects are the same as those of traditional modernist journalism. Aggregation is ostensibly "for" the audience: for giving them the same breadth of information while saving them time, for meeting their desires, and often for reinforcing their views. But all of those purposes are ultimately utilitarian, as the audiences are merely a means to an economic end. Journalists have struggled to resolve this tension, using norms like the divide between the news and business sides of a news organization in a largely unsuccessful effort to divorce themselves from an economic consideration of their audiences.[74] Aggregators have found it even more difficult. The futility of the clickbait norm in directing behavior, despite its ubiquity in journalistic discourse, is evidence of the difficulty of developing and upholding professional norms when dominated by an economic orientation. If journalism's audience is unequivocally a set of consumers rather than a citizenry or a public, there are few professional barriers limiting how nakedly their consumption can be pandered to.

CHAPTER FIVE

Atomization and the Breakdown (and Rebuilding) of News Narrative

Anthony De Rosa has found a potential news story, but he's trying to figure out where to put it.

De Rosa, Circa's editor-in-chief, is sitting at a small white table in the midst of the bright, bustling fifth-floor Manhattan office that Circa shares with an office messaging company, a 3D modeling startup, and two other small tech companies. De Rosa is a thirty-something man with dark, unkempt hair and a stubbly beard covering a tired face. He had little journalistic background other than blogging about the New York Mets and Giants when he moved from a technology position at Reuters into its editorial operation in 2010, eventually becoming its social media editor before moving to Circa in 2013. De Rosa is the only Circa employee who regularly comes into the startup's New York office; a couple of other editors who live in the New York area drop in occasionally, while most of his colleagues work from home, and the tech and business staff work from Circa's San Francisco headquarters.[1]

For most of the day, De Rosa plants himself in front of two screens: on one, he toggles between Circa's custom-made content management system and a stream of conversations with his coworkers on the office messaging platform Slack. The other is largely for monitoring the news. Here, De Rosa jumps back and forth between at least a half-dozen browser tabs, most often the unending flow of tweets on the Twitter application TweetDeck, along with news articles, his email inbox, and the workflow management system Trello, which the staff uses to organize its editorial process.

It's a Monday afternoon in January 2015, and a busy news day. Circa's eight editors on the job today will publish more than a hundred updates to news stories around the world in its mobile app by the end of the day. Those updates will be sent to users who have chosen to "follow" ongoing stories, often receiving push notifications when a new development occurs. When users open the app to read the update to the story they've followed, they are taken not to a full article but straight to the update itself—usually a couple of short paragraphs. The story that they have followed is a single, evolving text piecing together dozens of these updates over time, though the story's followers are only initially shown the new update they haven't yet read.

This "follow"-based updating system is Circa's most important feature. It's built on the idea that people who are trying to keep up with an ongoing story should only have to read whatever information is new rather than wading through paragraphs of rehashed background information in order to unearth a few slivers of actual news. Circa was launched in 2012 on this idea: skipping the elements of a news story that people already know and getting them straight to what's new circumvents the inefficiency of the one-size-fits-all news article.

The follow system also means that Circa editors' jobs are much more streamlined as well. When rebel groups are surrounding the U.S. embassy in Yemen and threatening to topple the government, as they are on the day of my visit, Circa's editor doesn't need to write a whole news article on the subject. Instead, he can summarize the action in a couple of paragraphs, push those out to the people following the ongoing story on civil unrest in Yemen, and rewrite the top of the story for any new readers. It's the kind of bare-bones efficiency that can allow a Circa editor at his home in Seattle to file updates on a dozen breaking stories around the world in an eight-hour workday.

Back in the Circa office, De Rosa is looking at a video of a British reporter cornering Louisiana governor and likely Republican presidential candidate Bobby Jindal about "no-go zones" in Europe—nonexistent Muslim-dominated areas that supposedly operate under Sharia law and exclude both police and non-Muslims. A Fox News anchor had made a false claim about the existence of such areas in Paris over the weekend, which Circa had ignored—"Just some Fox News idiot," De Rosa sighs—but now Jindal is fiercely defending their existence in an encounter that has aired on CNN.

This development is clearly more newsworthy in De Rosa's mind, but at Circa, the question isn't so much *whether* to do a story as *which* story to update. "Do we have a Jindal 2016 story?" De Rosa asks Circa's de facto politics editor, Adrian Arizmendi, in Slack. Arizmendi replies that they don't, and the two quickly decide it's too early to give Jindal his own campaign story. So without a story to put it in, De Rosa and Arizmendi hold off on publishing Jindal's "no-go zones" claim. Former Republican presidential nominee Mitt Romney already has his own 2016 campaign story, and if it were him or another prominent likely candidate like Jeb Bush, De Rosa says, the update might be worthwhile. But without an existing story to latch onto, the update dies.

The next day, the mayor of Paris threatens to sue Fox News for its claim, and this time De Rosa quickly green-lights a new story on claims about Muslim no-go zones. He now has enough of a narrative thread to justify a story that could be updated in the future—but the story is built around Fox News' claims, not Jindal's. "Now that we have a confluence of all these different things happening, we can use it as a way to track the lawsuit, which seems like something that's a lot more concrete than just Jindal popping off on TV," De Rosa says.

Several of the elements in De Rosa's calculation of newsworthiness are familiar to virtually any journalist: The prominence of a politician, the concreteness of a potential lawsuit, the inanity of a weekend cable news anchor's blather. But one element in that process made Circa distinct. It was not enough in this case for the story to be noteworthy; in order to be published, it had to be a story that fit more closely into one of the particular story structures Circa had built. Had Circa possessed a story on Jindal's potential candidacy in its system, it may have published Jindal's statements as an update to that story. Instead, since Circa didn't have a particular container for that story, it wasn't a story.

Circa's approach to news events as smaller blocks within sweeping stories influenced the way it presented news, but it also shaped the way its own editors saw the news themselves. Because news events had to be placed in those larger story structures, Circa's editors didn't fully see them as news until they could conceive of them as part of one of those structures. If news events didn't seem big enough to become the start of their own larger news story, they were left unpublished. Conversely, more negligible and incremental updates to stories were often deemed newsworthy because of their fit into an existing story structure. The decision about their newsworthiness "was made two years ago" when the story was formed, as technology editor Nicholas Deleon described one example.[2] Circa viewed news on a different narrative level than other organizations, and that meant that many news events were only fractions of stories, rather than stories in themselves.

Circa lived for just three years. In June 2015, five months after my visit, Circa shut down after running out of money and failing to find a buyer who would acquire both the company's technology and editorial team. But Circa was an audacious experiment in rethinking news as a narrative, in envisioning it as something different from the inverted pyramid-style article that has dominated news for more than a century. And it was ground zero for a larger movement to break news down into more granular, discrete "atomic units," allowing it to be organized and presented in new ways.

Circa sought to break down news narrative into its smallest possible parts, turning each news event into an update of a few dozen words that could stand on its own, without an article. But in doing so, Circa did not end up producing a series of disconnected, discrete chunks of news. Instead, Circa's "atomization" of news built narrative up, pushing its editors' focus toward broader story arcs and seeing individual events as necessarily tied to ongoing issues and other stories. Journalists have, of course, long seen news stories as part of larger narrative forms, though they have also routinely been criticized for ignoring context and treating events as isolated from one another.[3] But in making its news so small, Circa ended up making the big picture of news events its central organizing element, reflecting a shift evident in much of aggregation more broadly as well.

In journalists' ongoing bid for authority, narrative is a crucial tool. News stories do not function only as ways to communicate facts about events; in their very form they are also an argument for their own legitimacy. Presenting events in familiar news forms and narrative conventions communicates to readers that the author's account is a valid, definitive description that should be accepted as reality.[4] Journalism has historically built its narrative forms on a tension between the utility of conveying factual information and the aesthetic and cultural purposes of telling stories. News narratives, exemplified by the inverted pyramid and its variants, have been the often awkward embodiments of this tension, spewing rapid-fire facts while still using some storytelling devices to pull those facts together into narrative and imbue them with their value. That combination has been a potent one for journalists, providing a distinctive narrative form for news that allows audiences to immediately recognize it as such and frames themselves as dispassionate, authoritative chroniclers of the social world.[5]

Aggregation seems to break this form down by disregarding its more narrative components and stripping out virtually everything but basic facts in an effort to create news that's more efficiently produced and more quickly consumed. But in shifting toward shorter, more granular news, Circa and other aggregators in this study have adapted traditional narrative forms to bolster their case for authority. Many of them have doubled down on the unadorned, "just the facts" narrative style of much of modern journalism while also thinking of news on a broader narrative level, as something best understood as part of a larger web of events and discourse. In making this shift, they are vying for authority as contextualizers and sensemakers who can guide readers through a cacophonous digital news environment.

This chapter will explore the nature and consequences of that big-picture narrative shift, both at Circa and among other aggregators. I will start with an examination of the crucial and multifaceted role narrative has played in the way journalists conceive of and structure news. Specifically, we'll look at the development of both the "interpretive turn," which has lengthened news narrative, and the concept of "atomization," which has sought to break news narrative down. We will then look more closely at how Circa turned journalism's narrative conventions on their head and what those changes meant. Finally, we will examine other aggregative efforts to reframe news narrative around broader narrative arcs. In doing so, we'll see that aggregation may be about making news shorter and more digestible, but that there is room within that orientation for broader ways of producing news as narrative and potential for using those narrative reconceptions as a platform for authority.

CONCEPTUALIZING NEWS NARRATIVE

News is narrative. It's not *just* narrative, of course, but at its core, the act of communicating the news is recounting events, connecting them to one another, and thus giving them meaning. That is, the narrative theorists tell us, the definition of narrative: the selection and ordering of events allows people to read connection and even causality between them. "To tell what has happened," wrote the French philosopher Paul Ricœur, "is to tell why it has happened."[6] This gives narrative a central place in shaping our understanding of the world, in helping us communicate and make sense of reality. A narrative is not simply a chronicle of events; it is in itself a cognitive and even moral framework for understanding those events. By including and excluding, describing and connecting, and choosing beginnings and endings, we use narrative to show others how to see the world—and we make sense of the world for ourselves.[7]

Narrative does all these things for news, too, but in an even more direct way. Journalists collect pieces of information—facts, quotes, statistics, observations—but it isn't until those pieces are set into narrative form that we think of them as *news*. And the narrative form itself helps shape what journalists consider news. Journalists go through the newsgathering process with a sense of what "the story" is, then they gather facts to help fill that story out. That underlying story might change as new facts are gathered, but it determines how journalists know what kinds of facts to gather in the first place. This is how journalists understand events: when TV reporters approach a car accident, they don't just see a car accident. They see dramatic footage, sources, B-roll, sound bites, and perhaps a hero or villain. They see it first as a story. "It is not merely that news workers tell stories, but that they receive the world in a 'storied' way," observes sociologist Ronald Jacobs.[8]

The stories that journalists observe in the events they witness are not inherent in those events; there are many other ways to assemble events into narratives, each with their own set of meanings. That's why narrative is so important to journalistic authority: it produces a definitive account, tells us "what really happened," and makes that understanding seem foreknown in the events themselves. Journalistic narrative imposes a firm, authoritative stamp on its vision of reality, but it seeks to do so in a way that recedes from view, as if the narrative vision was simply part of reality itself and only discovered by the journalist.[9] This journalistic desire to produce an invisibly authoritative narrative has resulted in a style that eschews many of the characteristics we associate with narrative: setting, plot, rising action, climax, resolution. Instead, modernist news texts often unfold more as a series of propositions supporting assertions: a headline and first sentence stating the story's main assertion, then paragraph after paragraph backing up those assertions with evidence, something more akin to an argument. The traditional news story is more about conveying information efficiently and quietly persuading the reader of the author's legitimacy in defining that information than it is about building a narrative experience, but that doesn't mean it's not narrative. Historian Michael Schudson put news' disjointed narrative style best: "All news stories are stories, but some are more storylike than others."[10]

Some of this ambiguity regarding news as narrative stems from confusion about the term itself. We use the word *narrative* or *story* to refer to a wide variety of things about the news: we talk about news stories themselves as narratives—especially longer, more literary ones—but we also talk about narratives in broader senses as well. If news coverage has begun depicting a political campaign as clumsy and heavy-handed and its actions become interpreted in that light, we often speak of that image as a "media narrative." Journalists often refer to each individual piece they produce as a "story," but they also refer to a sequence of events that keeps an issue or person in the news over time as a story, as in a phrase like "the Hillary Clinton email story." To help clarify what we mean by news narrative and provide a framework for interpreting the narrative innovations of aggregators like Circa, it's helpful to break down news narrative into three levels: *macro*, *meso*, and *micro*.

The *macro*, or *myth*, level is the broadest of the three. It's the narrative canvas on which all occurrences are painted and given their basic meaning and moral color. Myths are the archetypal narratives that form the base level of how we interpret reality. They're informed by our cultural surroundings, religious beliefs, and a lifetime of hearing story after story with similar themes: the hero's journey, the crafty trickster, fall and redemption, exile and return. These myths are everywhere in our narratives and news stories, but they are so pervasive that they're often invisible, particularly because the moral interpretations they guide us to are consonant with our culture's dominant values.[11] Media scholar Jack Lule has argued that they reinforce journalists' unconscious biases by supplying them a stock of "types" through which they can interpret news events.[12] The macro level was at work among the aggregators I observed, just as it is for all journalists. But aggregators' mythical structures and archetypes didn't differ from those of other journalists, so the macro level will not be a significant part of my analysis here.[13]

The *meso*, or *story arc*, level is the one on which journalists view certain occurrences as news events and view certain news events as particular kinds of news stories—breaking news or features, scandals and nonstories. The meso level is where journalists perceive a house destroyed by fire as a mere event but a dangerous rescue during that house fire as a *story*. But it is also where journalists understand a months-long political campaign as a single story, perceiving narrative threads running through it as they construct them out of day-to-day campaign events and speeches.

Journalists see the world in terms of stories and nonstories—and particular types of stories—on the meso level. Ronald Jacobs has described the process by which journalists apply their narrative vision to news production as "narrative emplotment." Journalists come to news events with a set of thematic stories that they've become good at adapting to a wide variety of situations. These aren't as broad as the myths described earlier, nor are they as unconscious. Journalists might see news events as a "not in my backyard," or "stupid criminal," or maybe simply as an uplifting human interest story. They often expect that events will fit one of these story arcs, then find and organize facts to ensure that they do.[14] As journalists cover ongoing stories, they see these thematic narratives begin to develop as well; this is how we end up with a "media narrative" about an out-of-touch political candidate. When journalists talk about knowing what is a story and what is not, about getting to the bottom of a story, or about setting the narrative for a series of news events, they're talking about the meso level of narrative. The meso level can operate within a single news story, but at its most complex and robust, it stretches across multiple news events and texts, organizing them into a single cohesive storyline.

Finally, the *micro*, or *story form*, level refers to the textual and visual conventions through which a narrative is communicated. This is the narrowest sense of news as narrative: the news writer's lede and nutgraf, the TV journalist's sound bite and establishing shot, the visual journalist's bar chart and choropleth map. These narrative forms are more than just technical components or containers of content, though. They are how we make sense of news stories and what prompts us to recognize them as news stories in the first place.[15] For example, when we flip through channels on our TVs, we are immediately able to recognize the form of a local TV news broadcast because of the conventions—on-screen graphics, anchors at desks, reporter standups and voiceovers—that make up its news form. This is what prompts us to interpret its stories as representative of actual local happenings as opposed to fictional or far-away events. These forms help convey authority and credibility for the journalists and also give audiences a sense of what to expect from the types of news they're encountering. The micro level of narrative is the difference between flipping through summaries of a recently passed congressional bill on a news reader app and settling in to read a feature on the bill in the *New Yorker*.

These levels are conceptually distinct, but they function together when journalists produce news narratives. In producing a story about the aftermath of a tornado, for example, a reporter might be guided by macro-level narrative in coming to the event with myths to be reinforced about heroism of first responders and the expression of people's inherent goodness toward each other through volunteerism. She might be guided by meso-level narrative in seeking out an archetypal "next-day story" with anecdotes from eyewitnesses, estimates of damage, and descriptions of the cleanup effort. And she might also be guided by micro-level narrative through the directive from an editor to produce a 1,500-word feature story as well as several photos and a minute-long video for the web, all of which contain their own textual and visual narrative conventions. While all three narrative levels might function in tandem as a journalist constructs a news story, they may take on greater or lesser importance within particular cases or news practices as influences on news production.

The micro level is where news aggregation appears to diverge most significantly from traditional journalism. Aggregation is often about condensing news, stripping out unnecessary narrative elements to leave readers with just the pieces they need to understand it. Circa took that even further, breaking each story into minuscule factual pieces and showing users only the ones they hadn't seen yet. But as we'll see, Circa's greatest innovation was at the meso level, a new way of seeing news events as inherently connected to larger story arcs. Circa did this by building on a developing idea of how news narratives could be reconceived—the idea of the "atomic unit" of news.

SHORTFORM JOURNALISM AND THE "ATOMIC UNIT" OF NEWS

At the micro level of narrative, most news has been defined over the past century and a half by its brevity. The foundational narrative form of modern journalism is the inverted pyramid, which "appears to strip a story of everything but the 'facts,' " as media historian David Mindich put it.[16] The inverted pyramid begins with a lead that succinctly relays what the author sees as the most important element. The rest of the text is used not to develop a story around that information but simply to add facts and claims to the lead in an order organized around descending importance and thematic coherence.[17] The inverted pyramid is packed with facts, quotes, and attribution, and it is gutted of most everything else: narrative tension, opinion, rich description, ambiguity. Its purpose is to communicate news as efficiently as possible and to connote immediacy, factuality, and objectivity by the author. But in their insistence on the ruthless recitation of facts and little else, journalists end up focusing on communicating transient events to a fickle public mind rather than connecting them into a more holistic understanding of the world, as the sociologist Robert Park lamented in 1940.[18]

The inverted pyramid is in decline, a form being pulled apart in two directions, both longer and shorter, more complex and more granular. Over the past half-century, news writing has slowly but consistently moved toward more anecdotal leads, more narratively oriented structures, and a more analytical voice.[19] News stories in general have been becoming longer and more abstract for more than half a century, with events shifting toward the background in favor of more interpretive themes and trends.[20] Beyond that overall shift, the subgenre of narrative or literary journalism, which had roots in the muckraking of the late 1800s and early 1900s, has experienced a resurgence in recent years. This genre combines in-depth reporting with sophisticated narrative devices drawn from fictional storytelling, and it has been catalyzed by new multimedia and interactive storytelling techniques available online.[21]

Journalism has been getting shorter, too, and aggregation has been a significant part of that. Throughout the past two decades, numerous news organizations have made pushes for shorter, more digestible stories, perhaps none more prominently than the *Wall Street Journal* after it was bought by media magnate Rupert Murdoch in 2007.[22] The economic calculus behind these changes is simple: news media budgets are shrinking dramatically, leaving fewer journalists to do the kind of in-depth work that longer reports typically require. Shorter news accounts are often easier and cheaper to create, and audiences have migrated to smaller screens where they consume news in shorter increments of time.[23] Aggregation has suited this shift perfectly: it repackages longer work into shorter, more digestible chunks, it's well-suited for quick reading on mobile devices and social media, and it allows a small staff to quickly and inexpensively produce a large swath of content.

This condensation of news can also result in a product that's simplistic rather than simpler, that lacks even the baseline narrative sophistication of traditional news. But the implicit premise of shortform aggregation is that the conventional news narrative is an unnecessarily cumbersome package in which the true element of news is trapped. The work of aggregation, in this view, is an effort to free that core news element and set it on its own, with as little extraneous material as possible. At its root, this is an argument that news is best understood not by being assembled into narratives but by being disassembled into smaller, discrete units of information. Where journalists have understood the news by seeing it in the form of a news story, aggregation would seem to understand it by taking much of the story out.

This argument has become most explicit in the discussion, especially in the early 2010s, of the need to rethink the "atomic unit" of news. The argument, voiced by an assortment of digital journalists, news futurists, and tech entrepreneurs, goes like this: For the past century, the article has been the basic unit of news, but it was a product of the routines and requirements of industrial print journalism. Now that we're free of the constraints of space and time that the print production process imposes, journalists not only can but should free themselves from the article as news' default narrative form. Instead, journalists should find a different "atomic unit" for news: perhaps facts or quotes, which could be reorganized in a variety of new ways. Or news elements like the who/what/when/where/why/how, which could form a database of news events that could be analyzed to discover new connections and patterns. Or perhaps the basic unit could be a news issue, with articles replaced by Wikipedia-like continually updated topic pages that would combine the most recent facts with thorough background information.[24]

Some of these conceptions of atomized news took the term *atomic unit* more literally, as the smallest indivisible element of news. The former definition, in particular, was connected to the idea of news as structured data, a notion popularized by influential programmer–journalist Adrian Holovaty. In a 2006 blog post, Holovaty argued that while journalists conceive of their work essentially in story form, they are actually mostly gathering structured data—"information with attributes that are consistent across a domain"—that would be more usefully organized as such, as opposed to being hidden within the text of a story. When stored in this way, the information could be sorted and searched systematically, yielding all kinds of additional potential uses in addition to serving simply as an archive of news articles. "Information," Holovaty told one interviewer, "is exponentially more valuable if it's structured."[25]

Under a structured data model, for example, a journalist covers a house fire not only by producing an article but by entering a series of discrete pieces of data (address, cause, damage amount, fire departments involved, and so on) into a database so they can be accessed, recombined, and analyzed in other forms.[26] The notion of structured data ties the atomic unit discussion into data journalism, another ascendant journalistic form during the 2010s. It has also inspired other wide-ranging journalistic projects: the Pulitzer Prize–winning PolitiFact, which has used structured data to track the truth and falsehood of political statements; Homicide Watch, an effort to track and tell the story of every murder victim in Washington, DC; and Structured Stories, a more esoteric experiment in structuring news events through semantic language.[27] But in addition to being a way of approaching news computationally as data, it's also fundamentally a narrative phenomenon. It's a means of abstracting the micro level to the point where it essentially ceases to be narrative, in order to gain new insight on the meso level.

The atomization of news, then, is not simply about producing shorter forms of news. It's an attempt to develop a new way of conceiving what news is—not stories, at bottom, but facts. Within the atomization paradigm, readers can gain the most knowledge from news not when journalists use narrative to shape facts but when they strip narrative out. These granular facts may be given narratives to help produce meaning, but according to this view, they have to be seen and organized simply as facts before that meaning can be added. With a few exceptions like PolitiFact, the idea of atomizing news remained largely an intriguing thought experiment until one full-scale news organization was built from scratch on the notion of atomizing the news: Circa. But through its atomization, Circa ended up even more deeply embedded in narrative as a way of understanding the news than traditional journalists.

CIRCA'S ATOMIZATION OF NEWS

Ben Huh was not familiar with these early discussions of breaking news into granular parts and updating ongoing stories with new developments when he founded Circa.[28] But in early 2011, Huh, who ran a collection of popular absurdist humor websites as the media company Cheezburger, had an epiphany. He was following a massive earthquake and tsunami in Japan and became frustrated that the news articles he found online about it required him to dig through paragraph after paragraph of information he already knew in order to find out something new. The traditional news article, it seemed to him, was an incredibly inefficient vehicle for delivering information. It forced news consumers to wade through redundant background information, and it forced journalists to write that information over and over, creating a bloated package of hundreds of words around what might only be a couple of paragraphs of new information. "Why can't the reporters just write a short update on the latest news?" Huh wrote in a blog post. "If you don't understand what's happening, the update makes no sense. But if you're like me and are following the news closely, I feel like I wasted my time." Huh ended that blog post, titled "Why Are We Still Consuming News Like It's 1899?" with a call "to bring together great minds and passionate people around this problem," which he dubbed the Moby Dick of news.[29]

The people he called for came together quickly. Within a few months, Huh had made presentations about his "Moby Dick Project" at two tech conferences and had organized a workshop on it at Stanford. At one of those conferences, fellow entrepreneur Matt Galligan approached Huh afterward. Neither he nor Huh had any journalism background, but the problem Huh had described was bothering him, too. A few days later, they agreed to form a company together. Galligan's first significant contribution to the project was to move it exclusively to the smartphone. It wasn't enough to rethink the article for people following ongoing stories, Galligan thought. It needed to be rethought for people reading on their phones. "If it's mobile, then we're not just talking about less text, for example, just summaries," Galligan said later, "but there needed to be the fundamental shift in the way that that text was consumed."[30]

The notion of rethinking the news article for the smartphone seems like a bland insight today, but it was less obvious in 2011. Though smartphone ownership was growing quickly across age groups, it still trailed feature phones in the United States. Many news organizations' mobile presentation consisted of rudimentary restructured versions of their websites for smaller screens.[31] It didn't take a visionary to determine that news consumption was going to become substantially mobile. But the idea that a news organization's product would be available exclusively as a mobile app, and that the news article should be reconceived with a smartphone in mind, was a novel—and risky— venture.[32]

After a few early detours (prelaunch versions of the app had a network of user profiles and a comment stream with emoticon reactions to stories),[33] Circa launched in October 2012 with two key components: points and the follow. Stories were broken up into 300-character "points"— a single fact, statistic, quote, piece of background information, image, and so on—that appeared on small individual rectangles called "cards" within the app. Users could "follow" stories, which allowed them to be alerted when new points were added and to jump to those new points when opening the story. Initially, followers jumped through the new points in the story by tapping arrows that the Circa team called "Mario warp buttons" after the 1980s Nintendo game, but eventually the new points displayed at the top of the story for returning followers, while showing up in their normal places throughout the story for new readers.[34]

The Circa team soon discovered that the most powerful part of its design was not breaking up stories into points—after all, new readers would end up scrolling through points to read a story as a whole, much like a traditional inverted-pyramid-style news article—but the follow. With the follow, Circa was able to build a record of what information its readers had and had not been exposed to (at least within its own app) and only show them what was new. It also fostered loyalty within its users. A user's decision to follow a story was a tangible signal of interest in that story and a means for Circa to continue to pull that user into the app through push notifications that the user was likely to open. "It really solved in a lot of big ways the problem of engagement," said Arsenio Santos, Circa's cofounder and chief technical officer. "How do you get people to come back to the app or the website? How do you make this part of a daily consumption habit? Follow was the key to that."[35]

The shift toward the follow was not a move away from atomizing news but simply a way for that atomization to be made legible and useful to the user. The follow relied on Circa's points structure to be effective. A follower couldn't be shown only the new information in a story unless that story had been broken up into small units that could be classified as new or old, seen or unseen. Circa would add other features, like a daily review of the biggest story updates of the day and a bare-bones web version of its stories. But the points and the follow together formed the backbone of Circa's user experience.

That user experience was built around giving users a new, more efficient way of consuming ongoing news stories on their smartphones, but divergence from traditional news was much more drastic—and more revealing—internally. In order to break stories into points that the app could show individually to users, Circa developed its own content management system (CMS) that strung movable, removable points into stories. Each point needed to be tied to its own source, a URL that would show up with the point in the CMS and would be collected at the bottom of the story in the app.

For Circa editors, updating a story was a matter of adding new information as a new point, finding a place to slot that new point in the story to make it readable for new readers, and revising or deleting points rendered outdated by the new information. Editors wrote points in the detached reportorial style characteristic of most modern wire service or newspaper copy, with one key difference: since each point would be displayed on its own, outside the story, to followers, it couldn't refer to events in a way that relied on a previous reference elsewhere in the story. (A point could not begin by saying, for example, "The senator's visit is the first to this war-torn country since 2009. . . .") The result was a writing style that was even more staccato than the bloodless tone of most traditional news writing.

The final decision involved with an update, and one of the most important, was whether the update merited alerting followers through a push notification or even recasting the entire story. The most inconsequential changes were called "silent updates"—updates that were made without a push notification to followers. The standard story update was given a push notification for followers, but two other update types went beyond this: to "pwn" a story (a term drawn from online gaming and referring to domination) was to rewrite the storyline in light of new events, and to "republish" a story meant giving it a new headline reflecting the new development and publishing it to the app's main list of stories so nonfollowers could see it.

The four update types created a natural hierarchy of newsworthiness for Circa editors, with republishing at the top and silent updates at the bottom. The decision about an update's newsworthiness, then, was not based solely on its perceived importance but on how much it changed the broader story of which it was a part. If an update was so minor that it could be made by changing an existing point, it got a silent update. If it required a new point, it would often get an update with push notification. If it changed the entire trajectory of the story Circa had been building, it would get a "pwn," and if it did so with a significant enough development to interest a broader audience, it would get republished. The update's news value was never considered on its own; it was always in relation to a larger story.

Likewise, when Circa editors looked for news, they were not so much looking for stories to write as points to add or update. Virtually every news event, in their eyes, was an incremental development within a larger story, rather than a story in itself. Circa kept track of all these broader stories (they were originally called "storylines") in a semiformal system of "branches" organized through the task management system Trello. Each story was part of a "main branch" that split off into a variety of stories. The main branch for Spain, for example, was a Trello card with a linked list of every ongoing Circa story on Spain, a couple dozen of them in total, divided into categories like "politics" or "economy."

Trello also contained a parallel system organizing stories by time—specifically, the next time the story needed to be checked on for an update. De Rosa's days began with a cruise through the list of the few dozen stories set for an update check that day, and he often spent most of the day whittling down that list, checking stories and assigning and editing updates. When news events popped up outside this system of daily checks, De Rosa would use the topical branch system to find the story where an update would fit. He kept this branch system in Trello open most of the time that he worked, searching for and moving and categorizing stories at a furious pace.

David Cohn, Circa's first editor, developed the Trello branch system early in his time there, using it to replace a chaotic Google Doc where editors listed the stories they were working on each day. Trello's capabilities to search for and organize stories outpaced Circa's own CMS, so it quickly became more than a daily agenda. It was, in essence, a somewhat systematic taxonomy of every news story it had ever covered, virtually all of which were considered "active" or updateable. Circa had no centralized list of main branches, but every incoming news event was slotted somewhere into this existing structure or, in some cases, added to it as a new branch.

Most news organizations have a searchable archive for their journalists, but unlike those, Circa's stories were organized taxonomically by topic, and they formed the framework through which its editors made sense of every incoming news event. Each of Circa's branches was also alive and evolving, with almost every story in it capable of being revised, added to, or branched off from. For Circa's editors, news events themselves became part of this larger organic system of storylines rather than individual occurrences or stories, as Circa deputy editor Evan Buxbaum put it:

> [For] terrorist incidents where you have the actual event that becomes a story, and then maybe there's legal court cases if somebody gets caught, that's a new branch. If there's a fallout angle—mourning, candlelight vigils, or something—maybe that's another

branch. International reaction—if you have a bunch of world leaders all coming out and saying things, maybe that becomes a branch. So you wind up with this tree of news, this ecology of news kind of feeding off each other in our system.[36]

The fact that Circa was able to develop such a structure for news doesn't necessarily mean that a self-evident structure for news topics exists—another news organization could have structured its stories entirely differently. But it does indicate that new and more systematic ways of structuring news are feasible. Circa's staff largely consisted of generalists, with a technology editor taking on the only defined coverage area. Other editors had areas of interest or expertise, but without the beats through which journalistic work has been organized for the past 125 years or so,[37] the structure of Circa editors' news universe came from the branch system. Circa editors' work was similar in many ways to that of wire editors, the journalists, often at newspapers, who monitor information coming from wire services and select and edit it for publication. Circa editors used a wide range of feeds—wire services, social media, local and foreign news organizations—to survey an astonishing variety of news each day. Over the course of an hour or two, De Rosa monitored and edited stories on terrorism arrests in Paris, Netflix's quarterly earnings, a deadly bombing in Ukraine, and a crackdown on honey labeling by the U.S. Food and Drug Administration. But all of that news was contained and connected within the same branch system, the master list of stories that encompassed all the world's news that was fit for Circa to publish.

CIRCA AND THE NARRATIVE ARC OF NEWS

The confluence of Circa's branch system, its breakup of news stories into granular "points," and its emphasis on following and updating stories through time brought two elements of the newsgathering process to the forefront. First, Circa editors had a heightened sense of stories existing and evolving through time, and a keen ability to gauge how an individual development fit within the broader arc of an ongoing story. Second, Circa editors saw stories fundamentally in relationship to other stories, which changed their calculations of those stories' newsworthiness.

Because Circa's editors saw news in both temporal and spatial terms, they understood news narrative as existing at the meso level, particularly as that level encompasses multiple news events and texts. Modern journalists have always taken this level of news into account, but Circa's editors fundamentally considered news as existing at a level above and across the individual stories that journalists have focused on. More than anything else, it was Circa's atomized news structure that pushed them to this broader level.

Perhaps the core skill Circa's structure required of its editors was the ability to identify when new information about ongoing news topics constituted a concrete development and what the narrative thread was between those events. As Cohn explained, it's not enough to simply tag news events with a topic, such as "Hillary Clinton," and pile them up as part of that category, because "even that, for a reader who's following Hillary Clinton, becomes kind of meaningless after a while. It's not a narrative." Instead, Cohn said, there has to be a through-line for all those events, something that ties them together in a narrative arc and allows editors to identify and contextualize meaningful events.[38]

Criminal court cases are particularly easy stories to understand this way. An arrest is made, charges are filed, a trial date is set, pretrial hearings are held, the trial takes place, a verdict is pronounced, the defendant is sentenced or goes free. The narrative arc is known from the beginning, and each development is discrete and easy to place within that arc. The story has a relatively fixed crescendo and limited set of outcomes—guilty, not guilty, hung jury, plea deal. For Circa's editors, these were the beginner's stories, the ones that practically wrote themselves.

The paths of most stories are not so simply discerned. The narratives they appear to form can splinter, be absorbed, take sharp turns, and dissolve, leaving journalists and readers wondering if they ever constituted a coherent narrative to begin with. A legislative farm subsidy bill may be held up by an amendment changing the formula for food stamp qualifications, changing the story from one about agriculture to one about poverty policy. When the amendment is defeated, does it become an agriculture story again? A presidential campaign has the most fixed of all structures, yet few stories' narrative threads are as turbulent and undetermined. For much of the 2016 U.S. presidential general election, the story of the race centered on the spectacularly chaotic Trump campaign, its increasingly absurd scandals and tactics, and the uncertain long-term prospects of a Republican Party that had nominated such an unruly and cruel candidate. Within twenty-four hours on November 8, the story of the campaign had been transformed, entirely in retrospect. Now the campaign's narrative was about Trump tapping into a powerful populist sentiment that had previously been hidden, the tactical failings of the Clinton campaign, and the role of Russia's government in influencing the election in Trump's favor. The events of May through early November had not changed at all, but what we saw those events as being and meaning changed completely.

For every news event that occurred, Circa required its editors to understand it as part of one of these larger narrative structures and to understand precisely how it changed that structure. That narrative vision was the core skill of a Circa editor, and it was a difficult one to develop. Some editors didn't have it, and they left quickly. Every new incoming fact presented high-level questions for Circa editors. "You have to understand, 'Is this update big enough to change the scope of the story?' Which means that we get a new headline, and we would lead with different information," De Rosa said. "How do you integrate all those updates into the story, and what do you retire from the story? What's no longer part of the current scope of what's happening in the story?"[39]

It was easier for new editors to simply think about news events as being distinct, rather than tied to existing stories. It took a much longer view of news stories and a better knowledge of Circa's branch system to see events as developments in larger story arcs, but once they did, the difference was striking. "I just remember at the time, just kind of having my mind blown, of 'I have to stop thinking about stories in this way.' You have to begin to see this new way of compiling information," recalled one editor, Abraham Hyatt, after Circa had shut down. "That's the gist of what being a Circa reporter or editor was, was figuring that out."[40]

"Figuring that out" meant looking at stories almost exclusively at the meso narrative level, as part of that larger narrative arc. Circa editors used the terms "push the story forward" or "drive the story forward" to describe news facts that contributed substantially to a story arc. The question of how much a new fact pushed the story forward drove the decision of whether to write an update, but also, in a more fine-grained way, whether to send out a silent update or push notification, to republish or "pwn" a story. Circa editors needed to have finely tuned senses of just how much each fact moved a story forward and in which direction.

That sense was oriented around action. For Circa, almost all of the facts that constituted a story and drove it forward were events. The corollary question to "Does this drive the story forward?" was, according to editor Ted Trautman, "Did something really happen?" He added, "I guess that's kind of vague, but we definitely try to avoid stories like, 'This might happen soon.' "[41] In many cases, this ruled out speech itself as an event, unless the speaker had the political power to enact the course of which they speak, in which case speech could become action worthy of a story update. "It doesn't add anything if generic congressman says something about something," explained Evan Buxbaum. "But if you go to, like, a peace talk or the Iran nuclear conversation, there's people, their status affords them—whatever they say becomes the news, right?"[42] Quite naturally, this tended to lead Circa toward official sources—and beyond that, a subset of official sources with significant individual power.

This orientation toward events was at work in the Muslim "no-go zones" example at the beginning of the chapter. Bobby Jindal, a sitting U.S. governor and likely presidential candidate, had made some controversial and traditionally newsworthy comments by defending the existence of a false Islamophobic conspiracy theory. But for Circa, it wasn't clear whether it drove a story forward, or what story it could drive forward in the first place. The Paris mayor's threat to sue Fox News was only speech, too, and it stretched the "this might happen soon" standard of newsworthiness, but, crucially, it could be tied to action, and that's what set it apart from Jindal's statements.

Journalists' focus on events as the core elements for structuring stories and organizing reality for their audiences is nothing new, of course. For decades, scholars have pointed out journalists' tendency to build stories around events even if they aren't a ready fit, something journalists have often referred to themselves as "finding a news peg."[43] But even beyond this focus, Circa's fixation on events was distinct. To feed its atomized story structure, Circa needed small, discrete "points," and those points needed to advance a larger story in a tangible way. If something didn't check those boxes, it wasn't news in Circa's eyes. Circa's narrative structure was shifting the way it represented and even viewed the world, moving its focus further toward the concrete and the isolable.

Circa's distinct way of seeing the news—its meso-level map of ongoing news stories through its branch system in Trello, its rigid focus on events that drove those news stories forward—wasn't necessarily part of its purpose. The purpose of its atomized, follow-based structure was to save readers time by making the news more efficient for them. The idea that Circa could also use this structure to present a more longitudinal view of news was more of a byproduct, a function of the way its editors had to envision and organize news in order to feed the structure they had built.[44] That way of seeing each news event as part of a broader story that evolved through time became the most intriguing element of Circa for editors like Trautman:

> If you pick up a traditional newspaper, you might see, "Oh, this happened," and in spite of a little bit of explanation in the article, you don't really get the sense of where it really has been. And I think from Circa, when we are succeeding, what we're doing is presenting a given event as part of a larger chain of events, rather than just something that came out of nowhere.[45]

This longitudinal perspective added a key criterion to a story's news value: the likelihood that it would be updated over time. That factor helped drive decisions about whether certain events would become stories, such as when De Rosa encountered a *New York Times* investigative piece on animal abuse at a publicly funded Nebraska meat research center.[46] A 5,500-word report on the inner workings of an obscure organization didn't appear to mesh well with Circa's breaking-news approach to national and global significance. But when De Rosa explained why he chose to begin a new story based on it, he named as his second criterion (after the fact that it was federally funded animal abuse) the likelihood that the story would have an interesting update because of a government response to public outcry.[47] Given Circa's reliance on the follow feature, a one-off story with no follow-ups was essentially useless. The only real stories for Circa were the ones that continued over time or at least showed a real possibility for it.

With this news value came a specialized skill for Circa editors—the ability to anticipate whether a news event would spur future update-worthy news events and what form those events might take. It proved helpful in avoiding one-off stories and in understanding where to place a particular update. Circa editor Adrian Arizmendi gave an example of the usefulness of this skill in his decision of what to do with the 2015 brinksmanship surrounding the U.S. congressional Republicans' threat to defund the Department of Homeland Security over President Barack Obama's executive actions loosening immigration restrictions. As the conflict about the threat began to escalate, Arizmendi had to decide whether to keep it within the story on the immigration executive actions or branch it into its own separate story.

> I thought about it, and I thought about patterns that have come up in the past, and had to think about the way sort of these things develop over time, and I made the call to branch a story. . . . And luckily, I'm glad I did, because it's turned into its own monster, with its own questions and its own players and its own everything, and its own timeline. And I feel like had we kept that story with the immigration storyline, some of the core points or elements or units of the immigration storyline could have been lost.[48]

A major part of Arizmendi's consideration of the nature of the Republicans' funding threat as a news story was its expected arc over time—that is, in the future, not simply in the past. Virtually every reporter writes her stories with a sense in the back of her mind of where that story might be headed; this is part of the "narrative emplotment" that helps journalists see their stories as stories in the first place. But at Circa, the longitudinal emphasis was so important that this judgment of a story's expected arc became a deeply embedded skill that dictated coverage decisions on a daily basis.

The encompassing importance of meso-level narrative arcs for Circa meant that its editors evaluated every news event not only in a temporal dimension but also in a "spatial" dimension of its relationship to other related stories. Like the temporal dimension, the spatial dimension was ingrained in Circa's sense of newsworthiness. For most journalists, something becomes news when they can look at it and say, "Aha, that's a *story*!"[49] But for Circa editors, an event often didn't become news until they could say, "Aha, that's part of *this* story!"

This, too, was rooted in Circa's branch system, which led its editors to consider new events as part of an ecology of news narratives rather than narratives in themselves. "When there's a new piece of information that comes in, I'm trying to think of where that goes in our general coverage, rather than thinking of things as they're individual stories," said Circa senior editor Daniel Bentley.[50] This could be difficult to do in practice, especially for new editors. The branch system in Trello made things simpler, but because there was no central listing encompassing all the branches, it was also easy to miss an existing story because it was listed in a different area than an editor expected.

Circa editors were willing to begin new stories for any event that seemed genuinely new, even if it was related to another story (provided, of course, that it was likely to be updated in the future). But just as in the Bobby Jindal example that opened this chapter, it was more difficult to see the news value in an event that didn't tie into an existing story. It didn't make much sense to De Rosa and Arizmendi to develop an entirely new "Jindal 2016" story just to create a container to put his comments on Muslim "no-go zones." But if that story had already existed, it would have been easy to drop that comment in as a point or two near the bottom of the story and perhaps send it out as a silent update. The form of the narrative made (or unmade) the news of Jindal's comments.

To its users, Circa was about taking the traditional news story and making it smaller. Instead of showing users a full article, most of which was filled with information they had already seen, Circa would break the story down its smallest possible units and feed its users these 300-character atoms. By breaking it down like this, Circa could show users only the pieces of information they hadn't seen; that, Circa said, was what would save them time and frustration. But to its journalists, Circa's atomization of news only broadened that news. By requiring each new piece of information to fit into a complex map of ever-evolving news topics, Circa took the meso-level narrative arcs that operate in the back of every journalist's mind and moved them to the front. The result was a conception of the world of news that was more holistic, more integrated, and more systematically organized. It was a world where, in stark contrast to Robert Park's classic complaint about the news providing an ephemeral view of events,[51] every event's foremost quality was its connection to the past and future. It was a news system with blind spots and force-fits, where events without that connection could get lost, where oversights in past coverage could easily compound by making new developments harder to place. But Circa did more than break the news article into chunks; it pushed its journalists into a new way of seeing news as narrative, one that provided fresh perspectives on the chaotic jumble of the world's events.

In June 2015, less than three years after it launched and only four years after Ben Huh's original blog post, Circa shut down, having run so low on money that it couldn't make payroll.[52] As a business venture it was a failure. It was a venture capital–funded startup that took far too long to seek to generate revenue. It was a consumer app that at heart was more like a reinvented wire service. And it was a product that dramatically limited its audience by largely ignoring social media and the web and sticking mostly to eat-your-vegetables hard news.[53] Circa certainly isn't a resounding endorsement of news audiences' willingness to consume news in nontraditional narrative structures. Indeed, a shift away from news articles toward a string of 300-character nuggets added over time may have been too large of a divergence from the news many consumers were used to. But it would be hasty to conclude based on Circa's demise that a structured or atomized news form is necessarily unpalatable for audiences. Circa was only the first full-fledged effort at such a form, and it is certainly conceivable that a more sophisticated or fully realized structured-data form could capture its narrative potential while satisfying audiences' need for structural familiarity. In any event, Circa's greater significance was in its internal orientation, the way its structure led its journalists to look at news differently—as smaller, structured events that couldn't fully be made sense of unless they were inherently attached to a larger narrative arc. Circa was distinct in the particular way this broadened vision of news was borne out, but in much more informal and unstructured ways, other aggregators I spoke with have also found that their shorter and more incremental news coverage has come with a broader conception of news narrative beyond the individual story.

BUILDING AUTHORITY THROUGH
NARRATIVE EXPANSION

For the aggregators beyond Circa, the shift to a meso-level under-standing of their stories' narrative was fundamentally a solution to an authority problem. These aggregators were consistently, as an inherent condition of their work, arriving late to stories and further removed from the information in it than some other news source. They worked hard to keep that lateness and distance as minimal as possible, but in most cases it was the inevitable product of relying on published sources to build news accounts. This chipped away at their authority in presenting the news; they were linking to other sources that had already presented it more authoritatively than they could, by virtue of their having reported it first and through more direct means. There were economic effects of this derivativeness as well. It was difficult to draw significant traffic to an aggregated version of the story when the original was already making the rounds on social media and topping search results, especially since Google News' algorithms have long sought to determine and prioritize the original source of a story in search results.[54] But this problem was downstream from the lack of authority invested in news texts that are based on accounts that other journalists have already published.

One of the ways the aggregators I observed dealt with this prob-lem was to expand the scope of the story until it became something on which they could speak more authoritatively. If the story is narrowly tracking another organization's account, the aggregator's informational and authoritative deficit is easily observable. But if the aggregator can broaden the story beyond that original account, she can bring in other pieces of information as well as some expertise on either the subject matter or the way the story is developing throughout the media eco-system. The goal, then, is to broaden the story until those informational and authoritative disadvantages are blunted or even disappear to the audience. Aggregators often talked about this broadening as adding "context" and saw it as a significant part of their professional value. (Several of them talked about it in close connection with the standard of "adding value" discussed in chapter 3.) This context took on differ-ent dimensions based on the organization, and in some cases those dimensions were a key part of their efforts to professionally distinguish themselves from competitors. SportsPop's professional niche was being keenly aware of what sports conversation (specifically on social media) looked like *right now*.For its journalists, then, the arc of a particular story consisted not so much of the events of that story as it did the amount and characteristics of the online attention to that story. If the story was, say, a performance-enhancing drug scandal involving a prominent athlete, framing an account around the details of the scandal would have been a dead-end for SportsPop: it had no established base of knowledge around the issue, and its authority on the story would be minuscule compared with the organization that first reported those details. But by conceiving the story more broadly as the scandal and public opinion of it as expressed on social media, SportsPop's journalists could move it into their realm of expertise. The fact that people were talking about a story often became the story itself for SportsPop, with social media conversation dominating discussion among writers and editors about the story's development and forming a wrapper around the news events that became an inextricable part of the news narrative.

VidNews made the shift to conceiving a broader narrative arc a more explicit part of its mission. When I visited in 2015, VidNews had built its organizational identity around analyzing media coverage of an event as part of its coverage of the event itself. Its primary goal was to cover news events; it was not a media criticism site like the *Columbia Journalism Review* or *Media Matters for America.* But for VidNews journalists, the story was not strictly the event itself, but the event specifically and consciously as it was filtered through layers of media coverage. One VidNews editor's description of the organization's approach to thinking about narrative is a perfect definition of the broadest type of meso-level news coverage:

> I think to really do the [VidNews] treatment justice, what we need to do is look where this story is coming from and look where it's going. So you have this trajectory of the story. Not just, like, a story arc, but a trajectory of coverage. So we can kind of see who was the first to report this, who picked it up.[55]

Understanding this broader meta-media narrative was where VidNews' editors saw their expertise, and it served as the base on which they sought to build their authority. Across multiple slogans over the years, their branding has emphasized their ability to analyze multiple perspectives and explain the news in context.[56] Note how another VidNews editor described an ideal story for his organization: "Where there's a lot of perspectives, a lot of opinions, and a lot of sources that we can go through and tell people, 'OK, here's what the real story is, this is what all these different sources are saying.' "[57] The ideal story for him was one where the range of perspectives allowed him to take a broad enough narrative angle to assume an authoritative voice in defining and explaining the story.

Aside from Circa's notable exception, this narrative expansion on the meso level did not translate to significant change on the micro level of story form. The aggregators in this study were ambivalent on the whole about traditional story structures and the inverted pyramid in particular. Some emphasized their similarity to historically dominant story forms. "The way I look at curation, it's no different than the Journalism 101 that we all learned when we were in our freshman year of college, where it's, you've got your lead, you've got your transition, you've got your quote. But your quote is someone else's work, essentially," said SportsPop's editor.[58] Even Circa's stories bore a striking resemblance to a classic inverted-pyramid, neutral-tone news narrative when all of its "points" were read together, as a new reader was intended to do.[59] Others, especially at Social Post and Billy Penn, criticized traditional writing styles as dry and stodgy and said they preferred looser and more conversational story structures. "I feel like everyone else is kind of just giving it all away in the beginning because they're leading with the facts rather than emotion," said one Social Post writer.[60] Even these professed deviations from traditional style, though, amounted to a more casual variant of the feature-oriented writing style that has ascended in journalism since the late twentieth century.[61] The ambivalence resembled recent findings by Edson Tandoc, who has noted that while BuzzFeed's journalists said they eschewed the inverted pyramid in favor of more experimentation, they used the format more often than the *New York Times* in one sample.[62] A few aggregators made notable modifications to traditional micro-level story forms, such as the writers at social news sites who saw images and embedded social media posts as part of their main textual narrative, as opposed to being peripheral elements. ("It's like writing and photo editing are merged into one thing," said one.[63]) But this kind of thinking was rare, and on the whole, aggregators' primary intervention into narrative conventions was on the meso level.

Thinking about a news story primarily as part of an arc that spans beyond individual accounts and includes media coverage itself is not wholly new to journalists. When reporters cover, for example, a sub-committee vote on a legislative bill, the story will often be written with the narrative trajectory of the bill's full progress through the legislative process foregrounded. This larger arc, particularly for minor procedural events, is predominantly what gives the individual event its meaning. There is even a routine genre of news story—a "second-day story"— that is written to account for both the journalist's and the audience's knowledge of previous media coverage and takes a broader narrative approach as a result. Research on the interpretive or contextual turn in journalism indicates that journalists have increasingly been structuring their stories around these broader frames, a trend that stretches back to the mid-twentieth century across numerous Western media systems.[64]

There are a couple of key differences that are distinct to aggregators: the first is the nature of the narrative arc, which is often explicitly including media coverage and mediated public sentiment (that is, public opinion drawn from social media). The explicit involvement of mediated coverage and reactions in the basic story arc conceived by journalists and represented in news accounts isn't entirely new, but its prominence is notable in this case. It stems largely from the fact that those media accounts are aggregators' main sources, but it is also a product of a news distribution environment characterized by what Matt Carlson has called "mundane media criticism"—large-scale public commentary that circulates online alongside the story itself, forming an interpretive lens for the consumption of the story.[65] In aggregation, we see a form of news coverage that often explicitly incorporates that interpretive lens into the production and form of the story as well. The second difference is the reason for aggregators' move to narrative breadth: because aggregators are not originating the stories they write, they are typically unable to ini-tiate a meso-level story arc. This places on them an ever-present burden to consider where their own account is arriving within a pre-existing arc, which becomes necessary for them to differentiate themselves from the other news sources who have preceded them in the story's trajectory. Perceiving a story's narrative in broader terms and then presenting that framing in the news text itself thus fills a more urgent need for authority. Without that broader narrative framework, there simply isn't much reason for many aggregators' accounts to be regarded. In their study of Dutch and Belgian narrative journalists, Jan Boesman and Irene Costera Meijer find that they employ broader story angles as a way to distance themselves from repetitive aggregators.[66] But in this study at least, many of those aggregators are also expanding their narrative approach to do virtually the same thing—to distance themselves from a perception of their work as shallow, repetitive, and superfluous.

ANOTHER PATHWAY FOR THE INTERPRETIVE TURN

In Boesman and Costera Meijer's study, one Belgian newspaper journalist summarized the approach to narrative in news by saying, "The more remote you are from the news, the more important your style."[67] This reporter was a narrative journalist who was speaking about writing news without a timely "news peg," but the principle aptly applies to aggregation as well. To the extent that the aggregators I observed were engaging in narrative innovation, it was driven by their distance from the news itself. Their remoteness required them to find new ways to frame their stories in order to maintain a sense that the story was theirs to tell in the first place. If their authority couldn't come from their ability to originate news of important events or deeply explore the issues behind those events through reporting, they needed to shift the story's narrative angle enough for it to fit their distinctive claim to authority.

Researchers have long tied the interpretive turn in journalism to journalists' quest for authority.[68] As journalists have professionalized and sought to monopolize knowledge of the social and political worlds, they have assumed more of the work of defining those worlds by not only describing events in them but also explicitly interpreting the meanings of those events. By pulling that interpretive power away from audiences and political actors, journalists expand their own base of authority. The inverted pyramid connotes authority in other ways—through its assertive tone and a structure that allows journalists to define a precise hierarchy of importance to any set of occurrences.[69] But as journalists' ability to single-handedly define news events as reality have increasingly been questioned since the mid-twentieth century, the implicit authority claimed in the inverted pyramid has given way to a more explicitly interpretive form.

It's in this sense that aggregation's condensation of the news and the growth in longform narrative journalism are part of the same phenomenon. Both represent a shift in the claim to authority from voice-of-God describers and definers to sensemakers and analyzers, as part of the same interpretive turn. On the micro level of narrative, both are hanging onto some aspects of traditional news form and the inverted pyramid while transforming it in opposite ways: narrative journalism is becoming longer and more complex, and aggregation is becoming shorter and simpler. But at the meso level, the narrative shift is remarkably similar: more accounts are being conceived of and explicitly presented as part of larger story arcs that require the journalist to do more of the work of interpretation and contextualization. In more traditional interpretive journalism, this is accomplished through broader time horizons and more analytical explanations of how and why events are occurring.[70] In aggregation, this is done through references to news media coverage and social media discourse around events and, in Circa's case, more structured narratives that organize news stories into larger wholes. Both are fundamentally attempts to assert authority that they cannot easily claim through simple, assertive, descriptive accounts of events. But they are mirror-image versions of the same narrative repositioning.

Circa took a different route to its meso-level shift than the other aggregators I observed. Its divergence from traditional form was much greater at the micro level than any other aggregators, and its conception of stories as part of broader narrative arcs was much more deeply embedded in their thinking about those stories. And unlike the others, its meso-level broadening was driven by the structure it had chosen rather than where its stories fell within the news cycle. But the most significant difference revolved around how to treat news events. For Circa, broadening the narrative vision involved breaking a news story down to only events, which were conceived as news' "atomic unit," then chaining those events together with others to connect them into overarching narrative frameworks. For other aggregators, seeing stories solely as events was insufficient to establish authority. Instead, their narrative expansion involved conceiving of the media coverage and public commentary surrounding the events as being just as inherent to the story as the events themselves. In both cases, aggregators applied a wider-than-usual narrative lens to events to adhere a distinctive stamp of meaning to them. That distinctiveness originated from a form of knowledge they were seeking to claim—knowledge of how complex ongoing stories were developing, in Circa's case, or of how the media or the public were responding to those stories.

Aggregation's narrative latitude is limited. It's built on abbreviation and reducing micro-level form to a minimum, and it's constricted on the meso level as well, because aggregators cannot begin new story arcs but can only build on arcs that others have developed. Still, aggregators are working to use narrative within those restraints to foster a more interpretive approach that can support their authority and professional status as sensemakers of the social world. It's not clear how effective those efforts are; aggregators' authority is so enervated overall that their narrative reframing may only give them a bare minimum to be considered legitimate parts of the journalistic profession. But in Circa's case in particular, the process had value even beyond the strategic dimension. It altered Circa journalists' conception of news itself, encouraging a more holistic, connected view of the realm of current events they covered. Their news units became smaller and smaller, but the news universe they envisioned to create those units only became more expansive and fully integrated.

CHAPTER SIX

Conclusion

Aggregation, Authority, and Uncertainty

The work of aggregation is deeply embedded into journalistic practice. It has been a part of Western journalism for at least 250 years, and it has evolved in countless ways along with the broader journalistic culture. It has been woven into virtually every context of news production and every medium of news distribution, from the nineteenth-century newspaper exchange editor to the twentieth-century broadcast "rip and read" of newspaper headlines to the breezy email newsletter of the 2010s. These practices are widely divergent in their material environments and cultural milieux, but they are all, at bottom, the work of bringing together and repackaging published material for new audiences. The remarkable breadth of this type of work makes it difficult to draw conclusions from any particular sample of aggregation practice. In that spirit, I offer the following assessment cautiously, knowing that it is the product of a body of data that is only a snapshot of an ever-changing practice, a partial glimpse at a wide spectrum of news forms. Still, with some notable exceptions, the observations and accounts given throughout this study can be roughly sketched into a common picture.

Aggregation, as it appears among the journalists in this study, is a fundamentally imitative and secondary practice, one that derives its methods and epistemological warrants from reporting but lacks reporting's proximity to evidence. It is a practice that is continually grasping after the certainty and validity that will always be just out of reach. That foundational inferiority as a form of knowledge work, heightened by the dismal professional discourse around it, leaves aggregation perpetually bereft of professional legitimacy. The work of these aggregators is not fully accepted as journalism largely because it is so reliant on the work of other journalists, and many of the aggregators in this study felt that exclusion acutely, often responding with self-deprecation and defensiveness. That devaluation is compounded by the fact that aggregation is monotonous work that tends to burn out its practitioners quickly, especially if there are minimal professional or organizational rewards attached. The currently prevalent iterations of aggregation are often driven by economic logic that conceives of newswork as content production and audiences as consumers. The result is a practice that can cynically cater to audiences' baser desires in order to efficiently exploit them for clicks and financial gain. Aggregators' professional jurisdiction is consequently so constrained that their efforts to establish and enforce meaningful ethical standards are hampered by a lack of coherence or an insubstantial normative foundation.

The connective component among all of these deficiencies is aggregators' lack of authority. They have difficulty generating it through the knowledge they work to produce, and that deficiency tinges virtually every aspect of their practice. Much of their professional culture is infused with a sense of inferiority that stems from their lack of authority, and many of their practices constitute an attempt to grasp that authority through ethical norms, knowledge of their audiences, or narrative repositioning. A central question in understanding aggregation, then, is why it struggles so mightily to produce authority and what that difficulty might tell us about other forms of newswork.

Matt Carlson outlines three components of journalistic authority: group identity, textual practices, and metadiscourse.[1] Group identity is the means by which journalists understand themselves to be professionals, holding shared values, beliefs, and normative practices, and allowing them to determine who does and does not count as a legitimate knowledge producer. Journalists' professional identity undergirds the normative argument they make for their own social value, an important foundational element of their claim to authority. The values embedded in identity are enacted through textual practices—that is, journalistic discourse—and metadiscourse. The qualities of news texts encompass the conventions such as inverted pyramids and quoting sources that journalists use to perform their authority, as well as the cultural meanings they convey through the content of their accounts. And metadiscourse is the way journalists tell stories about what they do and what it means, supporting the news texts themselves by reinforcing their status as the ones with the authority to produce those texts. All three of these components work against aggregators' ability to generate authority. As we saw in chapter 3, aggregators' often anemic sense of professional identity forms a weak base for their attempts to articulate and enact values and standards for their work. And though aggregators are attempting to broaden the narrative scope of their news texts as I described in chapter 5, they are often limited in the ways they can do so because of the extreme brevity and simplicity of their form.[2] Meanwhile, journalistic metadiscourse has consistently undermined aggregators' authority by denigrating their work as morally and professionally substandard and questioning their status as journalists.

None of these factors, though, are central to aggregation's authority deficit. The two most damaging, group identity and metadiscourse, both follow in part from a fourth component: the practices of *knowledge work.* Carlson describes his model as a complex interplay between factors, and I would submit that knowledge work is an additional component that could be added to this model and that has been pivotal in this particular case. Knowledge work refers to the actual processes of newswork, specifically as they relate to knowledge production. The core practices of knowledge work consist of assembling, verifying and corroborating evidence, determining how that evidence congeals into news facts, and ordering and giving meaning to those facts to create knowledge. Knowledge work is linked with the textual practices Carlson describes, as the knowledge produced through this work is ultimately presented through the particular forms of news texts. News forms also impose on evidence-assembling practices, as journalists' vision of the story they will produce helps direct the ways they conceive of news facts.[3] But knowledge work precedes textual practices; knowledge work assembles the raw materials of news knowledge, and textual practices encode the knowledge into particular forms for presentation.

When it's functioning correctly, knowledge work supports authority by establishing a base for audiences, critics, and other professionals to understand knowledge as having been procedurally validated. In other words, it is the means by which audiences and others can feel confident that what journalists know is appropriately supported by how they know it. It is also enmeshed with the other components in influencing authority. In order to be made visible to other parties, knowledge work must be translated through textual practices and metajournalistic discourse. Since audiences can't see the work directly, they can't know about that work unless it is communicated through the news text itself or the discourse surrounding journalism.

It also plays an important role in sustaining professional identity in two primary ways—through professional mythmaking and epistemological confidence. Knowledge work forms the basis for the ideological myths that solidify a sense of professional distinction built on particular practices, such as the lionization of "shoe-leather reporting" within the journalistic ethos.[4] Journalists use their identity to demarcate the boundaries of their profession, and that process has often relied on the ideological value attached to particular forms of knowledge work, like reporting and the practices that constitute journalistic objectivity.[5] Epistemologically, this work generates certainty for journalists that the knowledge they're producing is valid, just as it does for their audiences. The confidence in the knowledge that these practices—and reporting in particular—produce help form a foundation for professional identity. If journalists are to understand themselves as a group of people with a distinctive claim to expertise in informing the public about current events, it is necessary for them to feel confident in the ability of their work practices to do just that. Matt Carlson rightly stresses the importance of discourse to communicating and maintaining authority; work must be translated through discourse to be performed as authority for other parties. Newswork does not produce authority unilaterally, as journalists might imply when they advocate for restoring the public's trust by simply doing good reporting.[6] But discourse also needs work to stand up behind it in order to properly support authority. Journalistic and metajournalistic discourse that is not built on robust knowledge work will end up feeling hollow, a sort of Potemkin village of journalistic practice.

The derivative nature of aggregation's knowledge work strains each of these relationships in a way that eats away at its authority. It damages aggregators' professional identity, both because they aren't able to participate in the mythology surrounding reporting and because their distance from evidence leaves them more uncertain about their work's efficacy. It constrains their textual practices as well: they may choose to hew to the same narrative forms as the sources on which they're basing their work, but if they do, they compound the unoriginality of their accounts and offer little reason to be seen as definitive. The sense of inferiority around aggregation also makes it difficult to translate through textual practices in a way that signifies authority. The actual work of aggregation is largely absent from the accounts it produces—you are unlikely to read a phrase like, "Through examination of dozens of tweets and Google News results, and close comparison of several media accounts, Social Post has learned . . ." in an aggregated article. There is one primary way aggregators represent their work through textual practices, though—hyperlinking can mirror the quoting conventions in traditional journalistic work and indicate the work aggregators have done in finding and comparing news sources. Hyperlinking thus operates as an important textual conduit for authority from aggregation work, though it is limited in that respect relative to quoting or textual indications of eyewitness observation because of its ambiguity and indirect relationship to the work behind it.[7] Aggregation's secondhand quality has also influenced a good deal of negative metajournalistic discourse, which has formed the backdrop for much of its perceived professional inferiority. All of these factors have combined to give the particular practices of knowledge work within aggregation a central role in eroding the authority of the aggregators in this study.

Knowledge work likely plays a more outsized role in influencing journalistic authority in this case than it might in other areas of journalism. But it's a factor that could be salient in many of those areas: fact-checking, investigative reporting, live blogging and livestreaming, media criticism, and journalists' use of social media to gather and disseminate information, to name just a few. As we consider the authority of various forms of journalism, it's worth adding a pair of questions to our examination: *What are the processes through which knowledge is produced and validated within this phenomenon? How do they reinforce or undermine journalistic authority, particularly in relation to the other components of authority?*

Though it is of course a singular phenomenon, the case of aggregation may also provide some guidance for understanding other forms of knockoff knowledge work in relation to authority and professional status. When the practices of knowledge production are inherently derivative, the functional relationship among the components of authority is set askew. Professional status is sharply curtailed, as those who engage in the original practices being imitated use public discourse to mark off the interlopers as being outside the boundaries of the profession, or at least on its fringes. Knockoff knowledge producers, like other interlopers, are then faced with several options regarding this professional downgrade: they can reject the profession entirely and build an identity based on their lack of professional conformity, they can build alternative professional structures and values (the conservative media ecosystem exhibits characteristics of this approach),[8] or they can fight for scraps of professional status within the field whose work they are drafting off of. The latter approach is the one the aggregators in this study took. But based on this study, at least, the traditional routes to accruing professional status building from an identity as members of a respected community of practitioners appear to be largely unavailable to producers of knockoff knowledge.

HOW AGGREGATION'S AUTHORITY IS BUILT

Aggregation's authority is certainly weakened by the breakdown of knowledge work and professional status, but it is not precluded altogether. Other knockoff knowledge producers find ways of bolstering their own authority that are ultimately destructive rather than additive. Conspiracy theorists and many in conservative and populist media spend a good deal of energy trying to tear down the authority of more established information sources in order to establish their own authority in opposition to them. The publishers of predatory academic journals and false news instead draft off the authority of the forms they imitate, relying on deception to allow the authority to transfer onto them. But the aggregators in this study are jostling for authority through many of same strategies as other journalists who are closer to the center of the profession in a way that doesn't diminish those journalists' authority but simply attempts to make room under its penumbra.

It's not hard to see the seeds that some of the aggregators I examined have planted for the growth of their own authority. These aggregators have built their practices on such similar strata to reporting that the two are frequently difficult to distinguish. They care deeply about producing accurate, engaging, and useful news, and they're eager to communicate those goals to others. They're socialized, formally and informally, into professional journalistic values, and they aim to abide by the same ethical standards as the rest of their profession. And in large part, they do. These aggregators deeply desire to be accepted by other journalists as professional equals and to be valued by their audiences, and they want to achieve both of those things by doing excellent work. They have adapted newsgathering techniques to a torrent of online information in novel ways, and they have modified traditional narrative forms in hopes of distinguishing themselves and helping audiences making sense of that informational rush. Even amid aggregation's rickety epistemological and professional foundations, there is still a means for authority to be constructed through viable knowledge work and meaningful professional identity. The question, then, is under what conditions this picture of aggregation emerges and aggregators may be able to accrue authority.

First, aggregation becomes more conducive to building authority when its work becomes more epistemologically viable. We saw this in cases where aggregation incorporated elements that have more traditionally been the domain of reporting, such as interviews that go beyond a simple confirmatory phone call and more extensive use of documents to corroborate and verify accounts. Aggregators also moved toward this with their use of technologically mediated forms of presence, such as watching live streams of news events and press conferences. This presence is limited and doesn't match the information-gathering capacity or authoritative weight of physical presence, but it is effective in reducing distance from the evidence aggregators use. It's also helpful when aggregators work in fields where certainty about the events that transpire is high, because those events are broadcast to audiences or followed by hordes of reporters. This applied to SportsPop when it covered major sports leagues that received a glut of reported coverage. "With the NFL in particular, every story is covered by everyone," said one SportsPop writer. "So there's very little [that's] a bad source in the NFL."[9] These environments, of course, make it more difficult for aggregators to distinguish their own work enough to be listened to above the din, but they're helpful in establishing certainty within the work they do.

Second, aggregation's capability for authority is closely tied to the professional value that is invested in it and its ability to root a strong sense of professional identity in that value. This value could be manifested through more positive metajournalistic discourse about aggregation, though we have yet to see enough of that to weigh its impact. Instead, differences in professional identity among the aggregators in this study appeared to be more closely tied to the degree to which their organizations valued their work and the organizations themselves enjoyed professional status. In organizations that valued aggregation as a professional activity in itself or as a useful task to combine with reporting, aggregators tended to exhibit a stronger sense of identity and shared more directly in their organizations' authority. This dynamic was accentuated in organizations that enjoyed heightened professional status. The *New York Times* is a good example of this phenomenon: Its journalists rotate through aggregation and breaking-news jobs regularly, with that work seen as a valuable complement to more traditional reporting work and useful experience for other positions in the newsroom. Its aggregators also draw substantial professional identity from the *Times'* lofty reputation. But less revered organizations can take other routes to developing this identity as well. Circa's work consisted almost exclusively of aggregation, but its journalists drew their identity from the technological and narrative innovation that was woven into that aggregation. Professional identity has long been criticized by scholars as a restrictive force in journalism—a tool for management to control employees' behavior or a shield journalists use against the public's involvement in their work and the necessary evolution of their practices.[10] Those assessments are valid. But in this case, a more robust professional identity was a liberating factor, serving as a pathway to stronger practice and greater satisfaction in aggregators' work.

Third, aggregation's potential for authority is greater when the commercial influence on it is lesser. When commercial logic is dominant over the logic of public service, it acts as an encompassing pressure pushing against authority, constraining the development of all of the components that produce it. In aggregation's case, a prevailing commercial logic erodes professional status and identity by superseding many of the norms and values that form the base for professionalism. It also constricts knowledge work through an emphasis on speed and sensationalism. Additionally, by encouraging an algorithmic aloofness toward the audience, it limits the parameters for a relationship with the audience through which authority might be built. This commercial influence hovered over much of the aggregation in this study like a heavy fog, stifling its efforts to accrue authority at every turn. There were no sites where it was absent, but at Billy Penn the focus on events rather than advertising as its main revenue source helped suppress commercial logic in journalists' routinized work contexts. The site's model pushed its journalists to view its audience as a community to build relationships with. Accordingly, they viewed aggregation as a complement to enterprise reporting to fill in the audience's information gaps, rather than a treadmill of production for production's sake. There remain few prominent examples of aggregation relatively untethered to commercial interests, but given the inverse relationship between commercial influence and authority-producing factors in this study, less commercialized forms of aggregation stand a greater chance of developing authority.[11]

Fourth, aggregators can gain more authority when their values and ethical standards are articulated and followed. Both the articulation and the enactment are necessary for the standards and values to produce authority. They must be articulated because of authority's relational nature—they have to be understood and recognized by others within the professional field as well as the public in order to derive authority from those realms. And they must be enacted because just like with knowledge work, discourse that is not supported by practice forms a hollow basis for authority. These standards are a link between group identity and knowledge work, as group identity gives them the weight they need to hold sway and improve work practices.

The final factor is secondary, but it can become more important in particular cases or situations. Aggregation can be aided by a distinct narrative framing that repositions its textual practices to allow for greater authority. Many aggregators did this by using references to other media or social media texts in order to broaden the narrative arc and set themselves up as sensemakers. Circa used this method more dramatically by re-envisioning the basic format of the news article and thus positioning itself as an arbiter to its audience of the broader structure of events as news stories, not to mention developing legitimacy within the field as an innovator. This narrative repositioning is a textual practice that may be particularly useful for aggregators, though it is a variant of the interpretive turn through which journalists have pursued authority for decades.

These avenues to authority for aggregators are deeply interrelated. Improving the viability of knowledge work bolsters professional identity, which provides crucial support for values and standards to be upheld, which in turn improves the practices of knowledge work. When functioning properly, these factors produce a sort of virtuous cycle that continues to reinforce them and strengthens journalists' case for authority as it does so. But their interconnectedness also contributes to their fragility: substantially weaken one element, and the whole cycle starts to break apart. Commercial logic is a corrosive influence across virtually all of them, constraining each relationship in the cycle. Aggregators are operating in a media environment in which commercial logic is often predominant and authority for journalists as a whole is already tenuous. Their challenges within that environment are compounded by the nature of their work and the derisive metajournalistic discourse around it. Yet to the extent that more authoritative, respected, and valued aggregation is possible, it is the collective strengthening of these factors that will bring it about.

AGGREGATION AS UNCERTAINTY ACCOMMODATION

One of the most fundamental elements of our political and cultural age that defines aggregation as a form is epistemological uncertainty. Creators of deliberately false news stories have used the decentralized structures of social media to disseminate deception and sow discord and confusion. False news has exploited the credulity with which many people absorb new information and left behind a trail of disillusionment and skepticism.[12] Meanwhile, cynical, politically motivated cries of "Fake news!" led by President Donald Trump and taken up by authoritarian leaders and millions in extremist movements worldwide have emboldened opponents of establishment news sources to disregard news that doesn't reinforce their beliefs without even examining it. Both have contributed to a declining trust in the ability of professional journalists to provide accurate and credible information. Trust in media is near an all-time low in many parts of the world, paralleling a decline in trust in institutions overall—though it's possible that the slight uptick in media trust shown in the late 2010s could reflect some pushback against these forces.[13] Meanwhile, Trump, along with some ascendant politicians in Western Europe—often populist and reactionary—have displayed a kind of open mendacity that is virtually without precedent in modern political times.[14] The widely attested science on climate change, vaccination, and genetically modified food has been undermined by misleading and often disingenuous skepticism, turning scientific consensus into wide-open matters of public debate. We are flooded with exponentially more information than ever, but our certainty about the reliability of any of that information has plummeted.[15]

Apropos of the age in which it has taken root, contemporary digitally based news aggregation is also defined by its uncertainty. Aggregation is a response to this glut of information, an attempt to pull coherence out of it and to direct attention within it. But it does so at a remove from the sources of evidence that form the basis for much of that information. It's a way of absorbing as much of that information as possible, of making sense of it (with varying degrees of success), but without getting deep enough into individual pieces of that information to be sure of their validity. At worst, it merely adds to the glut of information, compounding confusion. At its best, it imposes some order and sense on that information, but rarely does it add certainty to that information.

That stands in contrast to reporting, which has historically presented itself as a knowledge-generating machine—a method whose purpose is to produce indubitable, authoritative accounts of current events. The reported news article is its own assurance of the validity of the methods used to gather the information in it, as reporters obliquely indicate how they acquired information as they present it as authoritative fact. For decades, the form of news articles themselves—terse, impersonal, loaded with facts and organized around immediacy rather than narrative arc—was itself a sort of seal of the certainty of the article's contents.[16] That certainty in the authority of reporting has been eroded for half a century. In the United States during the 1960s and 1970s, the concerted misinformation reported as fact throughout the Vietnam War began to chip away at both journalists' and the public's certitude about the information reported through the news media. Conservative leaders' decades-long effort to discredit the "mainstream media," which began around the same time, had the same effect.[17] Meanwhile, the media sociologists of the 1970s and 1980s, particularly Gaye Tuchman, exposed the limitations of reporting in a more systematic way. They revealed a practice that is beset with uncertainty but elides it by relying on official accounts and the conventions of objectivity, such as quoting and the neutral, fact-packed structure of the inverted pyramid.[18]

Our current age of epistemological uncertainty has extended those challenges to the validity of information produced by reporting. It has deepened the mistrust of journalists as conduits of reliable information and fractured any public perception that existed of the reporting process as a vouchsafe for that reliability. The declaration of "fake news" has taken the longstanding "media bias" critique to an absurd extreme. Where complaints of bias characterize news as true in part but distorted in its presentation, the cry of "fake news" proclaims news completely false, its reporting process unable or unwilling to produce even a shred of substantially true information. It has been clear for decades that reporting is an extremely flawed vehicle for knowledge transmission, limited by time, access, organizational structure, and the strictures of routine. Today's political and cultural environment has exposed those flaws and exaggerated them, attempting to strip away journalists' authority through reporting to certify virtually any significant piece of information as incontrovertibly true.

Some journalists have responded to their loss of authority by attempting to reassert the certainty of their work more forcefully or precisely. In the face of pointed doubts and dismissal of its reporting by the Trump administration and conservatives, CNN launched an ad campaign in late 2017 typifying this sort of defiance. The ad depicted a red apple with a voiceover saying: "This is an apple. Some people might try to tell you that it's a banana. They might scream 'Banana, banana, banana,' over and over and over again. They might put 'BANANA' in all caps. You might even start to believe that this is a banana. But it's not. This is an apple." The ad closed with the words "Facts First" and a CNN logo.[19] CNN's campaign was an assertion of an absolutely certain, epistemologically untroubled view of its reporting. The news it reported was as simple, irrefutable, and self-evidently true as calling an apple an apple. There were no complexities or ambiguities to the core information it broadcast: reporting was a process of producing pure, incontrovertible facts.

CNN journalists' own view of their work is surely not so simplistic; the ad was a rhetorical response to unprecedentedly brazen attacks on the truthfulness of its reporting. But it exemplifies a more muscular certainty in the process and product of reporting, something that has driven other recent movements within journalism as well. In particular, fact-checking and data journalism are both meant to reassert a stronger sense of the certainty of journalism, and both build that assertion on a process modeled after that of science. In *Deciding What's True*, his study of fact-checking in journalism, Lucas Graves explains how fact-checking has emerged as a response to challenges and revisions to the journalistic objectivity norm in recent decades, one that leans on social science's principles of transparency and reproducibility as well as a more interpretive approach. The result is a form of journalism that makes more robust truth claims than previous practices while re-institutionalizing objectivity in new ways.[20] Likewise, C. W. Anderson's genealogy of data journalism, *Apostles of Certainty*, traces journalism's history of borrowing from the techniques and epistemological paradigms of social science, culminating in a form of data journalism that manages its uncertainty through precision and quasi-scientific processes.[21] As Graves and Anderson document, both forms of journalism are more self-aware and careful than the almost cavalier confidence many of their predecessors showed in journalistic objectivity nearly a century ago. But their core posture is one that defies, and belies, the uncertainty that has surrounded journalism since then. Anderson's warning of this reassertion of certainty rings true:

> The trouble lies when the rhetoric of scientific certainty is only embraced halfway; science is, in the end, a discipline of uncertainty and even humility. It is not a becoming posture for a more methodologically uncertain, provisional, off-the-cuff intellectual discipline like journalism to proclaim itself more scientific than science itself.[22]

Aggregation takes a dramatically different approach to uncertainty. Instead of fighting it, aggregation accommodates it. This might not seem evident from the sometimes overblown headlines atop aggregated articles, but aggregation's continual attunement to its uncertainty is primarily expressed in its knowledge work, more so than its textual practices.[23] The knowledge aggregation creates is provisional and incremental; it is rarely able to make any claims to be definitive. Aggregators' information comes secondhand, and the paths that information takes to be asserted as knowledge are circuitous. Aggregation is in a way a deliberative process, a means of responding to and building on the claims of other journalists. It implies a willingness to accept the claims and accounts of others as legitimate. The act of aggregation itself is an acknowledgement that there is another account that is at least as authoritative, if not more so, than one's own. In the immediate sense, this curtails the aggregator's own authority, and it also renders her work more unstable. If the original becomes less certain—a competing account emerges or the credibility of its source is questioned—then the aggregators' own certainty has to be revised downward. An aggregated news story is rather like a toy block near the top of a stack being built by a child: the more accounts it's stacked on top of, the more opportunities there are for a slight jostling near the bottom to cause it to fall. Aggregators recognize this, and their work continually accounts for this uncertainty accordingly.

This is not, of course, an encouraging analogy for the quality of news produced by aggregation. But this more intrinsic acknowledgement of uncertainty is a more tenable approach for journalism than a full-throated assertion of certainty in a world that simply doesn't accept that certainty anymore. I echo Anderson's call for "a more humble, provisional, and uncertain journalism" that uses "the open acknowledgement of the unknown as a spur to gain further (always provisional) knowledge."[24] Journalists should continue to do all they can to seek certainty about the information they gather, but at the same time, perhaps they should also produce and present news in light of an acceptance that uncertainty is likely to be a more prominent and permanent feature of the news environment going forward. Aggregation is clearly uneven in its ability to produce certain and reliable information, but it does model a more humble and provisional approach to knowledge than many journalists are used to working with. If we pair this epistemological humility with aggregation that pursues certainty through the most rigorous newsgathering and verification practices, we may have a fledgling model of one way to adapt journalistic practice to this radically uncertain age.

BRIDGING NEWS PRODUCTION AND CIRCULATION

The work of aggregation is at the same time some of the oldest and most quickly changing in journalism. Accordingly, this book has been an effort to integrate a close study of contemporary aggregation practices and their professional and cultural milieu with a few of journalism's enduring questions: How do journalists know what's true? How do they represent that knowledge to the public and make the case for their ability to determine it? What happens if others—within journalism or outside of it—don't buy that argument? We started in the introduction by pulling back to view the concepts that underlie those questions, establishing that journalism's epistemological practices and its professional identity work together to support its claims to authority. A look at aggregation's history showed that it is deeply entrenched in journalism but also, in its most recent incarnation, often subject to an encompassing and constraining commercial logic.

We then looked more closely at the nature of aggregation as a practice of knowledge production, and in doing so, found one of the roots of aggregators' difficulty in developing authority: The secondary nature of their work relative to reporting and the additional distance from the evidence on which they rely. Chapter 1 explored the relationship between aggregation and reporting and the ways in which aggregators often seek to gather evidence of reporting as another form of evidence-gathering, putting them at a further remove from the information about which they write. This can engender a good deal of epistemological uncertainty, and chapter 2 examined aggregators' means of mitigating and managing that uncertainty. Aggregators use technological tools to achieve a sense of reportorial presence and reduce their distance from the events they cover. They also use compressed versions of reportorial techniques, such as confirmatory phone calls, to negotiate the need for verification with the demand for speed, while giving their work the sheen of reporting.

Aggregators' secondariness to the work of reporting plays an important role in weakening their authority, not only through the uncertainty about the credibility of the information they produce, but also by diminishing their professional status and identity. This was the focus of chapter 3. Aggregators are often a young, precariously employed workforce whose work can be monotonous and tends to be assigned little value by their fellow journalists. The conditions of their work, combined with its secondary nature and the derisive professional discourse that surrounds it, produce a deep sense of professional inferiority among many aggregators that undermines their own authority as well as efforts to improve their work. There are factors working against this inferiority, though: a strong organizational identity in some cases, as well as a nascent set of ethical values that allow aggregators to articulate the value of their work and establish some professional boundaries around it.

Some of those values relate to aggregators' treatment of their audiences, which was the relationship we explored in chapter 4. It is in this relationship that the commercial forces driving much of aggregation take greatest hold, as its common click-based economic structure encourages a thinly quantified vision of the audience and a drive to pander to those audiences' desires and behaviors. The norm proscribing clickbait has been erected as a professional safeguard against the more cynical versions of these impulses, but the ambiguity surrounding its values leaves it too incoherent to have much power. Finally, chapter 5 examined one of the ways aggregators are extending journalism's horizons, through their reconceptualization of news narrative. Even as aggregators break news narrative down into smaller, more granulated pieces, the secondary nature of their work pushes them to conceive of news stories more fully as a broader arc across individual texts and events. This allows aggregators to distinguish themselves as providers of commentary and context, or, in the case of Circa, to find new ways to structure news stories to aid audiences' understanding. Across this examination of aggregation, we see a journalistic practice whose secondary epistemological nature and professional insecurity make for a weak foundation for cultural authority. But we also see the seeds of professional assertion, of innovation in knowledge production and news form, that may help some types of aggregation grow into professionally valued and socially useful journalistic practices.

There is still much we don't know about aggregation, especially as its practices and the surrounding digital news environment continue to change. Our knowledge of aggregation could be deepened with a more precise breakdown of the evidence constituting news reports—reported, aggregated, or in combination. Further analysis could then connect that evidence to the processes that gathered and verified it, building on the work of Yigal Godler and Zvi Reich, who have been to analyze the practice of verification this way.[25] We also have much to learn about how audiences experience aggregation—what role it plays within their media repertoires, how they weigh the evidence presented in it, and what factors influence the credibility they give it. As we begin to understand how aggregated work is interacted with and perceived by the people for whom it is intended, we move toward the realm of news circulation, where we might find particularly significant insight into the role of aggregation in contemporary news ecosystems.

This book, along with much of the journalism studies research conducted over the past two decades, has focused on the production of news. But in an era defined by an abundance of information (and misinformation) and its rapid spread through digital channels and communities, questions regarding news circulation are becoming increasingly central. We find ourselves asking these questions each time we encounter a viral news story or conspiracy theory, or ascendant political theme: Where did this information or idea originate? How did it find its way into so many media channels and conversations? What networks did it travel through? How did it evolve from its original form to the one it's in now, and what sort of meanings has it picked up along the way? These are questions regarding circulation, but they also edge into questions of production. That's because the circulation process is, in many ways, becoming the production process, as news is produced through the rapid accretion of information while it circulates among networks of people on social media and in online communities.

The study of news aggregation offers a key point of connection between news production and circulation. It is the process of that information accretion, a practice through which published news is added onto, reshaped, or stripped down, and its meanings reinterpreted or reinforced. News is continually remade each time it is repackaged or recharacterized throughout its circulation. This is the peril of aggregation as productive circulation, as we saw in the opening example of this book: Cameron Harris' haphazard fabrication of a news story of thousands of fraudulent votes continued to metastasize after it had been debunked, as credulous aggregators repackaged its claims for new audiences. But in an era in which news is defined by the meanings it takes on as it evolves along its path through various audiences and platforms, this is also aggregation's potential. It is a chance, however rarely realized, for news to be clarified and distilled at each step.

Notes

INTRODUCTION: UNDERSTANDING AGGREGATION IN CONTEXT

1. Scott Shane, "From Headline to Photograph, a Fake News Masterpiece," *New York Times*, Jan. 18, 2017, https://www.nytimes.com/2017/01/18/us/fake-news-hillary-clinton-cameron-harris.html?_r=0. The description of Harris in the preceding paragraphs is drawn from Shane's article. Harris's article and site have been taken down but have been archived at https://web.archive.org/web/20161001064328/http://christiantimesnewspaper.com/breaking-tens-of-thousands-of-fraudulent-clinton-votes-found-in-ohio-warehouse/.

2. Bill Mitchell (@mitchellvii), "Is this story real? Were these merely sample ballots to show 'how to vote'? What is this about? No idea." *Twitter*, Sept. 30, 2016, 1:00 p.m., https://twitter.com/mitchellvii/status/781946741503459328.

3. "Breaking: Fraudulent Clinton Votes Discovered by the 'Tens of Thousands,'" *I Love My Freedom*, Sept. 30, 2016, https://ilovemyfreedom.org/breaking-fraudulent-clinton-votes-discovered-tens-thousands/; Ray Starmann, "BREAKING: 'Tens of Thousands' of Fraudulent Clinton Votes Found in Ohio Warehouse," *US Defense Watch*, Sept. 30, 2016, http://usdefensewatch.com/2016/09/breaking-tens-of-thousands-of-fraudulent-clinton-votes-found-in-ohio-warehouse/.

4. Franklin County Board of Elections (press release), Oct. 1, 2016, http://files.constantcontact.com/b01249ec501/58eeb35a-7d61-4807-b168-765d27ca11cf.pdf.

5. Dan Evon, "Ballot Bluffing," *Snopes*, Sept. 30, 2016, http://www.snopes.com/clinton-votes-found-in-warehouse/.

6. Pamela Geller, "'Tens of Thousands' of Fraudulent Clinton Votes Found in Ohio Warehouse UPDATE: Investigation Launched," *Geller Report*, Oct. 1, 2016, https://pamelageller.com/2016/10/tens-of-thousands-of-fraudulent-clinton-votes-found-in-ohio-warehouse.html/.

7. E.g., Elliot Bougis, "Worker Accidentally Stumbles Upon Hidden Warehouse, THOUSANDS Found In Boxes," *Conservative Daily Post*, Oct. 3, 2016, https://conservativedailypost.com/worker-accidentally-stumbles-upon-hidden-warehouse-thousands-found-in-boxes/; David Icke, "'Ten of Thousands' of Fraudulent Clinton Votes Found in Ohio Warehouse," *David Icke* (blog post), Oct. 1, 2016, https://web.archive.org/web/20161021045135/https://www.davidicke.com/article/387457/tens-thousands-fraudulent-clinton-votes-found-ohio-warehouse; Rebel Pharmacist, "'Tens of Thousands' of Fraudulent Clinton Votes Found in Ohio Warehouse," *Awareness Act*, Oct. 2, 2016, http://awarenessact.com/tens-of-thousands-of-fraudulent-clinton-votes-found-in-ohio-warehouse/.

8. Golden State Times, "Thousands of Fraudulent Voter Ballots Have Been Found Marked for Hillary Clinton!!!!" YouTube video, 6:01, Oct. 1, 2016, https://www.youtube.com/watch?v=-8on9JJLoU8; #SeekingTheTruth, "Fake Ballot Slips Found Marked for Hillary Clinton in Columbus, Ohio," YouTube Video, 17:05, Oct. 5, 2016, https://www.youtube.com/watch?v=-Hv31mvOWtc.

9. Franklin County Board of Elections (press release).

10. WSYX/WTTE, "Board of Elections Pushes Back After Article Claiming Filled-Out Ohio Ballots Found," *WACH FOX 57*, Oct. 2, 2016, http://wach.com/news/election/board-of-elections-pushes-back-after-internet-article-claiming-ballots-were-found; "Election Board: Article Alleging Voter Fraud Is Fake," *Columbus Dispatch* (blog), Oct. 1, 2016, http://www.dispatch.com/content/blogs/the-daily-briefing/2016/10/fake-story.html; Rachel Gribble, "Franklin Co. Board of Elections Launches Investigation into 'Fraudulent' Ballots," *WCMH-TV*, Oct. 1, 2016, http://nbc4i.com/2016/10/01/franklin-co-board-of-elections-launches-investigation/.

11. Geller, "'Tens of thousands.'"

12. These numbers are according to the public page view counter on Harris's website, as captured by the Internet Archive Wayback Machine: https://web.archive.org/web/20160101000000*/http://christiantimesnewspaper.com/breaking-tens-of-thousands-of-fraudulent-clinton-votes-found-in-ohio-warehouse/.

13. "'Tens of Thousands' of Fraudulent Clinton Votes Found in Ohio Warehouse: Fake Story," *Global Research*, Oct. 3, 2017, http://www.globalresearch.ca/tens-of-thousands-of-fraudulent-clinton-votes-found-in-ohio-warehouse/5549137. Within a few more days, the post had been updated with a statement declaring the story false, linking to Snopes, and describing the origins of Harris's photo.

14. Martin Armstrong, "Worker Claims to Discover a Warehouse in Ohio Loaded with Ballots for Hillary Already Filled Out," *Armstrong Economics* (blog), Oct. 3, 2016, https://www.armstrongeconomics.com/international-news/north_america /2016-u-s-presidential-election/worker-claims-to-discover-a-warehouse-in -ohio-loaded-with-ballots-for-hillary-already-filled-out/.
15. #SeekingTheTruth, "Fake Ballot Slips Found Marked."
16. For examples of this type of work, see Emily Bell and Taylor Owen, *The Platform Press: How Silicon Valley Reengineered Journalism*, Tow Center for Digital Journalism, March 29, 2017, https://www.cjr.org/tow_center_reports /platform-press-how-silicon-valley-reengineered-journalism.php; Florian Buhl, Elisabeth Günther, and Thorsten Quandt, "Observing the Dynamics of the Online News Ecosystem: News Diffusion Processes among German News Sites," *Journalism Studies* 19, no. 1 (2018): 79–104.
17. Most notably, this definition draws on Kimberley Isbell's definition of an aggregator as a source that "takes information from multiple sources and displays it in a single place." Kimberley Isbell, "The Rise of the News Aggregator: Legal Implications and Best Practices," *Citizen Media Law Project*, Working Paper 2010–10 (2010), https://papers.ssrn.com/sol3/papers.cfm?abstract_id=1670339. See also an early influential definition in Stuart Madnick and Michael Siegel, "Seizing the Opportunity: Exploiting Web Aggregation," *MIS Quarterly Executive* 1, no. 1 (2002): 35–46; and a more recent definition citing Isbell in Angela M. Lee and Hsiang Iris Chyi, "The Rise of Online News Aggregators: Consumption and Competition," *International Journal on Media Management* 17, no. 1 (2015): 3–24.
18. In this study, I refer to news through Mitchell Stephens's definition: "new information about a subject of some public interest that is shared with some portion of the public." Mitchell Stephens, *A History of News: From the Drum to the Satellite*, (New York: Viking, 1988), 9.
19. The documents that reporters rely on have, of course, often been published by corporate or government entities, though often not in a form that is meant to be widely accessible or understandable to the public, unlike the published media and social media sources aggregators work with.
20. E.g., "Josh du Lac Named Editor of General Assignment News Desk," *Washington Post PR Blog* (press release), May 9, 2014, https://www.washingtonpost.com /pr/wp/2014/05/09/josh-du-lac-named-editor-of-general-assignment-news -desk/?utm_term=.29e3f54ba5e9; Margaret Sullivan, "Sweetheart, Get Me Readers," *New York Times*, Feb. 6, 2016, https://www.nytimes.com/2016/02/07/public -editor/new-york-times-express-team-margaret-sullivan-public-editor.html.
21. In academic research, a broader definition for curation has developed that refers more generally to filtering online information flows as both a consumer and producer, though this definition is not specifically news-related and is

relatively disconnected from the professional conversation around aggrega-tion (e.g., Kjerstin Thorson and Chris Wells, "Curated Flows: A Framework for Mapping Media Exposure in the Digital Age," *Communication Theory* 26, no. 3 [2016]: 309–28.).

22. E.g., Maria Popova, "In a New World of Informational Abundance, Content Curation Is a New Kind of Authorship," *Nieman Journalism Lab*, June 10, 2011, www.niemanlab.org/2011/06/maria-popova-in-a-new-world-of-informational -abundance-content-curation-is-a-new-kind-of-authorship/; Erin Scime, "The Content Strategist as Digital Curator," *A List Apart*, Dec. 8, 2009, https://alistapart .com/article/content-strategist-as-digital-curator.

23. Piet Bakker, "Mr. Gates Returns: Curation, Community Management and Other New Roles for Journalists," *Journalism Studies* 15, no. 5 (2014): 596–606; Jeff Jarvis, "Death of the Curator. Long Live the Curator," *BuzzMachine* (blog post), April 23, 2009, http://buzzmachine.com/2009/04/23/death-of-the -curator-long-live-the-curator/. For a more recent example of the term being used as part of a framing of the superiority of human aggregation, see Jack Nicas, "Apple News's Radical Approach: Humans Over Machines," *New York Times*, Oct. 25, 2018, https://www.nytimes.com/2018/10/25/technology/apple -news-humans-algorithms.html. A definition of *curation* as manual and *aggregation* as automated, as some academics have used (Bakker, "Mr. Gates Returns," 596–606; Fiona Martin, "The Case for Curatorial Journalism . . . or, Can You Really Be an Ethical Aggregator?" in *Ethics for Digital Journalists: Emerging Best Practices*, ed. Lawrie Zion and David Craig [New York: Rout-ledge, 2015], 87–102) is unhelpful as well, since so much aggregation work is a hybrid of manual and automated processes that can be difficult to peel apart, especially given the fundamentally human role in designing automated pro-cesses. This kind of binary use of the two terms ignores the complex interplay at work between human and technological actors in any form of aggregation.

24. Mathew Ingram, "It's Not Curation or Aggregation, It's Just How the Internet Works," *Gigaom*, March 13, 2012, https://gigaom.com/2012/03/13/its-not-curation -or-aggregation-its-just-how-the-internet-works/.

25. Sam Kirkland, "Has 'Curate' Replaced 'Aggregate' as the Default Term for Sum-marizing Other People's News?" *Poynter*, Jan. 29, 2014, https://www.poynter .org/reporting-editing/2014/has-curate-replaced-aggregate-as-the-default -term-for-summarizing-other-peoples-news/.

26. Quoted in Piet Bakker, "Aggregation, Content Farms and Huffinization: The Rise of Low-Pay and No-Pay Journalism," *Journalism Practice* 6, nos. 5–6 (2012): 627–37; "How News Happens: A Study of the News Ecosystem of One American City," *Project for Excellence in Journalism* (Washington, DC: Pew

Research Center, 2010), http://www.journalism.org/2010/01/11/how-news
-happens/.

27. Theodora Saridou, Lia-Paschalia Spyridou, and Andreas Veglis, "Churnalism
on the Rise? Assessing Convergence Effects on Editorial Practices," *Digital
Journalism* 5, no. 8 (2017): 1006–24.

28. Nic Newman, Richard Fletcher, Antonis Kalogeropoulos, David A. L. Levy,
and Rasmus Kleis Nielsen, "Reuters Institute Digital News Report 2017," *Reuters Institute for the Study of Journalism* (Oxford, 2017), https://reutersinsti-
tute.politics.ox.ac.uk/sites/default/files/Digital%20News%20Report%202017
%20web_0.pdf, 13; Nic Newman, Richard Fletcher, Antonis Kalogeropoulos,
David A. L. Levy, and Rasmus Kleis Nielsen, "Reuters Institute Digital News
Report 2018," *Reuters Institute for the Study of Journalism* (Oxford, 2018),
http://media.digitalnewsreport.org/wp-content/uploads/2018/06/digital-news
-report-2018.pdf?x89475, 15.

29. C. W. Anderson, *Rebuilding the News: Metropolitan Journalism in the Digital
Age* (Philadelphia, PA: Temple University Press, 2013), 52.

30. Dominic Boyer, *The Life Informatic: Newsmaking in the Digital Era* (Ithaca, NY:
Cornell University Press, 2013), 2.

31. Pablo J. Boczkowski, *News at Work: Imitation in an Age of Information Abun-
dance* (Chicago: University of Chicago Press, 2010); Angela Phillips, "Old
Sources: New Bottles," in *New Media, Old News: Journalism and Democracy in
the Digital Age*, ed. Natalie Fenton (Los Angeles: Sage, 2010): 87–101; Tamara
Witschge, "Transforming Journalistic Practice: A Profession Caught Between
Change and Tradition," in *Rethinking Journalism: Trust and Participation in a
Transformed News Landscape*, ed. Chris Peters and Marcel Broersma (London:
Routledge, 2013): 160–72.

32. Hsiang Iris Chyi, Seth C. Lewis, and Nan Zheng, "Parasite or Partner? Coverage
of Google News in an Era of News Aggregation," *Journalism & Mass Communication Quarterly* 93, no. 4 (2016): 789–815.

33. Alastair Dawber, "Murdoch Blasts Search Engine 'Kleptomaniacs,'" *The Independent*, Oct. 9, 2009, http://www.independent.co.uk/news/media/online
/murdoch-blasts-search-engine-kleptomaniacs-1800569.html; Bill Keller, "All the
Aggregation That's Fit to Aggregate," *New York Times Magazine*, March 10, 2011,
http://www.nytimes.com/2011/03/13/magazine/mag-13lede-t.html; Jane Schulze,
"Google Dubbed Internet Parasite by WSJ Editor," *The Australian*, April 6, 2009,
https://web.archive.org/web/20111016161951/http://www.theaustralian.com.au
/media/google-dubbed-internet-parasite/story-e6frg996-1225696931547.

34. On the connection in journalistic discourse between aggregators and newspapers' struggles, see Chyi, Lewis, and Zheng, "Parasite or Partner?"

35. "American Views: Trust, Media and Democracy." *Gallup/Knight Foundation* (Washington DC, 2018), https://knightfoundation.org/reports/american-views -trust-media-and-democracy, 8. Interestingly, though, a slight majority of Americans—and a larger majority of Democrats, young people, and people of color—said aggregators had had a positive impact on the overall news environment.

36. James Hamblin, "It's Everywhere, the Clickbait," *The Atlantic*, Nov. 11, 2014, https://www.theatlantic.com/entertainment/archive/2014/11/clickbait-what -is/382545/; Sam Sanders, "Upworthy Was One Of The Hottest Sites Ever. You Won't Believe What Happened Next," *All Tech Considered*, NPR, June 20, 2017, http://www.npr.org/sections/alltechconsidered/2017/06/20/533529538/upworthy -was-one-of-the-hottest-sites-ever-you-wont-believe-what-happened-next.

37. Ezra Klein, "How Vox Aggregates," *Vox*, April 13, 2015, https://www.vox.com /2015/4/13/8405999/how-vox-aggregates.

38. Keller, "All the Aggregation"; Bill Keller, "Postscript: Aggregation Aggro," *New York Times* (blog post), March 13, 2011, https://6thfloor.blogs.nytimes .com/2011/03/13/postscript-aggregation-aggro/.

39. Knight Center, "ISOJ 2018—Day 2—Afternoon Sessions" YouTube Video, 4:22:38, April 14, 2018, https://www.youtube.com/watch?v=V901_oZ1tTA.

40. Matthew Powers, "'In Forms that Are Familiar and Yet-to-Be Invented': American Journalism and the Discourse of Technologically Specific Work," *Journal of Communication Inquiry* 36, no. 1 (2012): 24–43.

41. Nikki Usher, *Interactive Journalism: Hackers, Data, and Code* (Urbana: University of Illinois Press, 2016).

42. See, e.g., Sheetal D. Agarwal and Michael L. Barthel, "The Friendly Barbarians: Professional Norms and Work Routines of Online Journalists in the United States," *Journalism* 16, no. 3 (2015): 376–91; Jannie Møller Hartley, "The Online Journalist Between Ideals and Audiences: Towards a (More) Audience-Driven and Source-Detached Journalism?" *Journalism Practice* 7, no. 5 (2013): 572–87; Tim P. Vos and Patrick Ferrucci, "Who Am I? Perceptions of Digital Journalists' Professional Identity," in *The Routledge Handbook of Developments in Digital Journalism Studies*, ed. Scott A. Eldridge II and Bob Franklin (New York: Routledge, 2018), 40–52.

43. For an example of these characteristics at work in conspiracy theories, see Michael J. Wood, "Propagating and Debunking Conspiracy Theories on Twitter During the 2015–2016 Zika Virus Outbreak," *Cyberpsychology, Behavior, and Social Networking* 21, no. 8 (2018): 485–90. For a critical analysis of predatory publishing as mimicry of the academic publishing process, see Kirsten Bell, "'Predatory' Open Access Journals as Parody: Exposing the Limitations of

'Legitimate' Academic Publishing," *TripleC: Communication, Capitalism & Critique* 15, no. 2 (2017): 651–62.

44. Matt Carlson, *Journalistic Authority: Legitimating News in the Digital Era* (New York: Columbia University Press, 2017), 13; see also C. W. Anderson, "Journalism: Expertise, Authority, and Power in Democratic Life," in *The Media and Social Theory*, ed. David Hesmondhalgh and Jason Toynbee (New York: Routledge, 2008), 248–64; Barbie Zelizer, *Covering the Body: The Kennedy Assassination, the Media, and the Shaping of Collective Memory* (Chicago: University of Chicago Press, 1992).

45. Carlson, *Journalistic Authority*; Zelizer, *Covering the Body*.

46. Paul Starr, *The Social Transformation of American Medicine* (New York: Basic Books, 1982); Max Weber, *The Theory of Social and Economic Organization*, trans. A. M. Henderson and Talcott Parsons (New York: Free Press, 1947).

47. Carlson, *Journalistic Authority*, 8. "A right to be listened to" is a quote from H. M. Höpfl, "Power, Authority and Legitimacy," *Human Resource Development International* 2, no. 3 (1999): 217–34.

48. Carlson, *Journalistic Authority*, 7.

49. Höpfl, "Power, Authority and Legitimacy"; Morten Skovsgaard and Peter Bro, "Preference, Principle and Practice: Journalistic Claims for Legitimacy," *Journalism Practice* 5, no. 3 (2011): 319–31; Starr, *The Social Transformation of American Medicine*.

50. Carlson, *Journalistic Authority*; Zelizer, *Covering the Body*; David L. Eason, "On Journalistic Authority: The Janet Cooke Scandal," *Critical Studies in Mass Communication* 3, no. 4 (1986): 429–47.

51. Carlson, *Journalistic Authority*; Tim P. Vos and Ryan J. Thomas, "The Discursive Construction of Journalistic Authority in a Post-Truth Age," *Journalism Studies* 19, no. 13 (2018): 2001–10.

52. Jingrong Tong, "Journalistic Legitimacy Revisited: Collapse or Revival in the Digital Age?" *Digital Journalism* 6, no. 2 (2018): 256–73; Zelizer, *Covering the Body*.

53. Mats Ekström, "Epistemologies of TV Journalism: A Theoretical Framework," *Journalism* 3, no. 3 (2002): 259–82, at 274.

54. This authority over knowledge-producing practices themselves has been characterized as "epistemic authority" in Matt Carlson and Jason T. Peifer, "The Impudence of Being Earnest: Jon Stewart and the Boundaries of Discursive Responsibility," *Journal of Communication* 63, no. 2 (2013): 333–50. See also Anderson, "Journalism."

55. Robert E. Park, "News as a Form of Knowledge: A Chapter in the Sociology of Knowledge," *American Journal of Sociology* 45, no. 5 (1940): 669–86. Park notably characterized the knowledge produced in news as transient, ephemeral, and incomplete.

56. Richard V. Ericson, Patricia M. Baranek, and Janet B. L. Chan, *Visualizing Deviance: A Study of News Organization* (Toronto, Canada: University of Toronto Press, 1987); Mark Fishman, *Manufacturing the News* (Austin: University of Texas Press, 1980); Gaye Tuchman, "Objectivity as Strategic Ritual: An Examination of Newsmen's Notions of Objectivity," *American Journal of Sociology* 77, no. 4 (1972): 660–69; Gaye Tuchman, *Making News: A Study in the Construction of Reality* (New York: Free Press, 1978).

57. Monika Krause, "Reporting and the Transformations of the Journalistic Field: US News Media, 1890–2000," *Media, Culture & Society* 33, no. 1 (2011): 89–104; Erik Neveu, "Revisiting Narrative Journalism as One of the Futures of Journalism," *Journalism Studies* 15, no. 5 (2014): 533–42.

58. Anderson, *Rebuilding the News*; Jay Rosen, "Good Old Fashioned Shoe Leather Reporting," *PressThink* (blog post), April 16, 2015, http://pressthink.org/2015/04/good-old-fashioned-shoe-leather-reporting/.

59. For an explication on the role of observation, interviews, and documents as fundamental objects of reporting, see C. W. Anderson, *Apostles of Certainty: Data Journalism and the Politics of Doubt* (Oxford: Oxford University Press, 2018), 187–92.

60. Anderson, "Journalism"; Carlson, *Journalistic Authority*; Michael Schudson and Chris Anderson, "Objectivity, Professionalism, and Truth Seeking in Journalism," in *The Handbook of Journalism Studies*, ed. Karin Wahl-Jorgensen and Thomas Hanitzsch (New York: Routledge, 2009), 88–101; Weber, *The Theory of Social and Economic Organization*.

61. Abbott refers to this link as jurisdiction. Andrew Abbott, *The System of Professions: An Essay on the Division of Expert Labor* (Chicago: University of Chicago Press, 1988), 20.

62. Seth C. Lewis, "The Tension Between Professional Control and Open Participation: Journalism and Its Boundaries," *Information, Communication & Society* 15, no. 6 (2012): 836–66.

63. Carlson, *Journalistic Authority*.

64. This question was first posed by Everett Hughes, *Men and Their Work* (Glencoe, IL: Free Press, 1958), but it has been applied to journalism by numerous scholars, including Lewis, "The Tension Between Professional Control," Schudson and Anderson, "Objectivity, Professionalism, and Truth Seeking," John Soloski, "News Reporting and Professionalism: Some Constraints on the Reporting of the News," *Media, Culture & Society* 11, no. 2 (1989): 207–28; and Zelizer, *Covering the Body*.

65. Patric Raemy, "Modelling the Constitution of Professional Identity and Its Impact for Journalism Studies" (2019), paper presented at the 2019 International

Communication Association conference, Washington, DC, May 24–28; Jenny Wiik, "Identities Under Construction: Professional Journalism in a Phase of Destabilization," *International Review of Sociology* 19, no. 2 (2009): 351–65.

66. Carlson, *Journalistic Authority*; Timothy E. Cook, *Governing with the News: The News Media as a Political Institution* (Chicago: University of Chicago Press, 1998).

67. Vos and Ferrucci, "Who Am I," 41; Zelizer, *Covering the Body*.

68. Meryl Aldridge, "The Tentative Hell-Raisers: Identity and Mythology in Contemporary UK Press Journalism," *Media, Culture & Society* 20, no. 1 (1998): 109–27.

69. This characterization of professional identity scholarship is borrowed from Merryn Sherwood and Penny O'Donnell, "Once a Journalist, Always a Journalist? Industry Restructure, Job Loss and Professional Identity," *Journalism Studies* 19, no. 7 (2018): 1021–38.

70. David M. Ryfe, *Can Journalism Survive? An Inside Look at American Newsrooms* (Cambridge: Polity, 2012), 19–20. See also Sherwood and O'Donnell, "Once a Journalist, Always a Journalist?" for more on this connection between practice and identity.

71. See Carlson, *Journalistic Authority*, for a thorough and illuminating examination of these factors.

72. See, e.g., Lewis, "The Tension Between Professional Control"; Tong, "Journalistic Legitimacy Revisited"; and Vos and Thomas, "The Discursive Construction of Journalistic Authority."

73. Kevin G. Barnhurst and John Nerone, *The Form of News: A History* (New York: The Guilford Press, 2001); Ellen Gruber Garvey, *Writing with Scissors: American Scrapbooks from the Civil War to the Harlem Renaissance* (Oxford: Oxford University Press, 2013).

74. Richard B. Kielbowicz, "Newsgathering by Printers' Exchanges Before the Telegraph," *Journalism History* 9, no. 2 (1982): 42–48.

75. The Berkman Klein Center for Internet & Society, "Joshua Benton on Journalisms Digital Transition." YouTube Video, 40:58, April 9, 2010, https://www.youtube.com/watch?v=inXaKU6Q7Q4; Meredith L. McGill, *American Literature and the Culture of Reprinting, 1834–1853* (Philadelphia: University of Pennsylvania Press, 2003), 107.

76. Kielbowicz, "Newsgathering by Printers' Exchanges," 47; Robert K. Stewart, "The Exchange System and the Development of American Politics in the 1820s," *American Journalism* 4, no. 1 (1987): 30–42.

77. Garvey, *Writing with Scissors*; Kielbowicz, "Newsgathering by Printers' Exchanges."

78. Anthony Smith, "The Long Road to Objectivity and Back Again: The Kinds of Truth We Get in Journalism," in *Newspaper History: From the Seventeenth Century to the Present Day*, George Boyce, James Curran, and Pauline Wingate (London: Constable, 1978), 153–71; Anthony Smith, *The Newspaper: An International History* (London: Thames & Hudson, 1979), 59.

79. Michael Schudson, *Discovering the News: A Social History of American Newspapers* (New York: Basic Books, 1978).

80. Daniel C. Hallin, "The Passing of the 'High Modernism' of American Journalism," *Journal of Communication* 42, no. 3 (1992): 14–25; Schudson, *Discovering the News*.

81. Johan Jarlbrink, "Mobile/Sedentary: News Work Behind and Beyond the Desk," *Media History* 21, no. 3 (2015): 280–93; Richard L. Kaplan, *Politics and the American Press: The Rise of Objectivity, 1865–1920* (Cambridge: Cambridge University Press, 2002), 107–108.

82. Richard K. Popp, "Information, Industrialization, and the Business of Press Clippings, 1880–1925," *The Journal of American History* 101, no. 2 (2014): 427–53.

83. W. Joseph Campbell, *Yellow Journalism: Puncturing the Myths, Defining the Legacies* (New York: Praeger, 2003), 115. Thanks to Jack Shafer for directing me to these instances.

84. Quoted in David E. Sumner, *The Magazine Century: American Magazines Since 1990* (New York: Peter Lang, 2010), 205.

85. Oswald Garrison Villard, *The Disappearing Daily* (New York: Knopf, 1944), 24. Thanks to Nikki Usher to pointing me to this statement.

86. See, e.g., Walter Gieber, "Across the Desk: A Study of 16 Telegraph Editors," *Journalism Quarterly* 33, no. 4 (1956): 423–32.

87. Justin Lewis, Andrew Williams, and Bob Franklin, "Four Rumours and an Explanation: A Political Economic Account of Journalists' Changing Newsgathering and Reporting Practices," *Journalism Practice* 2, no. 1 (2008): 27–45.

88. Jane B. Singer, "Still Guarding the Gate? The Newspaper Journalist's Role in an On-Line World," *Convergence* 3, no. 1 (1997): 72–89, at 87.

89. Isbell, "The Rise of the News Aggregator." Agence France-Presse and Google settled in 2007. For an example of the amazement and concern among journalists that marked Google News' arrival, see Michael Kinsley, "Computers Go Too Far; Hey—That's My Job You're Automating!" *Washington Post*, Nov. 29, 2002, retrieved from Factiva online database; and Leslie Walker, "Google News, Untouched by Human Hands," *Washington Post*, Sept. 26, 2002, retrieved from Factiva.

90. Kenneth Olmstead, Amy Mitchell, and Tom Rosenstiel, "The Top 25," Pew Research Center, May 9, 2011, http://www.journalism.org/2011/05/09/top-25/; The Pew Research Center for the People & the Press, "Audience Segments in a Changing News Environment," Aug. 17, 2008, Washington, DC.

91. Scott Rosenberg, *Say Everything: How Blogging Began, What It's Becoming, and Why It Matters* (New York: Crown, 2009).

92. Julie Moos, "Romenesko Resigns After 12 Years at Poynter," *Poynter*, Nov. 10, 2011, https://www.poynter.org/news/romenesko-resigns-after-12-years-poynter.

93. Bill Mitchell, "How the Romenesko Years Have Changed Journalism and Poynter," *Poynter*, Aug. 24, 2011, https://www.poynter.org/reporting-editing /2011/romenesko-impact-journalism-poynter/.

94. Rosenberg, *Say Everything*, 174–78.

95. Sydney Ember, "Gawker.com to Shut Down Next Week," *New York Times*, Aug. 18, 2016, https://www.nytimes.com/2016/08/19/business/media/gawkercom-to -shut-down-next-week.html.

96. There are scores of accounts of these developments, but two of the most succinctly useful are C. W. Anderson, Emily Bell, and Clay Shirky, *Post-industrial Journalism: Adapting to the Present*, Tow Center for Digital Journalism (2012), https://academiccommons.columbia.edu/doi/10.7916/D8N01JS7; and Rasmus Kleis Nielsen, "The Business of News," in *The Sage Handbook of Digital Journalism*, ed. Tamara Witschge, C. W. Anderson, David Domingo, and Alfred Hermida (Thousand Oaks, CA: Sage, 2016), 51–67.

97. Caitlin Petre, *The Traffic Factories: Metrics at Chartbeat, Gawker Media, and The New York Times*, Tow Center for Digital Journalism (2015), https:// academiccommons.columbia.edu/doi/10.7916/D80293W1; Edson C. Tandoc Jr., "Journalism Is Twerking? How Web Analytics Is Changing the Process of Gatekeeping," *New Media & Society* 16, no. 4 (2014): 559–75.

98. Bell and Owen, *The Platform Press*.

99. Dean Starkman, "The Hamster Wheel," *Columbia Journalism Review*, Sept./ Oct. 2010, http://archives.cjr.org/cover_story/the_hamster_wheel.php.

100. The observation in this study also includes a visit of a few hours to the *New York Times*, during which I interviewed two staffers, sat in on an editorial meeting, and briefly observed editors at work on its now-defunct aggregation app, NYT Now. I hesitate to describe this study as ethnographic in the traditional sense because, with a week at each field site, it lacks the cultural immersion over time that is the hallmark of ethnographic work. It does, however, bear many of the characteristics outlined by Usher (*Interactive Journalism*, 2016) as *hybrid ethnography*. Usher describes hybrid ethnography as a method that pulls together ethnographic field research and interviews in a structure built around extended case-study comparison as an attempt "to maximize ethnographic observation within a compressed time" (210). Other scholars of journalistic processes have also found that a substantial understanding of the organizational and social conventions and cultural meanings of particular types of newswork can be gained through shorter, more concentrated periods of fieldwork at several sites,

combined with interviews (David Domingo, "Ethnography for New Media Studies: A Field Report of Its Weaknesses and Benefits," Paper presented at the New Research for New Media: Innovative Research Methodologies conference, Minneapolis, MN, 2003, https://pdfs.semanticscholar.org/b4fb/44591fd7eb 156f536ab4104b44efb5d6aeb3.pdf; Karin Wahl-Jorgensen, "News Production, Ethnography, and Power: On the Challenges of Newsroom-centricity," in *The Anthropology of News and Journalism: Global Perspectives*, ed. S. Elizabeth Bird [Bloomington: Indiana University Press, 2010], 21–34.). These short-burst, hybrid techniques are especially helpful for work that is characterized by heavily routinized and repetitive processes, as aggregation is.

I approached data-gathering this way for several reasons, foremost among them a concern for capturing the breadth of an especially varied constellation of practices and social and professional contexts. Aggregation is an extremely wide-ranging form of newswork, and one of my goals in this project was to understand both its unifying characteristics across that range and the substantial ways it varies and reasons for that variance. Hybrid ethnography provided an appropriate approach to doing that, allowing me to select a wide range of practices for study while still achieving some depth in examining several of the cases within that range. The other reasons were related, and more practical: as I sought to capture the range of aggregation practice through multisite observation, I lacked the time and financial resources to engage in lengthy periods of fieldwork at those sites. Even if I had had those resources, access would have been a significant restriction as well. The news organizations I contacted for access to newsroom observation were loath to allow me there for any substantial length of time, and even gaining access for a week often took significant negotiation. Through hybrid ethnography, I was able to achieve some depth despite these limitations, as well as substantial breadth provided by the combination of observation-based fieldwork with interviews from within and outside of the organizations I observed.

My observation predominantly consisted of sitting alongside various journalists as they produced stories and asking numerous questions about both their specific current tasks and their work more generally. In only one case (a particularly busy day at SportsPop) I was asked not to sit with anyone but to observe the newsroom more generally; otherwise, I spent virtually all of my newsroom observation seated beside particular journalists. I attended most, though not all, staff meetings during my observation as well. There were two primary challenges with this type of work: one was that my presence and questions could slow down the journalist with whom I was sitting. Given the fast-paced nature of aggregation work, this was the main concern about my visits with most of the organizations I observed, and I tried to be conscientious about lessening my disruption by limiting my questions when journalists were up against a deadline. In one case at VidNews, though, a journalist began essentially narrating his story production process to me, something that was immensely useful to me but slowed him considerably. He turned in the story more than an hour late and apologized to his editor via chat message, saying he had an "observer." His editor responded, as I sat beside the journalist: "gotta learn to balance that, or hand the observer off." I worked to be as unobtrusive as possible in my observation, but my presence was inevitably a drag on the organizations' productivity.

The second challenge was the prevalence of group chat and office messaging programs such as Slack and Gchat for newsroom communication, which made it difficult to observe interpersonal interaction among newsroom staff. I was never given direct access to these systems (I asked in a few cases but was rejected each time), though I was often able to look over journalists' shoulders to see it unfold as they read it. Because I was sitting so close to journalists, it was quite clear to them when I was doing this. That doesn't mean it was clear to people with whom they were communicating that I was reading their messages, though in every newsroom except Circa's, I was visible to everyone in the group, so they could know when they were sending messages to someone I was observing. In some cases, when I felt as though reading messages directly would be intrusive or when I couldn't understand what was being said, I simply asked the journalist I was observing what she and her colleagues were saying to each other. Journalists responded amiably, either with a summary or an offer to see it for myself. In this way, I was able to characterize much of the relevant office-messaging discourse without accessing it directly myself. Still, given the ubiquity of these technologies in contemporary media organizations, news ethnographers would do well to begin developing a more robust approach to accessing, analyzing, and ethically approaching these forms of communication.

The form of my interviews varied as well. In some cases, my one-on-one observation of journalists at work morphed into the kind of "out in the open" interviews advocated by Usher (2016, 211) as part of a hybrid ethnographic approach. Most of the time, though, I conducted on-site interviews in offices and conference rooms, apart from the rest of the newsroom, largely in order to discuss sensitive topics. (Many of the aggregators worked in such close quarters that in situ interviews occasionally became a sort of group interview.) These interviews in the field were supplemented with many interviews over the phone. Some of these interviews were conducted with people from the organizations I observed after my time on site—to follow up on things I had observed or to talk with people I hadn't been able to interview in the newsroom. Many others were in other organizations where I didn't do fieldwork. I chose those interviewees largely to achieve variance in the types and contexts of aggregation represented in my data. That variance was along several dimensions: degree of professional status and socialization, platforms (apps, websites, email newsletters, videos, etc.), legacy media vs. digital-only settings, automated vs. manual forms, and organizational hierarchy (low-level workers and supervising editors). I determined whom to interview by developing lists of journalists at news organizations that did aggregation and selecting within those lists based on who helped fill out the dimensions of variance I was seeking, then using random selection within those groups. Interviews typically lasted about an hour and covered a wide range of questions and were semi-structured: each interview included very similar broad questions drawn from a basic interview outline but individualized follow-up questions.

As a former journalist, I was familiar with the newsroom setting and jargon—though not necessarily comfortable in the role of an observer. Many of the people I observed were close to my own age but a bit younger—I was between thirty and thirty-two at the time of the observation, and many were in their mid to late twenties—and I think this was helpful in gaining rapport and understanding many of the cultural references that ran throughout their conversations. I also brought with me experience as an aggregator, having written a "This Week in Review" column each week from 2010–2014 at the Nieman Journalism Lab aggregating news and analysis about the journalism and tech worlds. That experience was helpful in gaining access to wary news organizations, though I found that my experience as an aggregator was less intrusive an influence than I expected. I encountered almost no one who did aggregation in a form similar to my own previous work, and the work of aggregation turned out to be so much more varied and richly textured than I expected that my own work hardly ended up serving as a template for the work I observed.

101. Unlike journalistic work in which the default for information is on the record, this project was governed by principles of research ethics that tend to emphasize consent and agency of research participants to help determine their own role in research (see, e.g., Joan E. Sieber and Martin B. Tolich, *Planning Ethically Responsible Research*, 2nd ed. [Los Angeles: Sage, 2013]). This approach is often institutionalized through a university's institutional review board (IRB), which oversees research and encourages projects to be designed to maximize agency through the participants' ability to maintain confidentiality if they desire. These two factors—my own inclination toward participant agency and the guidelines set by my university's IRB—converged in this case. I encouraged participants to go on the record but did not pressure them to do so and didn't make it a necessary condition of their involvement. As a result, many of the participants chose not to allow their identity (or that of their news organization) to be revealed.

The anxiety among many participants about allowing their names to be used was palpable and, I think, notable. In some cases it was simply because the organization's public relations officials hadn't cleared the participants to talk to me, but in many others it seemed to stem from a wariness about how they and their work might be portrayed. As I discuss in chapter 3, many of the participants were used to being thought of as doing an inferior form of journalistic work, and I think they held some residual concern that I might not present them in a friendly light. I gave them no guarantees that I would characterize them favorably, though I often assured them that I understood aggregation's poor reputation in the news industry and was determined to transcend its stereotypes in my attempts to understand it. This reassurance was typically effective in securing their cooperation, though often not with their names attached. The fact that so many aggregators and their editors seemed to see the academic examination of their work practices as more likely to incur reputational harm than pride was itself a noteworthy indicator of the defensiveness and inferiority that attends aggregators' professional identity.

102. Dan Primack, "Exclusive: News App Circa Is Seeking a Buyer." *Fortune*, April 30, 2015, http://fortune.com/2015/04/30/news-app-circa-buyer/.

103. Much of the story of Circa's relaunch under Sinclair is well-explored in Laura Hazard Owen, "In Circa, Sinclair Sees a Way to Attract 'Independent-Minded' Millennials (and Sean Hannity)," *Nieman Journalism Lab*, July 5, 2017, http://www.niemanlab.org/2017/07/in-circa-sinclair-sees-a-way-to-attract-independent-minded-millennials-and-sean-hannity/. This information was also explained to me in a personal interview with John Solomon, who was at the time the chief operating officer of Circa under Sinclair, Sept. 29, 2016. Regarding its shutdown, see Laura Hazard Owen, "Circa, Sinclair's Millennial-Focused News Site (and the Final Remains of Some Interesting Mobile Ideas), Is Shutting Down," *Nieman Journalism Lab*, March 27, 2019, https://www.niemanlab.org/2019/03/circa-sinclairs-millennial-focused-news-site-and-the-final-remains-of-some-interesting-mobile-ideas-is-shutting-down/.

104. This prioritization of video has become influential enough that some publishers have begun using automation to produce web video based on text articles. See John Herrman, "As Online Video Surges, Publishers Turn to Automation," *New York Times*, July 10, 2016, https://www.nytimes.com/2016/07/11/business/media/as-online-video-surges-publishers-turn-to-automation.html.

105 Avi Wolfman-Arent, "WHYY Acquires Local News Site Billy Penn," *WHYY*, April 15, 2019, https://whyy.org/articles/whyy-acquires-local-news-site-billy-penn/.

106. There are some limits to this variance, of course. All of the organizations I observed, and many of the ones represented in interviews, consider themselves news organizations and operate with some degree of journalistic ethics and

professional identity as journalists. In other words, there are no aggregators in this study who are simply open plagiarists—fly-by-night sites and social media accounts that merely republish the work of others in its entirety. These sites rarely form established presences within the media environment, since they depend on the willingness of content creators to overlook or ignore their flagrant copyright violations merely to survive. But these aggregators, however ephemeral, do form a significant part of the contemporary infrastructure of online news distribution (as the false news example at the beginning of this introduction indicates). However, one of the major themes of this study is the interface between aggregation and professional journalistic values and practices, so I gathered data within a sample that was more oriented toward journalistic professionalism and thus provided opportunities to examine intersections among those values and practices. This approach was intended to produce a more focused and coherent study of aggregation, but it also necessarily leaves an incomplete picture of aggregation, one that largely eschews the aggregators who are least tethered to journalistic social structures and standards.

107. There are a few excellent studies of aspects of aggregation scattered around the world. See, e.g., Boyer, *The Life Informatic*; Andrew Duffy, Edson C. Tandoc, and Richard Ling, "Frankenstein Journalism," *Information, Communication & Society* 21, no. 10 (2018): 1354–68; Igor Vobič and Ana Milojević, "'What We Do Is Not Actually Journalism': Role Negotiations in Online Departments of Two Newspapers in Slovenia and Serbia," *Journalism* 15, no. 8 (2014): 1023–40. More studies from a variety of national and professional contexts such as these are needed, and despite its country-specific limitations, my hope is that this book will contribute to this growing body of data on aggregation in a wide range of international settings.

108. See Ryfe, *Can Journalism Survive?* for an extended discussion on the persistence of these professional norms in the face of organizational and institutional change.

1. GATHERING EVIDENCE OF EVIDENCE: AGGREGATION AS SECOND-ORDER NEWSWORK

1. Not her real name.

2. The description of Samantha's work on this story is drawn from the author's field notes, Feb. 4, 2015.

3. C. W. Anderson, *Rebuilding the News: Metropolitan Journalism in the Digital Age* (Philadelphia: Temple University Press, 2013), 56; Dominic Boyer, *The Life Informatic: Newsmaking in the Digital Era* (Ithaca, NY: Cornell University Press, 2013), 98. See also Natalie Fenton and Tamara Witschge, "'Comment Is Free, Facts Are Sacred,'" in *News Online: Transformations and Continuities*, ed. Graham Meikle and Guy Redden (Basingstoke, UK: Palgrave Macmillan, 2011), 148–63.

4. See, e.g., Michael Calderone, "AP Chair Takes on New Media," *Politico*, April 11, 2009, http://www.politico.com/story/2009/04/ap-chair-takes-on-new-media-021136; Simon Dumenco, "Thanks for the Apology, Huffington Post. Now Please Apologize to the Writer You Suspended," *Advertising Age*, July 12, 2011, http://adage.com/article/the-media-guy/apology-huffington-post/228664/; Bill Keller, "Postscript: Aggregation Aggro," *New York Times*, March 13, 2011, http://6thfloor.blogs.nytimes.com/2011/03/13/postscript-aggregation-aggro/; Jim Romenesko, "NYT Reporter Defends Forbes Writer Accused of Stealing His Work," *Jimromenesko.com* (blog post), Feb. 21, 2012, https://web.archive.org/web/20120221171108/http://jimromenesko.com/2012/02/21/nyt-reporter-defends-forbes-writer-accused-of-stealing-his-work/.

5. Richard V. Ericson, Patricia M. Baranek, and Janet B. L. Chan, *Visualizing Deviance: A Study of News Organization* (Toronto: University of Toronto Press, 1987); Jay Rosen, "Good Old Fashioned Shoe Leather Reporting," *PressThink* (blog post), April 16, 2015, http://pressthink.org/2015/04/good-old-fashioned-shoe-leather-reporting/. I will cover the professional mythology of reporting, especially as it relates to aggregation, more deeply in chapter 4.

6. Justin Lewis, Andy Williams, and Bob Franklin, "Four Rumours and an Explanation: A Political Economic Account of Journalists' Changing Newsgathering and Reporting Practice," *Journalism Practice* 2, no. 1 (2008): 27–45; Angela Phillips, "Faster and Shallower: Homogenisation, Cannibalisation and the Death of Reporting," in *Changing Journalism*, ed. Peter Lee-Wright, Angela Phillips, and Tamara Witschge (London: Routledge, 2012), 81–98; Michael Schudson, *Discovering the News: A Social History of American Newspapers* (New York: Basic Books, 1978).

7. Anderson, *Rebuilding the News*, 55–70.

8. The main way for aggregation to recoup this economic value is through immense amounts of web traffic, something that will be explored further in chapter 4.

9. Mats Ekström, "Epistemologies of TV Journalism: A Theoretical Framework," *Journalism* 3, no. 3 (2002): 259–82, at 260. See also James S. Ettema and Theodore L. Glasser, "On the Epistemology of Investigative Journalism," in *Mass Communication Review Yearbook*, ed. Michael Gurevitch and Mark R. Levy (Newbury Park, CA: Sage, 1987, vol. 6), 338–61.

10. Ekström, "Epistemologies of TV Journalism," 274; Frank Harbers and Marcel Broersma, "Between Engagement and Ironic Ambiguity: Mediating Subjectivity in Narrative Journalism," *Journalism* 15, no. 5 (2014): 639–54.

11. This is the purpose of journalism provided by Bill Kovach and Tom Rosenstiel, *The Elements of Journalism: What Newspeople Should Know and the Public Should Expect*, 2nd ed. (New York: Three Rivers, 2007.).

12. "2018 Edelman Trust Barometer: Global Report," *Edelman*, Jan. 21, 2018, https:// www.edelman.com/sites/g/files/aatuss191/files/2018-10/2018_Edelman_Trust _Barometer_Global_Report_FEB.pdf. There is some evidence of a slight uptick in the late 2010s, however. See Indira Lakshmanan and Rick Edmonds, "Finally Some Good News: Trust in News Is Up, Especially for Local Media," *Poynter*, Aug. 22, 2018, https://www.poynter.org/ethics-trust/2018/finally-some-good -news-trust-in-news-is-up-especially-for-local-media/; Nic Newman, Richard Fletcher, Antonis Kalogeropoulos, David A. L. Levy, and Rasmus Kleis Nielsen, "Reuters Institute Digital News Report 2018," *Reuters Institute for the Study of Journalism* (Oxford, 2018), http://media.digitalnewsreport.org/wp-content /uploads/2018/06/digital-news-report-2018.pdf?x89475.

13. The Media Insight Project, "A New Understanding: What Makes People Trust and Rely on News," *American Press Institute*, April 17, 2016, https://www.american pressinstitute.org/publications/reports/survey-research/trust-news/.

14. Kovach and Rosenstiel, *The Elements of Journalism*, 85–86.

15. This epistemology is essentially realism. See Yigal Godler and Zvi Reich, "How Journalists Think About Facts: Theorizing the Social Conditions Behind Epis-temological Beliefs," *Journalism Studies* 14, no. 1 (2013): 94–112; Robert A. Hackett, "Decline of a Paradigm? Bias and Objectivity in News Media Studies," *Critical Studies in Mass Communication* 1, no. 3 (1984): 229–59. For a historical overview of realism in news and its evolution into modernist epistemology, see Kevin G. Barnhurst, *Mister Pulitzer and the Spider: Modern News from Realism to the Digital* (Urbana: University of Illinois Press, 2016).

16. Lippmann's model can be found in Walter Lippmann, *Liberty and the News* (New Brunswick, NJ: Transaction, 1995, originally published 1920). Most nota-bly, Philip Meyer's "precision journalism" of the 1960s and 1970s applied social scientific techniques such as surveys to journalistic investigation. Precision journalism evolved into computer-assisted reporting, which became a forerun-ner of modern data journalism. For an examination of the relationship between journalism and social science and especially the role of precision journalism, see C. W. Anderson, *Apostles of Certainty: Data Journalism and the Politics of Doubt* (Oxford: Oxford University Press, 2018).

17. Walter Lippmann, *Public Opinion* (New York: Macmillan, 1961, originally pub-lished 1922), 358; Schudson, *Discovering the News*.

18. Carl Bernstein, "The Idiot Culture," *The New Republic* 206, no. 23 (June 8, 1992): 22–28; James S. Ettema and Theodore L. Glasser, *Custodians of Conscience: Investigative Journalism and Public Virtue* (New York: Columbia University Press, 1998); Kovach and Rosenstiel, *The Elements of Journalism*.

19. Ekström, "Epistemologies of TV Journalism," 270.

20. Mark Fishman, *Manufacturing the News* (Austin: University of Texas Press, 1980), 85–92.

21. Anderson, *Apostles of Certainty*, 187–92.

22. See, e.g., Rosen, "Good Old Fashioned Shoe Leather Reporting"; Barbie Zelizer, "On 'Having Been There': 'Eyewitnessing' as a Journalistic Key Word," *Critical Studies in Media Communication* 24, no. 5 (2007): 408–28.

23. Anderson, *Apostles of Certainty*, 188.

24. Fishman, *Manufacturing the News*, 92.

25. Allan Bell, *The Language of News Media* (Oxford: Blackwell, 1991); Michael Schudson, *The Power of News* (Cambridge, MA: Harvard University Press, 1995); Barbie Zelizer, "'Saying' as Collective Practice: Quoting and Differential Address in the News," *Text* 9, no. 4 (1989): 369–88.

26. Ericson et al., *Visualizing Deviance*; Ettema and Glasser, "On the Epistemology of Investigative Journalism"; Fishman, *Manufacturing the News*, 98–100. Fishman also notes that documents are particularly important as journalistic forms of evidence because thanks to their official imprimatur and the power of enforcement that lies behind them, they enact reality, rather than simply recording it. "Journalists love performative documents because these are the hardest facts they can get their hands on," Fishman writes (99).

27. Kovach and Rosenstiel, *The Elements of Journalism*, 79; Alfred Hermida, "Nothing But the Truth: Redrafting the Journalistic Boundary of Verification," in *Boundaries of Journalism: Professionalism, Practices and Participation*, ed. Matt Carlson and Seth C. Lewis (London: Routledge, 2015), 37–50; Ivor Shapiro, Colette Brin, Isabelle Bédard-Brûlé, and Kasia Mychajlowycz, "Verification as a Strategic Ritual: How Journalists Retrospectively Describe Processes for Ensuring Accuracy," *Journalism Practice* 7, no. 6 (2013): 657–73.

28. Ericson et al., *Visualizing Deviance*; Fishman, *Manufacturing the News*.

29. Ettema and Glasser, *Custodians of Conscience*; Shapiro et al., "Verification as a Strategic Ritual."

30. Richard V. Ericson, "How Journalists Visualize Fact," *The ANNALS of the American Academy of Political and Social Science* 560, no. 1 (1998): 83–95; Schudson, *Discovering the News*.

31. Kari Andén-Papadopoulos, "Media Witnessing and the 'Crowd-Sourced Video Revolution,'" *Visual Communication* 12, no. 3 (2013): 341–57; Zelizer, "On 'Having Been There.'" There are, however, substantial structural and institutional barriers to gaining widespread audiences online. While everyone is capable in theory of doing this, both the network effects of preferential attachment and the economic and institutional forces that reinforce the power of wealthy and politically powerful individuals and organizations drastically

limit the realistic potential audience of any given person in practice. See, e.g., Matthew Hindman, *The Myth of Digital Democracy* (Princeton, NJ: Princeton University Press, 2009).

32. See, e.g., Frank Bruni, "Who Needs Reporters?" *New York Times*, June 1, 2013, http://www.nytimes.com/2013/06/02/opinion/sunday/bruni-who-needs-reporters.html; Mark Coddington, "Clarifying Journalism's Quantitative Turn: A Typology for Evaluating Data Journalism, Computational Journalism, and Computer-Assisted Reporting," *Digital Journalism* 3, no. 3 (2015): 331–48; Mathew Ingram, "Is It Good for Journalism When Sources Go Direct?" *Gigaom*, Jan. 30, 2012, https://gigaom.com/2012/01/30/is-it-good-for-journalism-when-sources-go-direct/.

33. Nikki Usher, *Making News at* The New York Times (Ann Arbor: University of Michigan Press, 2014), 11; Pablo J. Boczkowski, *News at Work: Imitation in an Age of Information Abundance* (Chicago: University of Chicago Press, 2010); Boyer, *The Life Informatic*.

34. Kovach and Rosenstiel, *The Elements of Journalism*; Craig Silverman, ed., *Verification Handbook* (Maastricht, Netherlands: European Journalism Centre, 2014), http://verificationhandbook.com/downloads/verification.handbook.pdf.

35. Boczkowski, *News at Work*, 42–43.

36. Johan Jarlbrink notes this primacy of mediated observation in modern news-work and argues that it weakens the journalistic authority of physical presence itself because it's no longer necessary to validate important information. See Johan Jarlbrink, "Mobile/Sedentary: News Work Behind and Beyond the Desk," *Media History* 21, no. 3 (2015): 280–93, at 289.

37. C. W. Anderson, "What Aggregators Do: Towards a Networked Concept of Journalistic Expertise in the Digital Age," *Journalism* 14, no. 8 (2013): 1008–23.

38. Local news organizations were also considered quite reliable, provided they were reporting on stories in their geographical footprint. Local TV news was generally considered less reliable than local newspapers, though Social Post relied on it heavily, because it tended to cover the same sensational crime and offbeat news that Social Post was interested in. Its writers also appreciated local TV news because, as one writer told me, TV news had video that they could embed and fill their need for an image in their post.

39. Interview with the author, Feb. 25, 2015. Other researchers have found similar attitudes among Reddit users who collaboratively aggregate breaking news there. See Alex Leavitt and John J. Robinson, "Upvote My News: The Practices of Peer Information Aggregation for Breaking News on Reddit," *Proceedings of the ACM on Human-Computer Interaction* 1, no. 2 (2017), article 65.

40. Interviews with the author, Feb. 25, 2015, and March 6, 2015. In many cases, including both of these, the aggregators were employed by professional news

organizations, so their alignment with traditional professional journalistic values isn't surprising.

41. See, e.g., Matt Carlson, "Blogs and Journalistic Authority: The Role of Blogs in US Election Day 2004 Coverage," *Journalism Studies* 8, no. 2 (2007): 264–79; Sophie Lecheler and Sanne Kruikemeier, "Re-Evaluating Journalistic Routines in a Digital Age: A Review of Research on the Use of Online Sources," *New Media & Society* 18, no. 1 (2016): 156–71.

42. Interview with the author, Feb. 13, 2015.

43. This presents a conundrum for aggregators: the stories in which sourcing is unclear are the ones that are most in need of substantial verification, but verification is most difficult for those stories—precisely because the sourcing is unclear. In many cases, the verification process on a published news story for an aggregator would be easy, but that often means another news organization has already done it and made its sourcing clear, rendering substantial verification unnecessary.

44. Author's field notes, Jan. 19, 2015.

45. Author's field notes, Jan. 22, 2015.

46. Timothy E. Cook, *Governing with the News: The News Media as a Political Institution* (Chicago: University of Chicago Press, 1998); Fishman, *Manufacturing the News*; Herbert J. Gans, *Deciding What's News: A Study of CBS Evening News, NBC Nightly News, Newsweek, and Time* (New York, Pantheon, 1979); Gaye Tuchman, *Making News: A Study in the Construction of Reality* (New York: Free Press, 1978). Use of official sources has steadily increased since the 1950s, according to Barnhurst, *Mister Pulitzer and the Spider*, 55.

47. Interview with the author, Feb. 17, 2015.

48. Pew Research has found the percentage of Americans who say they trust the information they find on social media to be in the single digits. (Michael Barthel and Amy Mitchell, "Americans' Attitudes About the News Media Deeply Divided Along Partisan Lines," *Pew Research Center*, May 10, 2017, http://www.journalism.org/2017/05/10/americans-attitudes-about-the-news-media-deeply-divided-along-partisan-lines/. For a review of research on journalists' views on the credibility of information on social media, see Lecheler and Kruikemeier, "Re-Evaluating Journalistic Routines in a Digital Age."

49. Interview with the author, Jan. 30, 2015.

50. Not his real name. This description of Sean's source evaluation process and his statements about it are drawn from the author's field notes, Feb. 5, 2015, with some background clarification and explanation in an interview with the author, Feb. 20, 2015.

51. Kimberley Isbell, "The Rise of the News Aggregator: Legal Implications and Best Practices," *Citizen Media Law Project*, Working Paper 2010–10 (2010), https://papers.ssrn.com/sol3/papers.cfm?abstract_id=1670339; Alexander Barrett

Weaver, "Aggravated with Aggregators: Can International Copyright Law Help Save the Newsroom?" *Emory International Law Review* 26, no. 2 (2012): 1161–200.

52. Author's field notes, Feb. 5, 2015.

53. Interview with the author, March 13, 2015.

54. Emphasis mine. Reddit users aggregating breaking news also express a similar rationale in Leavitt & Robinson, "Upvote My News."

55. Interview with the author, Feb. 20, 2015.

56. For an excellent study in which journalists did precisely this, see Zvi Reich, "Source Credibility and Journalism: Between Visceral and Discretional Judgment," *Journalism Practice* 5, no. 1 (2011): 51–67.

57. Yigal Godler and Zvi Reich, "Journalistic Evidence: Cross-Verification as a Constituent of Mediated Knowledge," *Journalism* 18, no. 5 (2017): 558–74, at 570.

2. MAKING NEWS BY MANAGING UNCERTAINTY

1. Not her real name. The account of Morgan's newsgathering process for this story is drawn from the author's field notes, June 30, 2016, except quotes from field notes on other days where noted.

2. Author's field notes, June 27, 2016.

3. Author's field notes, June 27, 2016.

4. Charles R. Bantz, Suzanne McCorkle, and Roberta C. Baade, "The News Factory," *Communication Research* 7, no. 1 (1980): 45–68; Serena Carpenter, Seungahn Nah, and Deborah Chung, "A Study of US Online Community Journalists and Their Organizational Characteristics and Story Generation Routines," *Journalism* 16, no. 4 (2000): 505–20; Richard V. Ericson, Patricia M. Baranek, and Janet B. L. Chan, *Visualizing Deviance: A Study of News Organization* (Toronto: University of Toronto Press, 1987); Herbert J. Gans, *Deciding What's News: A Study of CBS Evening News, NBC Nightly News, Newsweek, and* Time (New York, Pantheon, 1979).

5. See, e.g., Pablo J. Boczkowski, *News at Work: Imitation in an Age of Information Abundance* (Chicago: University of Chicago Press, 2010); Ericson et al., *Visualizing Deviance,* 188–93; Gans, *Deciding What's News,* 176–81; and Ramona Vonbun, Katharina Kleinen von-Königslöw, and Klaus Schoenbach, "Intermedia Agenda-Setting in a Multimedia News Environment," *Journalism* 17, no. 8 (2016): 1054–73.

6. TweetDeck formed a wall of continually flowing Twitter feeds across the computer monitors of most of the aggregators I observed. Some of them reduced their description of the process by which they looked for stories as essentially "camping out on TweetDeck all day" (Interview with the author, Feb. 19, 2015).

The image of TweetDeck on an aggregator's screen is of a waterfall of information, with a half-dozen columns side-by-side, each pushing down the screen with new information almost literally every second. That continual flow helps reinforce a sense of relentless urgency, of constant "next-ness," as Dominic Boyer has called it in his study of German online journalists, that elevates timeliness as a condition of newsworthiness and inexorably orients aggregators toward the news values expressed by the prominent news organizations and professional journalists who dominate their feeds. (Dominic Boyer, *The Life Informatic: Newsmaking in the Digital Era* [Ithaca, NY: Cornell University Press, 2013], 69.)

7. Alicia and Christy are pseudonyms. The description of Alicia's search for stories is drawn from the author's field notes, June 28, 2016.

8. These tools, developed by companies like NewsWhip, Crowdtangle, and Dataminr, dig through millions of social media posts, likes, and shares in real time to determine what stories are generating the most conversation—and what emerging stories might be going viral soon.

9. "Amber Alert" is the name for a public missing-child alert in the United States.

10. Alicia did find a story that night—the 911 call was released in the shooting case with the Texas mom that evening, and she had the story up early the next morning. By midday, it had been viewed 129,000 times, according to Social Post's internal traffic numbers.

11. In many cases, these priorities bleed into other themes related to news production. Audience and traffic was a particularly significant factor for SportsPop (and Social Post), which we'll see in chapter 4, and narrative fit was a distinctly influential factor for Circa, something we'll examine more closely in chapter 5.

12. Johan Galtung and Mari Holmboe Ruge, "The Structure of Foreign News: The Presentation of the Congo, Cuba and Cyprus Crises in Four Norwegian Newspapers," *Journal of Peace Research* 2, no. 1 (1965): 64–90; Tony Harcup and Deirdre O'Neill, "What Is News? News Values Revisited (Again)," *Journalism Studies* 18, no. 12 (2016): 1470–88.

13. Craig Calcaterra, writer for NBC Sports' Hardball Talk baseball news site, interview with the author, March 5, 2015.

14. Cates Holderness, "What Colors Are This Dress?" *BuzzFeed*, Feb. 26, 2015, https://www.buzzfeed.com/catesish/help-am-i-going-insane-its-definitely-blue.

15. See, e.g., Megan Daley, "'The Dress' Debate and Other Misunderstood, Iconic Dresses," *Entertainment Weekly*, Feb. 27, 2015, http://ew.com/article/2015/02/27/dress-debate-and-other-misunderstood-iconic-dresses/; Adam Rogers, "The Science of Why No One Agrees on the Color of This Dress," *Wired*, Feb. 26, 2015, https://www.wired.com/2015/02/science-one-agrees-color-dress/.

16. Ben Fischer, "The Dress Phenomenon Didn't Happen By Accident. It Took Big Money," *New York Business Journal*, Feb. 27, 2015, http://www.bizjournals.com/newyork/blog/techflash/2015/02/the-dress-phenomenon-didnt-happen-by-accident.html.

17. Author's field notes, Feb. 4, 2015.

18. For more on this tension between intuitive and quantitative ways of knowing the audience, see chapter 4.

19. See, e.g., Ahmed Al-Rawi, "Viral News on Social Media," *Digital Journalism* 7, no. 1 (2019): 63–79; Jonah Berger and Katherine L. Milkman, "What Makes Online Content Viral?" *Journal of Marketing Research* 49, no. 2 (2012): 192–205; Stefan Stieglitz and Linh Dang-Xuan, "Emotions and Information Diffusion in Social Media—Sentiment of Microblogs and Sharing Behavior," *Journal of Management Information Systems* 29, no. 4 (2013): 217–48.

20. Interview with the author, March 13, 2015.

21. Dan Berkowitz, "Non-Routine News and Newswork: Exploring a What-a-Story," *Journal of Communication* 42, no. 1 (1992): 82–94; Carlin Romano, "The Grisly Truth About Bare Facts," in *Reading the News*, ed. Robert Karl Manoff and Michael Schudson (New York: Pantheon, 1986), 38–78; Gaye Tuchman, *Making News: A Study in the Construction of Reality* (New York: Free Press, 1978).

22. Tim P. Vos and Teri Finneman, "The Early Historical Construction of Journalism's Gatekeeping Role," *Journalism* 18, no. 3 (2017): 265–80.

23. Gaye Tuchman, "Objectivity as Strategic Ritual: An Examination of Newsmen's Notions of Objectivity," *American Journal of Sociology* 77, no. 4 (1972): 660–79, at 672.

24. Gans, *Deciding What's News*; Pamela J. Shoemaker and Stephen D. Reese, *Mediating the Message in the 21st Century: A Media Sociology Perspective*, 3rd ed. (New York: Routledge, 2014); Tuchman, "Objectivity as Strategic Ritual."

25. See, e.g., C. W. Anderson, "Between Creative and Quantified Audiences: Web Metrics and Changing Patterns of Newswork in Local US Newsrooms," *Journalism* 12, no. 5 (2011): 550–66; Boczkowski, *News at Work*; Angela M. Lee, Seth C. Lewis, and Matthew Powers, "Audience Clicks and News Placement: A Study of Time-Lagged Influence in Online Journalism," *Communication Research* 41, no. 4 (2012): 505–30.

26. Author's field notes, Jan. 20, 2015.

27. Interview with the author, Feb. 20, 2015.

28. Interview with the author, Feb. 25, 2015.

29. Interview with the author, Feb. 23, 2015.

30. Interview with the author, March 3, 2015.

31. Interview with the author, June 9, 2016.

32. Nikki Usher, *Making News at* The New York Times (Ann Arbor: University of Michigan Press, 2014), 63.

33. Interview with the author, June 17, 2016. About a year after this interview, Orso took a position with the *Inquirer* herself.

34. Interview with the author, March 18, 2015.

35. Interview with the author, March 18, 2015.

36. For more on the professionally driven ethical values behind this desire, see chapter 3.

37. I occasionally saw news organizations aggregate news stories based on single sources. In those cases, it was typically a long, investigative story by a reputable news organization—one that showed great evidence of reporting and would have been very difficult for other sources to match. In these cases, aggregators would add other sources for background information (to avoid a single-source story), but those additional sources didn't have anything to do with verifying the main source of the story.

38. James S. Ettema and Theodore L. Glasser, *Custodians of Conscience: Investigative Journalism and Public Virtue* (New York: Columbia University Press, 1998).

39. In this sense, the stories of both VidNews' Sean in the previous chapter and Social Post's Morgan in this chapter are exceptions. Though I saw aggregators almost always use multiple sources, those sources were often easy to find (unlike in Sean's case), and the discrepancies between them either fairly easy to resolve or nonexistent (unlike in Morgan's case).

40. Billy Penn's and SportsPop's writers were also calling people regularly, though that was largely part of reporting stories that were separate from their aggregated work. Social Post's writers also often contacted people who posted things on social media (typically through Facebook Messenger or email), though confirming the veracity of those posts was only a secondary purpose. The primary purpose was getting permission to write about them. The posts would often be intended only for the author's friends and family, and several of Social Post's writers and editors considered it a significant ethical issue to get people's permission before turning that post into a widely disseminated news story.

41. Interview with the author, June 23, 2016.

42. Interview with the author, March 6, 2015.

43. Interview with the author, June 9, 2016.

44. Interview with the author, Feb. 25, 2015.

45. Interview with the author, Feb. 18, 2015.

46. Interview with the author, June 27, 2016.

47. Barbie Zelizer, "Where Is the Author in American TV News? On the Construction and Presentation of Proximity, Authorship, and Journalistic Authority," *Semiotica* 80, no. 1/2 (1990): 37–48; Barbie Zelizer, "On 'Having Been There': 'Eyewitnessing' as a Journalistic Key Word," *Critical Studies in Media Communication* 24, no. 5 (2007), 408–28. For information on the decline in journalism and especially reporting jobs, see data in the United States and Europe, e.g., "Mapping Changes in Employment in the Journalism & Media Industry," *European Federation of Journalists*, Aug. 31, 2012, https://ia600603.us.archive.org/16/items /EFJ-EURO-MEI-Mapping-Project/EFJ_EURO-MEI_Mapping_Project.pdf; Alex T. Williams, "Employment Picture Darkens for Journalists at Digital Outlets," *Columbia Journalism Review*, Sept. 27, 2016, https://www.cjr.org /business_of_news/journalism_jobs_digital_decline.php.

48. Interview with the author, Feb. 17, 2015.

49. Author's field notes, Jan. 29, 2015.

50. Zelizer, "On 'Having Been There.'" See also Kari Andén-Papadopoulos, "Citizen Camera-Witnessing: Embodied Political Dissent in the Age of 'Mediated Mass Self-Communication,'" *New Media & Society* 16, no. 5 (2014): 753–69.

51. Interview with the author, Feb. 20, 2015.

52. Mats Ekström, "Epistemologies of TV Journalism: A Theoretical Framework," *Journalism* 3, no. 3 (2002), 259–82, at 270.

53. For an example of this accusation, see Jacob Silverman, *Terms of Service: Social Media and the Price of Constant Connection* (New York: Harper, 2015), 106–8.

54. Katherine Barner, "The Viral-Media Editor Who Says Cute Babies and Animals Are Her 'Bread and Butter,'" *New York*, April 13, 2017, http://nymag .com/thejob/2017/04/the-viral-media-editor-who-will-get-a-click-with-cute -babies-and-animals.html; John Herrman, "Inside Facebook's (Totally Insane, Unintentionally Gigantic, Hyperpartisan) Political-Media Machine," *New York Times Magazine*, Aug. 24, 2016, https://www.nytimes.com/2016/08/28/magazine /inside-facebooks-totally-insane-unintentionally-gigantic-hyperpartisan -political-media-machine.html?_r=0; Andrew Marantz, "The Virologist," *The New Yorker*, Jan. 5, 2015, https://www.newyorker.com/magazine/2015/01/05 /virologist.

55. Ivor Shapiro, Colette Brin, Isabelle Bédard-Brûlé, and Kasia Mychajlowycz, "Verification as a Strategic Ritual: How Journalists Retrospectively Describe Processes for Ensuring Accuracy," *Journalism Practice* 7, no. 6 (2013): 657–73; Tuchman, "Objectivity as Strategic Ritual."

56. Duffy et al. (Andrew Duffy, Edson C. Tandoc, and Richard Ling, "Frankenstein Journalism," *Information, Communication & Society* 21, no. 10 [2018]: 1354–68)

make a similar finding regarding aggregators' eagerness to incorporate rituals from traditional reporting work as a way to elevate their own.

57. Interview with the author, June 9, 2016.

58. In Sean's case, he had sources from the wire services reporting this information, so that alleviated his uncertainty somewhat in this particular situation. But he couldn't use those sources in his story, so his uncertainty about his ability to provide public evidence on the story remained.

59. Interview with the author, Jan. 22, 2015.

60. Interview with the author, June 23, 2015.

61. Leon V. Sigal, *Reporters and Officials: The Organization and Politics of News-making* (Lexington, MA: D.C. Heath and Co., 1973); Bartholomew H. Sparrow, *Uncertain Guardians: The News Media as a Political Institution* (Baltimore, MD: Johns Hopkins University Press, 1999).

62. Matt Carlson, *Journalistic Authority: Legitimating News in the Digital Era* (New York: Columbia University Press, 2017); Scott A. Eldridge II and Henrik Bødker, "Negotiating Uncertain Claims: Journalism as an Inferential Community," *Journalism Studies* 19, no. 13 (2018): 1912–22.

63. C. W. Anderson, *Apostles of Certainty: Data Journalism and the Politics of Doubt* (Oxford: Oxford University Press, 2018).

64. For other examples of journalists' routines of hedging information in the face of uncertainty, see Eldridge and Bødker, "Negotiating Uncertain Claims"; Shelly Rom and Zvi Reich, "Between the Technological Hare and the Journalistic Tortoise: Minimization of Knowledge Claims in Online News Flashes," *Journalism* (2017), published online before print.

65. Tuchman, "Objectivity as Strategic Ritual"; *Making News*.

66. Juliette De Maeyer and Avery E. Holton, "Why Linking Matters: A Metajournalistic Discourse Analysis," *Journalism* 17, no. 6 (2016): 776–94; Duffy et al., "Frankenstein Journalism."

67. Interview with the author, March 18, 2015.

68. Interview with the author, March 5, 2015. Notably, Calcaterra said he only engaged in this strategy for stories involving baseball transactions—what he considered minor news that relies primarily on anonymously sourced reports—and would not take this approach with more significant or sensitive stories.

69. Author's field notes, Jan. 30, 2015. This is somewhat similar to the phenomenon of subject/object switching characterized in Eldridge and Bødker, "Negotiating Uncertain Claims."

70. Author's field notes, June 30, 2016.

71. Author's field notes, Feb. 6, 2015.

3. INFERIORITY AND IDENTITY: AGGREGATORS AND THE JOURNALISTIC PROFESSION

1. Jennifer is a pseudonym. The description of Jennifer's demonstration of VidNews' old story is drawn from the author's field notes, Feb. 3, 2015.

2. See, e.g., Alastair Dawber, "Murdoch Blasts Search Engine 'Kleptomaniacs,'" *The Independent*, Oct. 9, 2009, http://www.independent.co.uk/news/media /online/murdoch-blasts-search-engine-kleptomaniacs-1800569.html; Bill Keller, "All the Aggregation That's Fit to Aggregate," *New York Times Magazine*, March 10, 2011, http://www.nytimes.com/2011/03/13/magazine/mag-13lede-t .html; Jane Schulze, "Google Dubbed Internet Parasite by WSJ Editor," *The Australian*, April 6, 2009, https://web.archive.org/web/20111016161951/http:// www.theaustralian.com.au/media/google-dubbed-internet-parasite/story -e6frg996-1225696931547. For an academic study on this discourse, see Hsiang Iris Chyi, Seth C. Lewis, and Nan Zheng, "Parasite or Partner? Coverage of Google News in an Era of News Aggregation," *Journalism & Mass Communication Quarterly* 93, no. 4 (2016): 789–815.

3. Seth C. Lewis, "The Tension Between Professional Control and Open Participation: Journalism and Its Boundaries," *Information, Communication & Society* 15, no. 6 (2012): 836–66; Michael Schudson and Chris Anderson, "Objectivity, Professionalism, and Truth Seeking in Journalism," in *The Handbook of Journalism Studies*, ed. Karin Wahl-Jorgensen and Thomas Hanitzsch (New York: Routledge, 2009), 88–101.

4. Jane B. Singer, "Who Are These Guys? The Online Challenge to the Notion of Journalistic Professionalism," *Journalism* 4, no. 2 (2003): 139–63; Barbie Zelizer, *Covering the Body: The Kennedy Assassination, the Media, and the Shaping of Collective Memory* (Chicago: University of Chicago Press, 1992).

5. Max Weber, *The Theory of Social and Economic Organization*, trans. A. M. Henderson and Talcott Parsons (New York: Free Press, 1947); Timothy E. Cook, *Governing with the News: The News Media as a Political Institution* (Chicago: University of Chicago Press, 1998); Schudson and Anderson, "Objectivity, Professionalism, and Truth Seeking in Journalism"; Singer, "Who Are These Guys?"

6. Matt Carlson, *Journalistic Authority: Legitimating News in the Digital Era* (New York: Columbia University Press, 2017); John Soloski, "News Reporting and Professionalism: Some Constraints on the Reporting of the News," *Media, Culture & Society* 11, no. 2 (1989): 207–28; Zelizer, *Covering the Body*.

7. Carlson, *Journalistic Authority*; Lewis, "The Tension Between Professional Control."

8. Cook, *Governing with the News*, 77.

9. Carlson, *Journalistic Authority*; Zelizer, *Covering the Body*. There have been exceptions to this: during particular historical periods such as the anti-establishment wave of the 1960s and among particular groups of journalists, such as young journalists and those on the margins of the field. See, e.g., Henrik Örnebring, "Journalists Thinking About Precarity: Making Sense of the "New Normal," *ISOJ* 8, no. 1 (2018), http://isoj.org/research/journalists-thinking-about -precarity-making-sense-of-the-new-normal/; and Michael Schudson, *Discovering the News: A Social History of American Newspapers* (New York: Basic Books, 1978).

10. Mark Deuze, "What Is Journalism? Professional Identity and Ideology of Journalists Reconsidered," *Journalism* 6, no. 4 (2005): 442–64; Merryn Sherwood and Penny O'Donnell, "Once a Journalist, Always a Journalist? Industry Restructure, Job Loss and Professional Identity," *Journalism Studies* 19, no. 7 (2018): 1021–38.

11. This was possibly partly because Social Post, as a relatively new startup and a conservative media organization, was less likely to be guided by the hiring precedents of traditional media.

12. Though I did not typically ask participants' ages, it was possible to deduce a reasonable estimate through their descriptions of their professional background, matched up with biographical information they had posted about themselves online on sites such as LinkedIn. (Several people volunteered their ages during the course fieldwork or interviews.) One notable exception to this youthful emphasis was the *New York Times*, which staffed its now-defunct aggregational features Watching and NYT Now with newsroom veterans, many with at least a decade of journalism experience.

13. Interview with the author, June 29, 2016.

14. Interview with the author, March 11, 2015.

15. For more on the flexibility and precarity that characterizes the modern journalistic work environment, see Mark Deuze, *Media Work* (Cambridge: Polity, 2007); Örnebring, "Journalists Thinking About Precarity."

16. Interview with the author, July 8, 2016. Snyder did note that there were exceptions: "I think there's definitely some people who just have this in their blood," he said. "They're very good at really churning out the daily news stuff. And they kind of get into their groove, and they like to stay there." I only talked to a couple of people who might have fit this description. Most notable was Craig Calcaterra, a baseball blogger for NBC Sports' Hardball Talk, who as of 2019 has been doing mostly aggregated writing about baseball full-time for ten years and part-time for two years before that. As long as technology didn't substantially change the job, he told me, "I could do it for a long, long time." (Interview with the author, May 8, 2015.)

17. Nikki Usher, *Making News at* The New York Times (Ann Arbor: University of Michigan Press, 2014), 11. See also Pablo J. Boczkowski, *News at Work: Imitation in an Age of Information Abundance* (Chicago: University of Chicago Press, 2010); Dominic Boyer, *The Life Informatic: Newsmaking in the Digital Era* (Ithaca, NY: Cornell University Press, 2013); Dean Starkman, "The Hamster Wheel," *Columbia Journalism Review*, Sept./Oct. 2010, http://archives.cjr.org/cover_story/the_hamster_wheel.php.

18. Interview with the author, March 11, 2015.

19. Boyer, *The Life Informatic*, 15–16, 130–31. For a description of a similar phenomenon and its connection to the cut-and-paste aggregation of the nineteenth and early twentieth centuries, see Johan Jarlbrink, "Mobile /Sedentary: News Work Behind and Beyond the Desk," *Media History* 21, no. 3 (2015): 280–93.

20. Interview with the author, March 9, 2015.

21. Interview with the author, Feb. 17, 2015.

22. Interview with the author, June 27, 2016.

23. Interview with the author, March 6, 2015.

24. Starkman, "The Hamster Wheel."

25. Author's field notes, Feb. 1, 2015.

26. Interview with the author, March 11, 2015.

27. Interview with the author, June 15, 2016.

28. Marjan de Bruin, "Gender, Organizational and Professional Identities in Journalism," *Journalism* 1, no. 2 (2000): 217–38, at 229.

29. Interview with the author, Feb. 24, 2015. The other descriptions and quotes in this description of SportsPop are drawn from the author's field notes, Jan. 28–Feb. 1, 2015.

30. Interview with the author, Feb. 26, 2015.

31. Interview with the author, Feb. 23, 2015.

32. Pamela J. Shoemaker and Stephen D. Reese, *Mediating the Message in the 21st Century: A Media Sociology Perspective*, 3rd ed.(New York: Routledge, 2014). For a description of this dynamic at work among digital journalists, see Tim P. Vos and Patrick Ferrucci, "Who Am I? Perceptions of Digital Journalists' Professional Identity," in *The Routledge Handbook of Developments in Digital Journalism Studies*, ed. Scott A. Eldridge II and Bob Franklin (New York: Routledge, 2018), 40–52.

33. Interview with the author, June 23, 2016. The *Times*' Express Team is probably not best described as aggregation, as much of it revolves around the core information-gathering elements of reporting—interviewing sources, in particular. It does largely involve following up on stories that have broken elsewhere and have become widely discussed online. But the reporting orientation of

the work plays an important role in the Express Team journalists' ability to identify their work as part of a substantial professional career.

34. Interview with the author, March 11, 2015.

35. Interview with the author, March 3, 2015.

36. Michael Arrington, "Everybody Forgets the Readers When They Bash News Aggregators," *TechCrunch*, Feb. 2, 2010, https://techcrunch.com/2010/02/02 /everybody-forgets-the-readers-when-they-bash-news-aggregators/; Alastair Dawber, "Murdoch Blasts Search Engine 'Kleptomaniacs,'" *The Independent*, Oct. 9, 2009, http://www.independent.co.uk/news/media/online/murdoch-blasts -search-engine-kleptomaniacs-1800569.html; Andrew Leonard, "If the Web Doesn't Kill Journalism, Michael Wolff Will," *Salon*, April 5, 2010, https://www .salon.com/2010/04/05/michael_wolff_the_wrap_and_newser/; Jane Schulze, "Google Dubbed Internet Parasite by WSJ Editor," *The Australian*, April 6, 2009, https://web.archive.org/web/20111016161951/http://www.theaustralian.com.au /media/google-dubbed-internet-parasite/story-e6frg996-1225696931547.

37. Mercedes Bunz, "Rupert Murdoch: 'There's No Such Thing as a Free News Story,'" *The Guardian*, Dec. 1, 2009, https://www.theguardian.com/media/2009 /dec/01/rupert-murdoch-no-free-news; Simon Dumenco, "What It's Like to Get Used and Abused by The Huffington Post," *Advertising Age*, July 11, 2011, http://adage.com/article/the-media-guy/abused-huffington-post/228607/; Bill Keller, "All the Aggregation That's Fit to Aggregate," *New York Times Magazine*, March 10, 2011, http://www.nytimes.com/2011/03/13/magazine/mag-13lede-t .html; Leonard, "If the Web Doesn't Kill Journalism."

38. Dumenco, "What It's Like to Get Used and Abused."

39. Katherine Barner, "The Viral-Media Editor Who Says Cute Babies and Animals Are Her 'Bread and Butter,'" *New York*, April 13, 2017, http://nymag.com/thejob /2017/04/the-viral-media-editor-who-will-get-a-click-with-cute-babies-and -animals.html; James King, "My Year Ripping Off the Web With the Daily Mail Online," *Gawker*, March 4, 2015, http://tktk.gawker.com/my-year-ripping-off -the-web-with-the-daily-mail-online-1689453286; Jason McIntyre, "Low Morale at CBS Sports.com as it Eschews Reporting in Favor of Aggregation," *The Big Lead*, Feb. 3, 2016, http://thebiglead.com/2016/02/03/low-morale-at-cbs-sports -com-as-it-eschews-reporting-in-favor-of-aggregation/; Sam Stecklow, "The Chicago End-Times," *The Awl*, Oct. 8, 2015, https://www.theawl.com/2015/10 /the-chicago-end-times/.

40. When I asked aggregators how they'd like to be perceived within the news industry, several gave answers like Billy Penn managing editor Shannon Wink's: "Anytime somebody's going to shake their fist at me because something's in list form, I'm just going to dismiss them. . . . My all-caps answer is, *I do not care*" (Author's field notes, June 15, 2016).

41. Interview with the author, March 9, 2015.

42. The more immediate and prominent cause, though, was a change in ownership. VidNews was purchased by a large media organization that sought to professionalize its new property by moving toward more standardized and "original" aggregation practices. This was tied to the response to criticism, though, as the new owner proved more concerned about external criticism than the previous one had.

43. Interview with the author, Feb. 6, 2015.

44. Interview with the author, June 30, 2016.

45. See, e.g., Kit Eaton, "News App Circa Is One of the Top Apps of the Year," *Fast Company*, Dec. 18, 2013, https://www.fastcompany.com/3023729/news -app-circa-is-one-of-the-top-apps-of-the-year; Mathew Ingram, "Circa Wants to Rethink the Way We Consume the News on a Sub-Atomic Level," *Gigaom*, Oct. 15, 2012, https://gigaom.com/2012/10/15/circa-wants-to-rethink-the-news -at-a-sub-atomic-level/; Cade Metz, "Man Reinvents Daily News in the Image of Open Source Software," *Wired*, Oct. 3, 2013, https://www.wired.com /2013/10/78301/.

46. Billy Penn's journalists were also universally proud of their work, but their pride had little to do with their aggregation. Instead, it was rooted in their enterprise reporting work, their innovative reputation, and their young, hip audience. Aggregation was tangential to their identity at best.

47. Interview with the author, June 9, 2016.

48. Author's field notes, June 28, 2016.

49. Interview with the author, June 30, 2016.

50. Gerald J. Baldasty, *The Commercialization of News in the Nineteenth Century* (Madison: University of Wisconsin Press, 1992); James T. Hamilton, *All the News That's Fit to Sell: How the Market Transforms Information into News* (Princeton, NJ: Princeton University Press, 2004); Ekaterina Ognianova and James W. Endersby, "Objectivity Revisited: A Spatial Model of Political Ideology and Mass Communication," *Journalism & Communication Monographs* 159 (1996): 1–32.

51. Interview with the author, Feb. 20, 2015.

52. Author's field notes, Jan. 29, 2015.

53. Interview with the author, Feb. 17, 2015.

54. Interview with the author, March 11, 2015.

55. Interview with the author, March 13, 2015.

56. Jay Rosen, "Good Old Fashioned Shoe Leather Reporting," *PressThink* (blog post), April 16, 2015, http://pressthink.org/2015/04/good-old-fashioned-shoe-leather -reporting/; see also Mark Coddington, "Defending Judgment and Context in 'Original Reporting': Journalists' Construction of Newswork in a Networked Age,"

Journalism 15, no. 6 (2014): 678–95. This veneration of reporting is an important part of the identity even of digital journalists, who have historically been less tied to that work (Vos and Ferrucci, "Who Am I," 49).

57. C. W. Anderson, *Rebuilding the News: Metropolitan Journalism in the Digital Age* (Philadelphia, PA: Temple University Press, 2013); David M. Ryfe, *Can Journalism Survive? An Inside Look at American Newsrooms* (Cambridge: Polity, 2012); Sherwood and O'Donnell, "Once a Journalist, Always a Journalist?"

58. Interview with the author, Jan. 30, 2015.

59. Interview with the author, June 17, 2016.

60. Interview with the author, June 27, 2016.

61. As of early 2019, the site was still doing aggregation almost exclusively. (This editor had left the organization.)

62. Circa was not able to secure this round of funding, leading it to close within a few months of my visit there. For more details on Circa's shutdown and financial struggles, see chapter 6.

63. Interview with the author, July 20, 2016.

64. Edson C. Tandoc and Cassie Yuan Wen Foo, "Here's What BuzzFeed Journalists Think of Their Journalism," *Digital Journalism* 6, no. 1 (2018): 41–57; Konstantin Valerievich Toropin, "Gawker, BuzzFeed, and Journalism: Case Studies in Boundaries, News Aggregation, and Journalistic Authority," unpublished master's thesis, Hubbard School of Journalism, University of Minnesota (2016).

65. Author's field notes, Jan. 21, 2015.

66. Interview with the author, Jan. 30, 2015.

67. Interview with the author, July 8, 2016.

68. Interview with the author, Feb. 16, 2015.

69. Interview with the author, June 29, 2016.

70. Interview with the author, March 9, 2015.

71. Interview with the author, July 8, 2016.

72. Interview with the author, Feb. 23, 2015.

73. Singer, "Who Are These Guys?"; Jane B. Singer, "Out of Bounds: Professional Norms as Boundary Markers," in *Boundaries of Journalism: Professionalism, Practices and Participation*, ed. Matt Carlson and Seth C. Lewis (London: Routledge, 2015), 21–36. To see an example of the role of ethics in establishing legitimacy for an organization with roots in aggregation, see Tandoc and Foo, "Here's What BuzzFeed Journalists Think."

74. Interview with the author, Feb. 25, 2015.

75. Billy Penn's content management system made it literally impossible to post a link to the homepage without citing a source for it. Attribution was thus a paramount principle in the design of the website and content management system, though it became almost invisible in the daily work of its reporter/curators.

76. Mark Coddington, "Normalizing the Hyperlink: How Bloggers, Professional Journalists, and Institutions Shape Linking Values," *Digital Journalism* 2, no. 2 (2014): 140–55; Andrew Duffy, Edson C. Tandoc, and Richard Ling, "Frankenstein Journalism," *Information, Communication & Society* 21, no. 10 (2018): 1354–68.

77. Steve Buttry, "Aggregation Guidelines: Link, Attribute, Add Value," *The Buttry Diary* (blog post), May 16, 2012, https://stevebuttry.wordpress.com/2012/05/16/aggregation-guidelines-link-attribute-add-value/.

78. This question about adding to an overarching narrative leads aggregation into a broader conception of narrative than individual stories, as chapter 5 will address in detail.

79. Interview with the author, March 13, 2015.

80. Scott A. Eldridge II, *Online Journalism from the Periphery: Interloper Media and the Journalistic Field* (London: Routledge, 2018), 30, 92. Note that this is a sense of "adding value" that would not be distinct to aggregation.

81. Ryfe, *Can Journalism Survive?*

82. I am indebted to an anonymous reviewer for articulating this point.

83. For an analysis of deprofessionalization as applied to digital journalism, see Henrik Örnebring, "Reassessing Journalism as a Profession," in *The Routledge Companion to News and Journalism,* ed. Stuart Allan (London: Routledge, 2010), 568–77.

84. Carlson, *Journalistic Authority*; Jingrong Tong, "Journalistic Legitimacy Revisited: Collapse or Revival in the Digital Age?" *Digital Journalism* 6, no. 2 (2018): 256–73.

85. C. W. Anderson, "What Aggregators Do: Towards a Networked Concept of Journalistic Expertise in the Digital Age," *Journalism* 14, no. 8 (2013): 1008–23; Carlson, *Journalistic Authority*; Patrick Ferrucci and Tim Vos, "Who's In, Who's Out? Constructing the Identity of Digital Journalists," *Digital Journalism* 5, no. 7 (2017): 868–83.

4. CLICKBAIT, ANALYTICS, AND GUT FEELINGS: HOW AGGREGATORS UNDERSTAND THEIR AUDIENCES

1. This account is drawn from the author's field notes, Jan. 28–Feb. 1, 2015.

2. Matt Carlson, *Journalistic Authority: Legitimating News in the Digital Era* (New York: Columbia University Press, 2017).

3. Mark Deuze, "What Is Journalism? Professional Identity and Ideology of Journalists Reconsidered," *Journalism* 6, no. 4 (2005): 442–64; Jane B. Singer, "Who Are These Guys? The Online Challenge to the Notion of Journalistic Professionalism," *Journalism* 4, no. 2 (2003): 139–63. Journalists' professional status also depends on public acceptance of their exclusive control over an area of

knowledge, just as it does for their authority. See John Soloski, "News Reporting and Professionalism: Some Constraints on the Reporting of the News," *Media, Culture & Society* 11, no. 2 (1989): 207–28.

4. C. W. Anderson, *Rebuilding the News: Metropolitan Journalism in the Digital Age* (Philadelphia, PA: Temple University Press, 2013).

5. C. W. Anderson, "Deliberative, Agonistic, and Algorithmic Audiences: Journalism's Vision of Its Public in an Age of Audience Transparency," *International Journal of Communication* 5 (2011): 529–47.

6. Mark Coddington, "The Wall Becomes a Curtain: Revisiting Journalism's News-Business Boundary," in *Boundaries of Journalism: Professionalism, Practices and Participation*, ed. Matt Carlson and Seth C. Lewis (London: Routledge, 2015), 67–82.

7. Rasmus Kleis Nielsen, "The Business of News," in *The Sage Handbook of Digital Journalism*, ed. Tamara Witschge, C. W. Anderson, David Domingo, and Alfred Hermida (Thousand Oaks, CA: Sage, 2016), 51–67.

8. Interview with the author, Feb. 24, 2015.

9. Interview with the author, June 27, 2016.

10. See, e.g., Randal A. Beam, Bonnie J. Brownlee, David H. Weaver, and Damon T. Di Cicco, "Journalism and Public Service in Troubled Times," *Journalism Studies* 10, no. 6 (2009): 734–53; Bill Kovach and Tom Rosenstiel, *The Elements of Journalism; What Newspeople Should Know and the Public Should Expect*, 2nd ed. (New York: Three Rivers, 2007); Monika Krause, "Reporting and the Transformations of the Journalistic Field: US News Media, 1890–2000," *Media, Culture & Society* 33, no. 1 (2011): 89–104.

11. Herbert J. Gans, *Deciding What's News: A Study of CBS Evening News, NBC Nightly News, Newsweek, and* Time (New York, Pantheon, 1979); Philip Schlesinger, *Putting "Reality" Together: BBC News* (London: Constable, 1978); Randall S. Sumpter, "Daily Newspaper Editors' Audience Construction Routines: A Case Study," *Critical Studies in Media Communication* 17, no. 3 (2000): 334–46.

12. Ien Ang, *Desperately Seeking the Audience* (London: Routledge, 1991); James T. Hamilton, *All the News That's Fit to Sell: How the Market Transforms Information into News* (Princeton, NJ: Princeton University Press, 2004); Joseph Turow, *Breaking Up America: Advertisers and the New Media World* (Chicago: University of Chicago Press, 1997); Doug Underwood, *When MBAs Rule the Newsroom: How the Marketers and Managers Are Reshaping Today's Media* (New York: Columbia University Press, 1992).

13. Anthony M. Nadler, *Making the News Popular: Mobilizing U.S. News Audiences* (Urbana: University of Illinois Press, 2016). See also Ang, *Desperately Seeking the Audience*; Turow, *Breaking Up America*.

14. For the roots, flaws, and effects of this market research-driven approach to audiences, see Nadler, *Making the News Popular*.

15. Kevin G. Barnhurst, *Mister Pulitzer and the Spider: Modern News from Realism to the Digital* (Urbana: University of Illinois, 2016), 72; Gans, *Deciding What's News*; Schlesinger, *Putting "Reality" Together*.

16. Richard V. Ericson, Patricia M. Baranek, and Janet B. L. Chan, *Visualizing Deviance: A Study of News Organization* (Toronto: University of Toronto Press, 1987); Gans, *Deciding What's News*; Schlesinger, *Putting "Reality" Together*; Sumpter, "Daily Newspaper Editors' Audience Construction Routines."

17. Ericson et al., *Visualizing Deviance*; Sumpter, "Daily Newspaper Editors' Audience Construction Routines."

18. See, e.g., Ang, *Desperately Seeking the Audience*; Hamilton, *All the News That's Fit to Sell*.

19. See, e.g., Tanni Haas and Linda Steiner, "Public Journalism: A Response to Critics," *Journalism* 7, no. 2 (2006): 238–54; Jay Rosen, *What Are Journalists For?* (New Haven, CT: Yale University Press, 1999).

20. Seth C. Lewis, "The Tension Between Professional Control and Open Participation: Journalism and Its Boundaries," *Information, Communication & Society* 15, no. 6 (2012): 836–66; Joyce Y. M. Nip, "Exploring the Second Phase of Public Journalism," *Journalism Studies* 7, no. 2 (2006): 212–36; Jay Rosen, "The People Formerly Known as the Audience," *PressThink* (blog post), June 27, 2006, http://archive.pressthink.org/2006/06/27/ppl_frmr.html.

21. Pablo J. Boczkowski, *News at Work: Imitation in an Age of Information Abundance* (Chicago: University of Chicago Press, 2010); Edson C. Tandoc Jr., "Journalism Is Twerking? How Web Analytics Is Changing the Process of Gatekeeping," *New Media & Society* 16, no. 4 (2014): 559–75; Nikki Usher, "Going Web-First at *The Christian Science Monitor*: A Three-Part Study of Change," *International Journal of Communication* 6 (2012): 1898–917, http://ijoc.org/index.php/ijoc/article/view/1404.

22. Boczkowski, *News at Work*; Caitlin Petre, *The Traffic Factories: Metrics at Chartbeat, Gawker Media, and* The New York Times, Tow Center for Digital Journalism (2015), https://academiccommons.columbia.edu/doi/10.7916/D80293W1; Usher, "Going Web-First at *The Christian Science Monitor*."

23. Anderson, "Deliberative, Agonistic, and Algorithmic Audiences"; Angela M. Lee, Seth C. Lewis, and Matthew Powers, "Audience Clicks and News Placement: A Study of Time-Lagged Influence in Online Journalism," *Communication Research* 41, no. 4 (2012): 505–30.

24. Rodrigo Zamith, "Quantified Audiences in News Production: A Synthesis and Research Agenda," *Digital Journalism* 6, no. 4 (2018): 418–35.

25. Interview with the author, Feb. 23, 2015.

244 *4. Clickbait, Analytics, and Gut Feelings*

26. Interview with the author, Jan. 30, 2015.

27. Interview with the author, March 13, 2015.

28. Interview with the author, Feb. 25, 2015.

29. All of these statements are taken from the author's field notes, June 27–July 1, 2016.

30. This sort of cynicism is often ascribed to aggregators or purveyors of clickbait more generally, but it's rare for those sentiments to be voiced publicly by those writers themselves. There are a few exceptions in areas of aggregation that are focused purely on virality without any reverence for a journalistic sense of news value. For an example of these statements of more naked catering to audience desires, see Katherine Barner, "The Viral-Media Editor Who Says Cute Babies and Animals Are Her 'Bread and Butter,'" *New York*, April 13, 2017, http://nymag.com/thejob/2017/04/the-viral-media-editor-who-will-get-a-click-with-cute-babies-and-animals.html.

31. Author's field notes, Jan. 30, 2015.

32. Meryl Aldridge, "The Tentative Hell-Raisers: Identity and Mythology in Contemporary UK Press Journalism," *Media, Culture & Society* 20, no. 1 (1998): 109–27.

33. Pamela J. Shoemaker and Stephen D. Reese, *Mediating the Message in the 21st Century: A Media Sociology Perspective*, 3rd ed.(New York: Routledge, 2014), 170.

34. C. W. Anderson, "Between Creative and Quantified Audiences: Web Metrics and Changing Patterns of Newswork in Local US Newsrooms," *Journalism* 12, no. 5 (2011): 550–66, at 561. Emphasis in original.

35. Anderson, *Rebuilding the News*; Tandoc, "Journalism Is Twerking?"; Usher, "Going Web-First at *The Christian Science Monitor.*"

36. For a thorough review of this literature, see Zamith, "Quantified Audiences in News Production."

37. Interview with the author, Feb. 6, 2015. By the following year, VidNews had indeed changed substantially on that front. It had hired a full-time staff member focusing on data and audience analysis who had worked to centralize VidNews' disparate data and produce weekly reports for newsroom managers (Interview with the author, July 20, 2016).

38. Author's field notes, Jan. 30, 2015.

39. Author's field notes, June 28, 2016.

40. Interview with the author, March 13, 2015.

41. Interview with the author, Feb. 25, 2015.

42. For more detail on this factor as a criterion of newsworthiness, see chapter 2.

43. Interview with the author, Feb. 25, 2015.

44. Interview with the author, Jan. 30, 2015.

45. This unknowability echoes the findings of Dominic Boyer in his study of German online journalists. As Boyer noted, journalists couldn't *not* look at analytics reports, but the reports, and the strategies derived from them, never alleviated the ultimately mysterious nature of the user. "In a sense," Boyer writes, "the more that is known about the user, the less that remains unknown seems knowable" (83). See Dominic Boyer, *The Life Informatic: Newsmaking in the Digital Era* (Ithaca, NY: Cornell University Press, 2013), 79–84.

46. Both quotes are from the author's field notes, Jan. 29, 2015.

47. Anderson, "Between Creative and Quantified Audiences"; Petre, *The Traffic Factories*; Usher, "Going Web-First at *The Christian Science Monitor.*"

48. Interview with the author, Jan. 30, 2015.

49. Interview with the author, Feb. 26, 2015.

50. Kovach and Rosenstiel, *The Elements of Journalism*; Tim P. Vos and Stephanie Craft, "The Discursive Construction of Journalistic Transparency," *Journalism Studies* 18, no. 12 (2017): 1505–22.

51. The term *clickbait* dates back to at least 1999, when it appeared in a *Network* magazine article on mobile code security (Jonathan Angel, "Mobile Code Security," *Network* 14, no. 12 (Dec. 1999), retrieved from the Factiva database). It took on greater use in the blogosphere in 2010 and 2011 and began appearing in traditional news sources in late 2011, according to searches of Google and the Factiva database.

52. *Oxford English Living Dictionaries*, s.v. "clickbait (*n.*)," accessed Feb. 20, 2019, https://en.oxforddictionaries.com/definition/us/clickbait.

53. *Oxford English Dictionary*, s.v. "clickbait (*n.*)," accessed Feb. 20, 2019, http:// www.oed.com/view/Entry/37263110?redirectedFrom=clickbait&. Merriam -Webster has a similar definition, saying it's especially for "content of dubi- ous value or interest." (*Merriam-Webster Online Unabridged Dictionary*, s.v. "clickbait (*n.*)," accessed Feb. 20, 2019, https://www.merriam-webster.com /dictionary/clickbait)

54. Ben Smith, "Why BuzzFeed Doesn't Do Clickbait," *BuzzFeed*, Nov. 6, 2014, https://www.buzzfeed.com/bensmith/why-buzzfeed-doesnt-do-clickbait?utm _term=.fjv1DNKooL#.yj0enYG22A. The insufficiency of this definition is evident in that it led Smith to declare that "clickbait stopped working around 2009," a statement that, a decade after that point, seems absurd on its face.

55. Alex Peysakhovich and Kristin Hendrix, "Further Reducing Clickbait in Feed," *Facebook Newsroom*, Aug. 4, 2016, https://newsroom.fb.com/news/2016/08 /news-feed-fyi-further-reducing-clickbait-in-feed/.

56. See, e.g., Laura Klinger and Kelly McBride, "Stop Calling Every News Article Clickbait," *Poynter*, Feb. 22, 2016, https://www.poynter.org/educators-students /2016/clickbait/.

57. Tim Marchman, "Shut Up About 'Clickbait,'" *Deadspin*, March 26, 2014, http://theconcourse.deadspin.com/shut-up-about-clickbait-1551902024.

58. Dolors Palau-Sampio, "Reference Press Metamorphosis in the Digital Context: Clickbait and Tabloid Strategies in Elpais.com," *Communication & Society* 29, no. 2 (2016): 63–79.

59. S. Elizabeth Bird, "Storytelling on the Far Side: Journalism and the Weekly Tabloid," *Critical Studies in Mass Communication* 7, no. 4 (1990): 377–89; David Elliot Berman, "Breaking Babel: A Comparative Historical Analysis of Yellow Journalism and Clickbait," Paper presented at the AEJMC 2018 annual conference, Aug. 6–9, Washington, DC.

60. Interview with the author, June 30, 2016.

61. Interview with the author, Feb. 24, 2015.

62. Interviews with the author, Feb. 27, 2015 and March 11, 2015.

63. Interview with the author, Feb. 17, 2015.

64. Interview with the author, March 11, 2015.

65. Jane B. Singer, "Out of Bounds: Professional Norms as Boundary Markers," in Carlson and Lewis, *Boundaries of Journalism*, 21–36.

66. Interview with the author, Jan. 30, 2015.

67. Author's field notes, Jan. 29, 2015. Other journalists have made similar arguments publicly. See, e.g., Chris Cillizza, "In Defense of Clickbait—and Why Journalists Should Stop Being So Snobby," *Washington Post*, Aug. 17, 2015, https://www.washingtonpost.com/news/the-fix/wp/2015/08/17/in-defense -of-clickbait-and-why-journalists-should-stop-being-so-snobby/?utm_term =.5890974eae2b.

68. Adriana Amado and Silvio Waisbord, "Divided We Stand: Blurred Boundaries in Argentine Journalism," in Carlson and Lewis, *Boundaries of Journalism*, 51–66.

69. Elizabeth and Oscar are pseudonyms. This account is drawn from the author's field notes, June 29, 2016.

70. This headline has been changed slightly to preserve the anonymity of Elizabeth's story. The substance and style of the headline remain the same, however.

71. Author's field notes, Jan. 28, 2015.

72. Nadler, *Making the News Popular*, 2.

73. Ángel Arrese, "From Gratis to Paywalls: A Brief History of a Retro-Innovation in the Press's Business," *Journalism Studies* 17, no. 8 (2016): 1051–67.

74. For more on the tension inherent in journalism's news-business divide, see Coddington, "The Wall Becomes a Curtain."

5. ATOMIZATION AND THE BREAKDOWN (AND REBUILDING) OF NEWS NARRATIVE

1. This description of De Rosa at work with Circa is drawn from the author's field notes, Jan. 19–20, 2015.

2. Interview with the author, Feb. 19, 2015. This was not a universal rule, of course; Circa started new stories regularly, and its editors noted that they tried not to be too concerned about starting a new story. But editors typically first attempted to find existing stories to fit a news development with, especially since a new story started with zero followers, while an existing story had a built-in audience.

3. Shanto Iyengar, *Is Anyone Responsible? How Television Frames Political Issues* (Chicago: University of Chicago Press, 1991); Robert E. Park, "News as a Form of Knowledge: A Chapter in the Sociology of Knowledge," *American Journal of Sociology* 45, no. 5 (1940): 669–86; Thomas E. Patterson, *Out of Order* (New York: Vintage, 1993).

4. Marcel Broersma, "Journalism as Performative Discourse: The Importance of Form and Style in Journalism," in *Journalism and Meaning-Making: Reading the Newspaper*, ed. Verica Rupar (Cresskill, NJ: Hampton, 2010), 15–35; Matt Carlson, *Journalistic Authority: Legitimating News in the Digital Age* (New York: Columbia University Press, 2017), 53.

5. James S. Ettema and Theodore L. Glasser, *Custodians of Conscience: Investigative Journalism and Public Virtue* (New York: Columbia University Press, 1998); Michael Schudson, *Discovering the News: A Social History of American Newspapers* (New York: Basic Books, 1978); Paul H. Weaver, "Newspaper News and Television News," in *Television as a Social Force: New Approaches to TV Criticism*, ed. Douglas Cater and Richard Adler (New York: Praeger, 1975), 81–94.

6. Paul Ricœur, *Time and Narrative* (Chicago, University of Chicago Press, 1984/1990), 152. See also Sarah Kozloff, "Narrative Theory and Television," in *Channels of Discourse, Reassembled: Television and Contemporary Criticism*, ed. Robert Clyde Allen (London: Routledge, 2005), 21–83.

7. Ettema and Glasser, *Custodians of Conscience*, 111–13; Walter R. Fisher, "Narration as a Human Communication Paradigm: The Case of Public Moral Argument," *Communication Monographs* 51, no. 1 (1984): 1–22; Hayden White, "The Value of Narrativity in the Representation of Reality," in *On Narrative*, ed. W. J. T. Mitchell (Chicago: University of Chicago Press, 1980), 1–23.

8. Ronald N. Jacobs, "Producing the News, Producing the Crisis: Narrativity, Television and News Work," *Media, Culture & Society* 18, no. 3 (1996): 373–397, at 381. See also Mats Ekström, "Information, Storytelling and Attractions:

TV Journalism in Three Modes of Communication," *Media, Culture & Society* 22, no. 4 (2000): 465–92; Ettema and Glasser, *Custodians of Conscience*, 131–37; Itzhak Roeh and Sharon Ashley, "Criticizing Press Coverage of the War in Lebanon: Toward a Paradigm of News as Storytelling," in *Communication Yearbook*, 9th ed., ed. Margaret L. McLaughlin (Beverly Hills, CA: Sage, 1986), 117–41.

9. Ettema and Glasser, *Custodians of Conscience*, 112; Robert A. Hackett, "Decline of a Paradigm? Bias and Objectivity in News Media Studies," *Critical Studies in Mass Communication* 1, no. 3 (1984): 229–59; Hayden White, *The Content of the Form: Narrative Discourse and Historical Representation* (Baltimore, MD: Johns Hopkins University Press, 1987), 178.

10. Michael Schudson, *The Sociology of News*, 2nd ed. (New York: W.W. Norton & Co., 2011), 186. For more on the argument of news articles as a series of propositions rather than a narrative, see Elizabeth A. Thomson, Peter R.R. White, and Philip Kitley, "'Objectivity' and 'Hard News' Reporting Across Cultures: Comparing the News Report in English, French, Japanese and Indonesian Journalism," *Journalism Studies* 9, no. 2 (2008): 212–28; and Teun A. van Dijk, *News as Discourse* (New York: Longman, 1986), 15.

11. Robert E. Gutsche Jr. and Erica Salkin, "Who Lost What? An Analysis of Myth, Loss, and Proximity in News Coverage of the Steubenville Rape," *Journalism* 17, no. 4 (2016): 456–73.

12. Jack Lule, *Daily News, Eternal Stories: The Mythological Role of Journalism* (New York: The Guilford Press, 2001), 15–17; S. Elizabeth Bird and Robert W. Dardenne, "Myth, Chronicle, and Story: Exploring the Narrative Qualities of News," in *Media, Myths, and Narratives: Television and the Press*, ed. James W. Carey (Newbury Park, CA: Sage, 1988), 67–86. There is a mountain of literature on the role of myth and archetype in narrative more broadly, including, most notably, Roland Barthes, *Mythologies* (New York: Hill and Wang, 1957/1978) and Joseph Campbell, *The Hero with a Thousand Faces* (New York: Pantheon, 1949).

13. One notable (and explicit) exception to this came when the editor of a social news site said his organization considers archetypal narratives as a way to ensure that its stories connect emotionally with readers and increase their chances of being shared more widely: "Something that we're specific about is Hollywood narratives—you know, the basic outline of the way stories work, like hero versus villain and overcoming obstacles, like six or eight basic Hollywood narratives. Thinking about those kinds of things, and thinking about, 'Can we frame this, or tell this story in a way that the reader can understand clearly why we're telling this story, and what they're walking away from this story thinking?'" (Interview with the author, March 13, 2015).

14. Jacobs, "Producing News, Producing the Crisis," 383. See also S. Elizabeth Bird, Storytelling on the Far Side: Journalism and the Weekly Tabloid," *Critical Studies in Mass Communication* 7, no. 4 (1990): 377–89; Gaye Tuchman, *Making News: A Study in the Construction of Reality* (New York: Free Press, 1978), 215.

15. Marcel Broersma, "Form, Style and Journalistic Strategies: An Introduction," in *Form and Style in Journalism: European Newspapers and the Representation of News 1880–2005* (Leuven, Belgium: Peeters, 2007), ix-xxix; Broersma, "Journalism as Performative Discourse."

16. David T. Z. Mindich, *Just the Facts: How "Objectivity" Came to Define American Journalism* (New York: New York University Press, 1998), 65.

17. For explications of the inverted pyramid and its changes over time, see Thomson et al., " 'Objectivity' and 'Hard News' Reporting Across Cultures"; and Espen Ytreberg, "Moving Out of the Inverted Pyramid: Narratives and Descriptions in Television News," *Journalism Studies* 2, no. 3 (2001): 357–71.

18. Park, "News as a Form of Knowledge," 646.

19. Katherine Fink and Michael Schudson, "The Rise of Contextual Journalism, 1950s–2000s," *Journalism* 15, no. 1 (2014): 3–20; Jane Johnston and Caroline Graham, "The New, Old Journalism: Narrative Writing in Contemporary Newspapers," *Journalism Studies* 13, no. 4 (2012): 517–33. Michele Weldon, *Everyman News: The Changing American Front Page* (Columbia: University of Missouri Press, 2008).

20. Kevin G. Barnhurst and Diana Mutz, "American Journalism and the Decline in Event-Centered Reporting," *Journal of Communication* 47, no. 4 (1997): 27–53; Fink and Schudson, "The Rise of Contextual Journalism"; Svennik Høyer and Hedda A. Nossen, "Revisions of the News Paradigm: Changes in Stylistic Features Between 1950 and 2008 in the Journalism of Norway's Largest Newspaper," *Journalism* 16, no. 4 (2015): 536–52.

21. For more on the growth of interactive and longform news stories, see David Dowling and Travis Vogan, "Can We 'Snowfall' This? Digital Longform and the Race for the Tablet Market," *Digital Journalism* 3, no. 2 (2015): 209–24; Nikki Usher, *Interactive Journalism: Hackers, Data, and Code* (Urbana: University of Illinois Press, 2016). For a historical review of the origins of literary journalism in the United States, see John Hartsock, *A History of American Literary Journalism: The Emergence of a Modern Narrative Form* (Amherst: University of Massachusetts Press, 2000).

22. Ryan Chittum, "The Shorter-Form *Journal*," *Columbia Journalism Review*, Oct. 10, 2011, http://www.cjr.org/the_audit/the_shorter-form_journal.php; Project for Excellence in Journalism, *The Changing Newsroom: What Is Being Gained and What Is Being Lost in America's Daily Newspapers?* (Washington, DC: Pew Research Center, 2008), http://www.journalism.org/2008/07/21/the

-changing-newsroom-2/; Jack Shafer, "In Today's News, One Size Fits All," *Reuters*, May 14, 2014, http://blogs.reuters.com/jackshafer/2014/05/14/in-todays -news-one-size-fits-all/; Dean Starkman, "Major Papers' Longform Meltdown," *Columbia Journalism Review*, Jan. 17, 2013, http://www.cjr.org/the_audit/major _papers_longform_meltdown.php?page=all; Weldon, *Everyman News*.

23. Erik Neveu, "Revisiting Narrative Journalism as One of the Futures of Jour-nalism," *Journalism Studies* 15, no. 5 (2014): 533–42. Regarding mobile news consumption and reduced attention and time spent per story, a good review of research has been conducted by Johanna Dunaway, *Mobile vs. Computer: Implications for News Audiences and Outlets* (Cambridge, MA: Shorenstein Center on Media, Politics and Public Policy, 2016), https://shorensteincenter .org/mobile-vs-computer-news-audiences-and-outlets/.

24. Sean Blanda, "We Need to Reinvent the Article," *SeanBlanda.com* (blog post), May 25, 2012 https://web.archive.org/web/20141004141907/http://seanblanda. com/we-need-to-reinvent-the-article/; Jonathan Glick, "The News Article Is Breaking Up," *Business Insider*, June 1, 2011, http://www.businessinsider.com /the-news-article-is-breaking-up-2011-6; Jeff Jarvis, "The Article as Luxury or Byproduct," *BuzzMachine* (blog post), May 28, 2011, http://buzzmachine .com/2011/05/28/the-article-as-luxury-or-byproduct/; Bill Kovach and Tom Rosenstiel, *Blur: How to Know What's True in the Age of Information Overload* (New York: Bloomsbury, 2010), 192–94.

25. Adrian Holovaty, "A Fundamental Way Newspaper Sites Need to Change," *holovaty.com* (blog post), Sept. 6, 2006, http://www.holovaty.com/writing /fundamental-change/; Robert Niles, "The Programmer as Journalist: A Q&A with Adrian Holovaty," *OJR: The Online Journalism Review*, June 5, 2006, https://web.archive.org/web/20130208020127/http://www.ojr.org/ojr/stories /060605niles/.

26. The fire analogy is borrowed from Dan Conover, "The 'Lack of Vision' Thing? Well, Here's a Hopeful Vision for You," *Xark* (blog post), May 11, 2009, http:// xark.typepad.com/my_weblog/2009/05/the-lack-of-vision-thing-well-heres-a -vision-for-you.html.

27. Regarding PolitiFact, see Matt Waite, "To Build a Digital Future for News, Developers Have to Be Able to Hack at the Core of the Old Ways," *Nieman Journalism Lab*, March 8, 2011, http://www.niemanlab.org/2011/03/matt-waite -to-build-a-digital-future-for-news-developers-have-to-be-able-to-hack-at -the-core-of-the-old-ways/; Matt Waite, "Finding Stories in the Structure of Data," *Nieman Journalism Lab*, May 2, 2013, https://source.opennews.org/en -US/learning/finding-stories-structure-data/. For a description of Structured Stories' approach, see David Caswell and Konstantin Dörr, "Automated Jour-nalism 2.0: Event-Driven Narratives: From Simple Descriptions to Real Stories,"

Journalism Practice 12, no. 4 (2018): 477–96. Regarding Homicide Watch and other structured journalism projects, see Chava Gourarie, " 'Structured Journalism' Offers Readers a Different Kind of Story Experience," *Columbia Journalism Review*, July 30, 2015, https://www.cjr.org/innovations/structured_journalism .php.

28. Interview with the author, July 21, 2016.

29. Ben Huh, "Why Are We Still Consuming the News Like It's 1899?" *BenHuh. com* (blog post), May 23, 2011, https://web.archive.org/web/20110527023136 /https://benhuh.com/2011/05/23/why-are-we-still-consuming-the-news -like-its-1899/.

30. Interview with the author, July 28, 2016.

31. Jakob Nielsen, "Generation App: 62% of Mobile Users 25–34 Own Smart-phones," Nov. 3, 2011, http://www.nielsen.com/us/en/insights/news/2011 /generation-app-62-of-mobile-users-25-34-own-smartphones.html. For an example of a critique of news app design circa 2011, see Jakob Nielsen, "Why WSJ Mobile App Gets ** Customer Reviews," *Nielsen Normal Group*, July 5, 2011, https://www.nngroup.com/articles/why-wsj-mobile-app-gets-bad-reviews/.

32. Circa wasn't the only mobile-only news venture at this time. News Corp. famously launched a daily iPad-only news app called *The Daily* in Feb. 2011. It shut down in Dec. 2012, having suffered from technical problems and bloated costs. Peter Kafka, "News Corp. Shutters The Daily iPad App," *All Things Digital*, Dec. 3, 2012, http://allthingsd.com/20121203/news-corp-shutters-the-daily-ipad-app/.

33. Matt Galligan, "Blast from the Past: Looking Back to Early 2012 at Circa News 1.0 Pre-Launch," *Medium* (blog post), May 13, 2016, https://medium.com/@mg /blast-from-the-past-looking-back-to-early-2012-at-circa-news-1-0-pre -launch-e8fe961cbeee#.izrzhxgsx.

34. Interview with the author (David Cohn), Oct. 19, 2015.

35. Interview with the author, July 20, 2016. Santos noted that Circa's leadership came to this realization based on metrics that showed a strong relationship between users following stories and repeat visits to the app.

36. Interview with the author, Feb. 17, 2015.

37. See, e.g., Mark Fishman, *Manufacturing the News* (Austin: University of Texas Press, 1980); Tuchman, *Making News.*

38. Interview with the author, March 11, 2015.

39. Interview with the author, Jan. 22, 2015.

40. Interview with the author, June 9, 2016.

41. Interview with the author, Feb. 24, 2015.

42. Interview with the author, Feb. 17, 2015. Buxbaum was describing what some scholars have referred to as the "performativity" of speech—the notion that speech-acts themselves enact reality, rather than simply describe it. For a

discussion of the powerful hold of performativity on journalists within the realm of documents, see Fishman, *Manufacturing the News*, 98–100.

43. See, e.g., Walter Lippmann, *Public Opinion* (New York: Macmillan, 1922/1961); Harvey Molotch and Marilyn Lester, "News as Purposive Behavior: On the Strategic Use of Routine Events, Accidents, and Scandals," *American Sociological Review* 39, no. 1 (1974): 101–12; Tuchman, *Making News*, 134. Note, however, that there is evidence that journalists are moving away from structuring virtually all stories around particular events as they become more interpretive (Kevin G. Barnhurst, *Mister Pulitzer and the Spider: Modern News from Realism to the Digital* (Urbana: University of Illinois Press, 2016).

44. Because this longitudinal perspective wasn't part of Circa's primary initial purpose, little of the structure that helped Circa editors make sense of the news, such as the branch system, was available to their readers.

45. Interview with the author, Feb. 24, 2015.

46. Michael Moss, "U.S. Research Lab Lets Livestock Suffer in Quest for Profit," *New York Times*, Jan. 19, 2015, https://www.nytimes.com/2015/01/20/dining /animal-welfare-at-risk-in-experiments-for-meat-industry.html.

47. Author's field notes, Jan. 21, 2015.

48. Interview with the author, Feb. 26, 2015.

49. See, e.g., Ettema and Glasser, *Custodians of Conscience*; Jacobs, "Producing the News, Producing the Crisis." The classic typology of values by which journalists recognize events or issues as newsworthy includes the value of "continuity," which might apply here; for Circa editors, this particular form of continuity is both more systematic and more prominent in making something "news." Johan Galtung and Mari Holmboe Ruge, "The Structure of Foreign News: The Presentation of the Congo, Cuba and Cyprus Crises in Four Norwegian Newspapers," *Journal of Peace Research* 2, no. 1 (1965): 64–90.

50. Interview with the author, Feb. 18, 2015.

51. Park, "News as a Form of Knowledge," 646.

52. This detail is drawn from interviews with several former Circa staffers. Six months later, Sinclair Broadcasting Group, a conservative-leaning company that owns local TV stations around the United States, announced it had bought Circa's brand and its technology for an undisclosed amount of money. By the following summer, Sinclair had relaunched Circa as a different product—a mobile and social video-based platform that also supplied content for the websites of Sinclair's local stations.

53. David Cohn has referred to Circa as "a wire service 2.0," a traditionally more business-to-business approach that is difficult to translate into a direct-to-consumers app. Circa had plans to develop native advertising or paid services, but they never materialized. The mobile advertising market was quite sluggish

at the time, and Circa's user base was too small by tech standards to attract new investors or significant ad interest. Circa was extremely cagey about its user numbers—it was the only thing I was not allowed to report on as part of the terms of my visit there—but after it shut down, Matt Galligan talked about his numbers a few times publicly on Twitter, largely to defend the size of Circa's user base. He reported an average of 270,000 monthly active users and 50,000 daily active users. Matt Galligan (@mg), "Avg of 270k MAU / 50k DAU. Will report back with peaks." *Twitter*, Aug. 18, 2016, 1:44 p.m., https://twitter.com /mg/status/766375159133380608.

54. Joshua Benton, "SEO Lessons from Google News: How to Promote Your Stories, Straight from the Bot's Mouth," *Nieman Journalism Lab*, Sept. 3, 2009, http://www.niemanlab.org/2009/09/how-to-push-stories-high-in-google -news-straight-from-the-bots-mouth/; Frederic Filloux, "Google News: The Secret Sauce," *Guardian*, Feb. 25, 2013, https://www.theguardian.com/technology/2013 /feb/25/1.

55. Interview with the author, Feb. 13, 2015.

56. This approach was gradually de-emphasized internally as VidNews shifted toward reporting its own stories. It was even more central in the years before I visited there, and seemed to have faded as a form of institutional identity when I interviewed the senior news editor in mid-2016. But as of early 2019, it remained a central part of VidNews' branding.

57. Author's field notes, Feb. 4, 2015.

58. Interview with the author, Jan. 30, 2015.

59. This was by design, so that new readers would not be jarred by an unfamiliar story structure. "We still want to make it as normal a story for a regular reader as we possibly can," said Circa editor Anthony De Rosa "It would be silly for us to try to create something that people don't recognize as a traditional story, because then people wouldn't understand what we're trying to get across" (Author's field notes, Jan. 19, 2015).

60. Author's field notes, June 30, 2016.

61. Johnston and Graham, "The New, Old Journalism"; Weldon, *Everyman News*.

62. Edson C. Tandoc Jr., "Five Ways BuzzFeed Is Preserving (or Transforming) the Journalistic Field," *Journalism* 19, no. 2 (2018): 200–16; Edson C. Tandoc and Cassie Yuan Wen Foo, "Here's What BuzzFeed Journalists Think of Their Journalism," *Digital Journalism* 6, no. 1 (2018): 41–57.

63. Interview with the author, March 18, 2015.

64. Barnhurst, *Mister Pulitzer and the Spider*; Barnhurst and Mutz, "American Journalism and the Decline"; Frank Esser and Andrea Umbricht, "The Evolution of Objective and Interpretative Journalism in the Western Press:

Comparing Six News Systems Since the 1960s," *Journalism & Mass Communication Quarterly* 91, no. 2 (2014): 229–49; Fink and Schudson, "The Rise of Contextual Journalism."

65. Matt Carlson, "Embedded Links, Embedded Meanings: Social Media Commentary and News Sharing as Mundane Media Criticism," *Journalism Studies* 17, no. 7 (2016): 915–24.

66. Jan Boesman and Irene Costera Meijer, "'Don't Read Me the News, Tell Me the Story': How News Makers and Storytellers Negotiate Journalism's Boundaries When Preparing and Presenting News Stories," *#ISOJ* 8, no. 1 (2018), http://isoj.org/research/dont-read-me-the-news-tell-me-the-story-how-news -makers-and-storytellers-negotiate-journalisms-boundaries-when-preparing -and-presenting-news-stories/.

67. Jan Boesman and Irene Costera Meijer, "Nothing But the Facts? Exploring the Discursive Space for Storytelling and Truth-Seeking in Journalism," *Journalism Practice* 12, no. 8 (2018): 997–1007, at 998.

68. Kevin G. Barnhurst, "The Makers of Meaning: National Public Radio and the New Long Journalism, 1980–2000," *Political Communication* 20, no. 1 (2003): 1–22; Barnhurst and Mutz, "American Journalism and the Decline in Event-Centered Reporting"; Lucas Graves, *Deciding What's True: The Rise of Political Fact-Checking in American Journalism* (New York: Columbia University Press, 2016), 65–66.

69. Svennik Høyer, "Why Study Journalistic Genres?" in *Journalism at the Crossroads: Perspectives on Research*, ed. Juha Koivisto and Epp Lauk (Tartu, Estonia: Tartu University Press, 1997), 65–77; Ytreberg, "Moving Out of the Inverted Pyramid."

70. Fink and Schudson, "The Rise of Contextual Journalism"; Høyer and Nossen, "Revisions of the News Paradigm"; Susana Salgado and Jesper Strömbäck, "Interpretive Journalism: A Review of Concepts, Operationalizations and Key Findings," *Journalism* 13, no. 2 (2012): 144–61.

6. CONCLUSION: AGGREGATION, AUTHORITY, AND UNCERTAINTY

1. The description of these components is drawn from Matt Carlson, *Journalistic Authority: Legitimating News in the Digital Era* (New York: Columbia University Press, 2017), 183–5.

2. Circa was a notable exception to this, as it used its novel textual form to achieve some distinction. The degree to which it actually converted the distinctiveness of its form to authority is unclear, though.

3. See S. Elizabeth Bird, "Storytelling on the Far Side: Journalism and the Weekly Tabloid," *Critical Studies in Mass Communication* 7, no. 4 (1990): 377–89; Ronald N. Jacobs, "Producing the News, Producing the Crisis: Narrativity, Television and News Work," *Media, Culture & Society* 18, no. 3 (1996): 373–97.

4. C. W. Anderson, *Rebuilding the News: Metropolitan Journalism in the Digital Age* (Philadelphia, PA: Temple University Press, 2013); Brian Creech, "Disciplines of Truth: The 'Arab Spring,' American Journalistic Practice, and the Production of Public Knowledge," *Journalism* 16, no. 8 (2015): 1010–26; Jay Rosen, "Good Old Fashioned Shoe Leather Reporting," *PressThink* (blog post), April 16, 2015, http://pressthink.org/2015/04/good-old-fashioned-shoe-leather -reporting/.

5. You can see the role of such practices in journalistic boundary work in a variety of studies, including Ronald Bishop, "From Behind the Walls: Boundary Work by News Organizations in Their Coverage of Princess Diana's Death," *Journal of Communication Inquiry* 23, no. 1 (1999): 90–112; Mark Coddington, "Defending a Paradigm by Patrolling a Boundary: Two Global Newspapers' Approach to WikiLeaks," *Journalism & Mass Communication Quarterly* 89, no. 3 (2012): 377–96; Matthias Revers, "Journalistic Professionalism as Performance and Boundary Work: Source Relations at the State House," *Journalism* 15, no. 1 (2014): 37–52.

6. This point can be found in Matt Carlson, "The Information Politics of Journalism in a Post-Truth Age," *Journalism Studies* 19, no. 13 (2018): 1879–88.

7. The literature on the journalistic functions of the hyperlink is robust. For research exploring the role of hyperlinks in establishing legitimacy and making journalistic evidence-gathering visible, see, e.g., Juliette De Maeyer, "Citation Needed: Investigating the Use of Hyperlinks to Display Sources in News Stories," *Journalism Practice* 8, no. 5 (2014): 532–41; Juliette De Maeyer and Avery E. Holton, "Why Linking Matters: A Metajournalistic Discourse Analysis," *Journalism* 17, no. 6 (2016): 776–94; Andrew Duffy, Edson C. Tandoc, and Richard Ling, "Frankenstein Journalism," *Information, Communication & Society* 21, no. 10 (2018): 1354–68.

8. For an example of the formation of alternate structures of authority among far-right political video producers on YouTube, see Rebecca Lewis, "Alternative Influence: Broadcasting the Reactionary Right on YouTube," *Data & Society* (New York, 2018), https://datasociety.net/wp-content/uploads/2018/09/DS _Alternative_Influence.pdf.

9. Interview with the author, Feb. 17, 2015.

10. Meryl Aldridge and Julia Evetts, "Rethinking the Concept of Professionalism: The Case of Journalism," *British Journal of Sociology* 54, no. 4 (2003): 547–64;

Seth C. Lewis, "The Tension Between Professional Control and Open Participation: Journalism and Its Boundaries," *Information, Communication & Society* 15, no. 6 (2012): 836–66; John Soloski, "News Reporting and Professionalism: Some Constraints on the Reporting of the News," *Media, Culture & Society* 11, no. 2 (1989): 207–28.

11. One possible example may be the myriad personal email newsletters that began to crop up in the mid-2010s, many of which are intended as hobbies or efforts to burnish professional reputations rather than moneymakers. The best of these newsletters could be developing an authoritative voice on niche areas of interest through aggregation and commentary, though of course many of those are inevitably being turned into commercial vehicles. For an overview of this subgenre of aggregation, see Andrew Jack, "Editorial Email Newsletters: The Medium Is Not the Only Message," *Reuters Institute for the Study of Journalism* (working paper), Nov. 2016, https://reutersinstitute.politics.ox.ac.uk/our-research/editorial-email-newsletters-medium-not-only-message.

12. Of course, people have long been willing to believe most anything that fits with their pre-existing beliefs, as many observers have noted and reams of social psychology research have indicated. And media and political sources have long been happy to oblige them with misleading information meant to reinforce those views and mobilize emotion. What's new is the widespread skepticism about information that false news has helped engender, along with a more tribal political environment and the rise of institutional structures (such as Facebook) working to aid that flow. See, e.g., Alexis C. Madrigal, "What Facebook Did to American Democracy," *The Atlantic*, Oct. 12, 2017, https://www.theatlantic.com/technology/archive/2017/10/what-facebook-did/542502/; David Ryfe, "What Is the Problem with Fake News?" *Iowa City Press-Citizen*, Oct. 13, 2017, http://www.press-citizen.com/story/opinion/contributors/guest-editorials/2017/10/13/what-problem-fake-news/751323001/.

13. For an overview of the overall global distrust in media as well as this small bounce in trust, see "2019 Edelman Trust Barometer: Global Report," *Edelman*, Jan. 20, 2019, https://www.edelman.com/sites/g/files/aatuss191/files/2019-02/2019_Edelman_Trust_Barometer_Global_Report_2.pdf. See also Indira Lakshmanan and Rick Edmonds, "Finally Some Good News: Trust in News Is Up, Especially for Local Media," *Poynter*, Aug. 22, 2018, https://www.poynter.org/news/finally-some-good-news-trust-news-especially-local-media; Nic Newman, Richard Fletcher, Antonis Kalogeropoulos, David A. L. Levy, and Rasmus Kleis Nielsen, "Reuters Institute Digital News Report 2018," *Reuters Institute for the Study of Journalism* (Oxford, 2018), http://media.digitalnewsreport.org/wp-content/uploads/2018/06/digital-news-report-2018.pdf?x89475.

14. See, e.g., Toril Aalberg, Frank Esser, Carsten Reinemann, Jesper Strömbäck, and Claes H. de Vreese, eds., *Populist Political Communication in Europe* (London: Routledge, 2017); Sven Engesser, Nayla Fawzi, and Anders Olof Larsson, eds., "Populist Online Communication," Special Issue, *Information, Communication & Society* 20, no. 9 (2017).

15. The term *post-truth* is often used to describe this era, and Carlson rightly argues that while the term implies a sudden and total rift with a previous era, it does aptly "suggest a shift in which facticity and rigor lose their epistemic bearing." Carlson, "The Information Politics of Journalism," 1880.

16. Helen Fulton, "Print News as Narrative," in *Narrative and Media* (Cambridge, UK: Cambridge University Press, 2005), 218–44; Gaye Tuchman, *Making News: A Study in the Construction of Reality* (New York: Free Press, 1978); Paul H. Weaver, "Newspaper News and Television News," in *Television as a Social Force: New Approaches to TV Criticism*, ed. Douglas Cater and Richard Adler (New York: Praeger, 1975), 81–94.

17. Nicole Hemmer, *Messengers of the Right: Conservative Media and the Transformation of American Politics* (Philadelphia: University of Pennsylvania Press, 2016); Michael Schudson, *Discovering the News: A Social History of American Newspapers* (New York: Basic Books, 1978).

18. Mark Fishman, *Manufacturing the News* (Austin: University of Texas Press, 1980); Gaye Tuchman, "Objectivity as Strategic Ritual: An Examination of Newsmen's Notions of Objectivity," *American Journal of Sociology* 77, no. 4 (1972): 660–79; Tuchman, *Making News*.

19. Meghann Farnsworth, "CNN's New 'This Is an Apple' Ad Targets Trump," *Recode*, Oct. 23, 2017, https://www.recode.net/2017/10/23/16524594/cnn-new-ad-apple-banana-trump-fake-news-mainstream-media.

20. Lucas Graves, *Deciding What's True: The Rise of Political Fact-Checking in American Journalism* (New York: Columbia University Press, 2016), 63–79.

21. C. W. Anderson, *Apostles of Certainty: Data Journalism and the Politics of Doubt* (Oxford, UK: Oxford University Press, 2018).

22. Anderson, *Apostles of Certainty*, 182.

23. There are, of course, textual practices that aggregators use to express uncertainty, including hyperlinks, as mentioned earlier in this chapter, and attributing information, challenging the veracity of a source, or re-angling a story, as discussed in chapter 2. But these practices do not match the depth of uncertainty that exists in the elemental work of aggregation itself.

24. Anderson, *Apostles of Certainty*, 183.

25. Yigal Godler and Zvi Reich, "Journalistic Evidence: Cross-Verification as a Constituent of Mediated Knowledge," *Journalism* 18, no. 5 (2017): 558–74.

Selected Bibliography

Abbott, Andrew. *The System of Professions: An Essay on the Division of Expert Labor.* Chicago: University of Chicago Press, 1988.

Agarwal, Sheetal D., and Michael L. Barthel. "The Friendly Barbarians: Professional Norms and Work Routines of Online Journalists in the United States." *Journalism* 16, no. 3 (2015): 376–91.

Aldridge, Meryl. "The Tentative Hell-Raisers: Identity and Mythology in Contemporary UK Press Journalism." *Media, Culture & Society* 20, no. 1 (1998): 109–27.

Aldridge, Meryl, and Julia Evetts. "Rethinking the Concept of Professionalism: The Case of Journalism." *British Journal of Sociology* 54, no. 4 (2003): 547–64.

Amado, Adriana, and Silvio Waisbord. "Divided We Stand: Blurred Boundaries in Argentine Journalism." In *Boundaries of Journalism: Professionalism, Practices and Participation*, ed. Matt Carlson and Seth C. Lewis (London: Routledge, 2015), 51–66.

"American Views: Trust, Media and Democracy." *Gallup/Knight Foundation.* Washington DC, 2018. https://knightfoundation.org/reports/american-views -trust-media-and-democracy.

Andén-Papadopoulos, Kari. "Media Witnessing and the 'Crowd-Sourced Video Revolution.'" *Visual Communication* 12, no. 3 (2013): 341–57.

Anderson, C. W. *Apostles of Certainty: Data Journalism and the Politics of Doubt.* Oxford: Oxford University Press, 2018.

——. "Between Creative and Quantified Audiences: Web Metrics and Changing Patterns of Newswork in Local US Newsrooms." *Journalism* 12, no. 5 (2011): 550–66.

——. "Deliberative, Agonistic, and Algorithmic Audiences: Journalism's Vision of Its Public in an Age of Audience Transparency." *International Journal of Communication* 5 (2011): 529–47.

——. "Journalism: Expertise, Authority, and Power in Democratic Life." In *The Media and Social Theory*, ed. David Hesmondhalgh and Jason Toynbee (New York: Routledge, 2008), 248–64.

——. *Rebuilding the News: Metropolitan Journalism in the Digital Age*. Philadelphia, PA: Temple University Press, 2013.

——. "What Aggregators Do: Towards a Networked Concept of Journalistic Expertise in the Digital Age." *Journalism* 14, no. 8 (2013): 1008–23.

Ang, Ien. *Desperately Seeking the Audience*. London: Routledge, 1991.

Bakker, Piet. "Aggregation, Content Farms and Huffinization: The Rise of Low-Pay and No-Pay Journalism." *Journalism Practice* 6, nos. 5–6 (2012): 627–37.

Baldasty, Gerald J. *The Commercialization of News in the Nineteenth Century*. Madison: University of Wisconsin Press, 1992.

Bantz, Charles R., Suzanne McCorkle, and Roberta C. Baade. "The News Factory." *Communication Research* 7, no. 1 (1980): 45–68.

Barner, Katherine. "The Viral-Media Editor Who Says Cute Babies and Animals Are Her 'Bread and Butter.' " *New York*, April 13, 2017. http://nymag.com/thejob /2017/04/the-viral-media-editor-who-will-get-a-click-with-cute-babies-and -animals.html.

Barnhurst, Kevin G. *Mister Pulitzer and the Spider: Modern News from Realism to the Digital*. Urbana: University of Illinois, 2016.

Barnhurst, Kevin G., and Diana Mutz. "American Journalism and the Decline in Event-Centered Reporting." *Journal of Communication* 47, no. 4 (1997): 27–53.

Barnhurst, Kevin G., and John Nerone. *The Form of News: A History*. New York: The Guilford Press, 2001.

Bell, Allan. *The Language of News Media*. Oxford: Blackwell, 1991.

Bell, Emily, and Taylor Owen. *The Platform Press: How Silicon Valley Reengineered Journalism*. Tow Center for Digital Journalism, March 29, 2017. https://www .cjr.org/tow_center_reports/platform-press-how-silicon-valley-reengineered -journalism.php

Berkowitz, Dan. "Non-Routine News and Newswork: Exploring a What-a-Story." *Journal of Communication* 42, no. 1 (1992): 82–94.

Bird, S. Elizabeth. "Storytelling on the Far Side: Journalism and the Weekly Tabloid." *Critical Studies in Mass Communication* 7, no. 4 (1990): 377–89.

Bird, S. Elizabeth, and Robert W. Dardenne. "Myth, Chronicle, and Story: Exploring the Narrative Qualities of News." In *Media, Myths, and Narratives: Television and the Press*, ed. James W. Carey (Newbury Park, CA: Sage, 1988), 67–86.

Boczkowski, Pablo J. *News at Work: Imitation in an Age of Information Abundance.* Chicago: University of Chicago Press, 2010.

Boesman, Jan, and Irene Costera Meijer. " 'Don't Read Me the News, Tell Me the Story': How News Makers and Storytellers Negotiate Journalism's Boundaries When Preparing and Presenting News Stories." *#ISOJ* 8, no. 1 (2018). http://isoj .org/research/dont-read-me-the-news-tell-me-the-story-how-news-makers-and -storytellers-negotiate-journalisms-boundaries-when-preparing-and-presenting -news-stories/.

——. "Nothing But the Facts? Exploring the Discursive Space for Storytelling and Truth-Seeking in Journalism." *Journalism Practice* 12, no. 8 (2018): 997–1007.

Boyer, Dominic. *The Life Informatic: Newsmaking in the Digital Era.* Ithaca, NY: Cornell University Press, 2013.

Broersma, Marcel. "Form, Style and Journalistic Strategies: An Introduction." In *Form and Style in Journalism: European Newspapers and the Representation of News 1880–2005* (Leuven, Belgium: Peeters, 2007), ix–xxix.

——. "Journalism as Performative Discourse: The Importance of Form and Style in Journalism." In *Journalism and Meaning-Making: Reading the Newspaper,* ed. Verica Rupar (Cresskill, NJ: Hampton, 2010), 15–35.

Buhl, Florian, Elisabeth Günther, and Thorsten Quandt. "Observing the Dynamics of the Online News Ecosystem: News Diffusion Processes among German News Sites." *Journalism Studies* 19, no. 1 (2018): 79–104.

Buttry, Steve. "Aggregation Guidelines: Link, Attribute, Add Value." *The Buttry Diary* (blog post), May 16, 2012. https://stevebuttry.wordpress.com/2012/05/16/ aggregation-guidelines-link-attribute-add-value/.

Carlson, Matt. "Blogs and Journalistic Authority: The Role of Blogs in US Election Day 2004 Coverage." *Journalism Studies* 8, no. 2 (2007): 264–79.

——. "Embedded Links, Embedded Meanings: Social Media Commentary and News Sharing as Mundane Media Criticism." *Journalism Studies* 17, no. 7 (2016): 915–24.

——. "The Information Politics of Journalism in a Post-Truth Age." *Journalism Studies* 19, no. 13 (2018): 1879–88.

——. *Journalistic Authority: Legitimating News in the Digital Era.* New York: Columbia University Press, 2017.

Carlson, Matt, and Jason T. Peifer. "The Impudence of Being Earnest: Jon Stewart and the Boundaries of Discursive Responsibility." *Journal of Communication* 63, no. 2 (2013): 333–50.

Chyi, Hsiang Iris, Seth C. Lewis, and Nan Zheng. "Parasite or Partner? Coverage of Google News in an Era of News Aggregation." *Journalism & Mass Communication Quarterly* 93, no. 4 (2016): 789–815.

Coddington, Mark. "Defending Judgment and Context in 'Original Reporting': Journalists' Construction of Newswork in a Networked Age." *Journalism* 15, no. 6 (2014): 678–95.

———. "Normalizing the Hyperlink: How Bloggers, Professional Journalists, and Institutions Shape Linking Values." *Digital Journalism* 2, no. 2 (2014): 140–55.

———. "The Wall Becomes a Curtain: Revisiting Journalism's News-Business Boundary." In *Boundaries of Journalism: Professionalism, Practices and Participation*, ed. Matt Carlson and Seth C. Lewis (London: Routledge, 2015), 67–82.

Conover, Dan. "The 'Lack of Vision' Thing? Well, Here's a Hopeful Vision for You." *Xark* (blog post), May 11, 2009. http://xark.typepad.com/my_weblog/2009/05/the-lack-of-vision-thing-well-heres-a-vision-for-you.html.

Cook, Timothy E. *Governing with the News: The News Media as a Political Institution*. Chicago: University of Chicago Press, 1998.

de Bruin, Marjan. "Gender, Organizational and Professional Identities in Journalism." *Journalism* 1, no. 2 (2000): 217–38.

De Maeyer, Juliette, and Avery E. Holton. "Why Linking Matters: A Metajournalistic Discourse Analysis." *Journalism* 17, no. 6 (2016): 776–94.

Deuze, Mark. *Media Work*. Cambridge: Polity, 2007.

———. "What Is Journalism? Professional Identity and Ideology of Journalists Reconsidered." *Journalism* 6, no. 4 (2005): 442–64.

Duffy, Andrew, Edson C. Tandoc, and Richard Ling. "Frankenstein Journalism." *Information, Communication & Society* 21, no. 10 (2018): 1354–68.

Eason, David L. "On Journalistic Authority: The Janet Cooke Scandal." *Critical Studies in Mass Communication* 3, no. 4 (1986): 429–47.

Ekström, Mats. "Epistemologies of TV Journalism: A Theoretical Framework." *Journalism* 3, no. 3 (2002): 259–82.

———. "Information, Storytelling and Attractions: TV Journalism in Three Modes of Communication." *Media, Culture & Society* 22, no. 4 (2000): 465–92.

Eldridge II, Scott A. *Online Journalism from the Periphery: Interloper Media and the Journalistic Field*. London: Routledge, 2018.

Eldridge II, Scott A., and Henrik Bødker. "Negotiating Uncertain Claims: Journalism as an Inferential Community." *Journalism Studies* 19, no. 13 (2018): 1912–22.

Ericson, Richard V. "How Journalists Visualize Fact." *The ANNALS of the American Academy of Political and Social Science* 560, no. 1 (1998): 83–95.

Ericson, Richard V., Patricia M. Baranek, and Janet B. L. Chan. *Visualizing Deviance: A Study of News Organization*. Toronto, Canada: University of Toronto Press, 1987.

Ettema, James S., and Theodore L. Glasser. *Custodians of Conscience: Investigative Journalism and Public Virtue*. New York: Columbia University Press, 1998.

——. "On the Epistemology of Investigative Journalism." In *Mass Communication Review Yearbook*, ed. Michael Gurevitch and Mark R. Levy (Newbury Park, CA: Sage, 1987, vol. 6), 338–61.

Fenton, Natalie, and Tamara Witschge. " 'Comment Is Free, Facts Are Sacred.' " In *News Online: Transformations and Continuities*, ed. Graham Meikle and Guy Redden (Basingstoke, UK: Palgrave Macmillan, 2011), 148–63.

Fink, Katherine, and Michael Schudson. "The Rise of Contextual Journalism, 1950s–2000s." *Journalism* 15, no. 1 (2014): 3–20.

Fishman, Mark. *Manufacturing the News*. Austin: University of Texas Press, 1980.

Galtung, Johan, and Mari Holmboe Ruge. "The Structure of Foreign News: The Presentation of the Congo, Cuba and Cyprus Crises in Four Norwegian Newspapers." *Journal of Peace Research* 2, no. 1 (1965): 64–90.

Gans, Herbert J. *Deciding What's News: A Study of CBS Evening News, NBC Nightly News, Newsweek, and Time*. New York, Pantheon, 1979.

Garvey, Ellen Gruber. *Writing with Scissors: American Scrapbooks from the Civil War to the Harlem Renaissance*. Oxford: Oxford University Press, 2013.

Godler, Yigal, and Zvi Reich. "How Journalists Think About Facts: Theorizing the Social Conditions Behind Epistemological Beliefs." *Journalism Studies* 14, no. 1 (2013): 94–112.

——. "Journalistic Evidence: Cross-Verification as a Constituent of Mediated Knowledge." *Journalism* 18, no. 5 (2017): 558–74.

Graves, Lucas. *Deciding What's True: The Rise of Political Fact-Checking in American Journalism*. New York: Columbia University Press, 2016.

Gutsche Jr., Robert E., and Erica Salkin. "Who Lost What? An Analysis of Myth, Loss, and Proximity in News Coverage of the Steubenville Rape." *Journalism* 17, no. 4 (2016): 456–73.

Hackett, Robert A. "Decline of a Paradigm? Bias and Objectivity in News Media Studies." *Critical Studies in Mass Communication* 1, no. 3 (1984): 229–59.

Hallin, Daniel C. "The Passing of the 'High Modernism' of American Journalism." *Journal of Communication* 42, no. 3 (1992): 14–25.

Hamblin, James. "It's Everywhere, the Clickbait." *The Atlantic*, Nov. 11, 2014. https://www.theatlantic.com/entertainment/archive/2014/11/clickbait-what-is/382545/.

Hamilton, James T. *All the News That's Fit to Sell: How the Market Transforms Information into News*. Princeton, NJ: Princeton University Press, 2004.

Harbers, Frank, and Marcel Broersma. "Between Engagement and Ironic Ambiguity: Mediating Subjectivity in Narrative Journalism." *Journalism* 15, no. 5 (2014): 639–54.

Harcup, Tony, and Deirdre O'Neill. "What Is News? News Values Revisited (Again)." *Journalism Studies* 18, no. 12 (2016): 1470–88.

Hartley, Jannie Møller. "The Online Journalist Between Ideals and Audiences: Towards a (More) Audience-Driven and Source-Detached Journalism?" *Journalism Practice* 7, no. 5 (2013): 572–87.

Hermida, Alfred. "Nothing But the Truth: Redrafting the Journalistic Boundary of Verification." In *Boundaries of Journalism: Professionalism, Practices and Participation*, ed. Matt Carlson and Seth C. Lewis (London: Routledge, 2015), 37–50.

Höpfl, H. M. "Power, Authority and Legitimacy." *Human Resource Development International* 2, no. 3 (1999): 217–34.

"How News Happens: A Study of the News Ecosystem of One American City." *Project for Excellence in Journalism*. Washington, DC: Pew Research Center, 2010. http://www.journalism.org/2010/01/11/how-news-happens/

Høyer, Svennik, and Hedda A. Nossen. "Revisions of the News Paradigm: Changes in Stylistic Features Between 1950 and 2008 in the Journalism of Norway's Largest Newspaper." *Journalism* 16, no. 4 (2015): 536–52.

Isbell, Kimberley. "The Rise of the News Aggregator: Legal Implications and Best Practices." *Citizen Media Law Project*, Working Paper 2010–10 (2010). https://papers.ssrn.com/sol3/papers.cfm?abstract_id=1670339

Jacobs, Ronald N. "Producing the News, Producing the Crisis: Narrativity, Television and News Work." *Media, Culture & Society* 18, no. 3 (1996): 373–97.

Jarlbrink, Johan. "Mobile/Sedentary: News Work Behind and Beyond the Desk." *Media History* 21, no. 3 (2015): 280–93.

Johnston, Jane, and Caroline Graham. "The New, Old Journalism: Narrative Writing in Contemporary Newspapers." *Journalism Studies* 13, no. 4 (2012): 517–33.

Kielbowicz, Richard B. "Newsgathering by Printers' Exchanges Before the Telegraph." *Journalism History* 9, no. 2 (1982): 42–48.

Kovach, Bill, and Tom Rosenstiel. *The Elements of Journalism: What Newspeople Should Know and the Public Should Expect*, 2nd ed. New York: Three Rivers, 2007.

Krause, Monika. "Reporting and the Transformations of the Journalistic Field: US News Media, 1890–2000." *Media, Culture & Society* 33, no. 1 (2011): 89–104.

Leavitt, Alex, and John J. Robinson. "Upvote My News: The Practices of Peer Information Aggregation for Breaking News on Reddit." *Proceedings of the ACM on Human-Computer Interaction* 1, no. 2 (2017), article 65.

Lecheler, Sophie, and Sanne Kruikemeier, "Re-Evaluating Journalistic Routines in a Digital Age: A Review of Research on the Use of Online Sources," *New Media & Society* 18, no. 1 (2016): 156–71.

Lee, Angela M., and Hsiang Iris Chyi. "The Rise of Online News Aggregators: Consumption and Competition." *International Journal on Media Management* 17, no. 1 (2015): 3–24.

Lee, Angela M., Seth C. Lewis, and Matthew Powers. "Audience Clicks and News Placement: A Study of Time-Lagged Influence in Online Journalism." *Communication Research* 41, no. 4 (2012): 505–30.

Lewis, Justin, Andrew Williams, and Bob Franklin. "Four Rumours and an Explanation: A Political Economic Account of Journalists' Changing Newsgathering and Reporting Practices." *Journalism Practice* 2, no. 1 (2008): 27–45.

Lewis, Rebecca. "Alternative Influence: Broadcasting the Reactionary Right on YouTube." *Data & Society*. New York, 2018. https://datasociety.net/wp-content/uploads/2018/09/DS_Alternative_Influence.pdf.

Lewis, Seth C. "The Tension Between Professional Control and Open Participation: Journalism and Its Boundaries." *Information, Communication & Society* 15, no. 6 (2012): 836–66.

Lippmann, Walter. *Liberty and the News*. New Brunswick, NJ: Transaction, 1995, originally published 1920.

——. *Public Opinion*. New York: Macmillan, 1961, originally published 1922.

Lule, Jack. *Daily News, Eternal Stories: The Mythological Role of Journalism*. New York: The Guilford Press, 2001.

Madnick, Stuart, and Michael Siegel. "Seizing the Opportunity: Exploiting Web Aggregation." *MIS Quarterly Executive* 1, no. 1 (2002): 35–46.

McGill, Meredith L. *American Literature and the Culture of Reprinting, 1834–1853*. Philadelphia: University of Pennsylvania Press, 2003.

The Media Insight Project. "A New Understanding: What Makes People Trust and Rely on News." *American Press Institute*, April 17, 2016. https://www.americanpressinstitute.org/publications/reports/survey-research/trust-news/.

Mindich, David T. Z. *Just the Facts: How "Objectivity" Came to Define American Journalism*. New York: New York University Press, 1998.

Nadler, Anthony M. *Making the News Popular: Mobilizing U.S. News Audiences*. Urbana: University of Illinois Press, 2016.

Neveu, Erik. "Revisiting Narrative Journalism as One of the Futures of Journalism." *Journalism Studies* 15, no. 5 (2014): 533–42.

Newman, Nic, Richard Fletcher, Antonis Kalogeropoulos, David A. L. Levy, and Rasmus Kleis Nielsen. *Reuters Institute Digital News Report 2017*. Reuters Institute for the Study of Journalism. Oxford, 2017. https://reutersinstitute.politics.ox.ac.uk/sites/default/files/Digital%20News%20Report%220201%20web_0.pdf.

——. *Reuters Institute Digital News Report 2018*. Reuters Institute for the Study of Journalism. Oxford, 2018. http://media.digitalnewsreport.org/wp-content/uploads/2018/06/digital-news-report-2018.pdf?x89475.

Nielsen, Rasmus Kleis. "The Business of News." In *The Sage Handbook of Digital Journalism*, ed. Tamara Witschge, C. W. Anderson, David Domingo, and Alfred Hermida (Thousand Oaks, CA: Sage, 2016), 51–67.

Örnebring, Henrik. "Journalists Thinking About Precarity: Making Sense of the "New Normal." *ISOJ* 8, no. 1 (2018). http://isoj.org/research/journalists-thinking-about-precarity-making-sense-of-the-new-normal/.

——. "Reassessing Journalism as a Profession." In *The Routledge Companion to News and Journalism*, ed. Stuart Allan (London: Routledge, 2010), 568–77.

Palau-Sampio, Dolors. "Reference Press Metamorphosis in the Digital Context: Clickbait and Tabloid Strategies in Elpais.com." *Communication & Society* 29, no. 2 (2016): 63–79.

Park, Robert E. "News as a Form of Knowledge: A Chapter in the Sociology of Knowledge." *American Journal of Sociology* 45, no. 5 (1940): 669–86.

Petre, Caitlin. *The Traffic Factories: Metrics at Chartbeat, Gawker Media, and The New York Times*. Tow Center for Digital Journalism (2015). https://academiccommons.columbia.edu/doi/10.7916/D80293W1.

Phillips, Angela. "Faster and Shallower: Homogenisation, Cannibalisation and the Death of Reporting." In *Changing Journalism*, ed. Peter Lee-Wright, Angela Phillips, and Tamara Witschge (London: Routledge, 2012), 81–98.

——. "Old Sources: New Bottles." In *New Media, Old News: Journalism and Democracy in the Digital Age*, ed. Natalie Fenton (Los Angeles: Sage, 2010), 87–101.

Popp, Richard K. "Information, Industrialization, and the Business of Press Clippings, 1880–1925." *The Journal of American History* 101, no. 2 (2014): 427–53.

Powers, Matthew. "'In Forms that Are Familiar and Yet-to-Be Invented': American Journalism and the Discourse of Technologically Specific Work." *Journal of Communication Inquiry* 36, no. 1 (2012): 24–43.

Reich, Zvi. "Source Credibility and Journalism: Between Visceral and Discretional Judgment." *Journalism Practice* 5, no. 1 (2011): 51–67.

Ricoeur, Paul. *Time and Narrative*. Chicago, University of Chicago Press, 1984/1990.

Roeh, Itzhak, and Sharon Ashley. "Criticizing Press Coverage of the War in Lebanon: Toward a Paradigm of News as Storytelling." In *Communication Yearbook*, 9th ed., ed. Margaret L. McLaughlin (Beverly Hills, CA: Sage, 1986), 117–41.

Rom, Shelly, and Zvi Reich. "Between the Technological Hare and the Journalistic Tortoise: Minimization of Knowledge Claims in Online News Flashes." *Journalism* (2017), published online before print.

Romano, Carlin. "The Grisly Truth About Bare Facts." In *Reading the News*, ed. Robert Karl Manoff and Michael Schudson (New York: Pantheon, 1986), 38–78.

Rosen, Jay. "Good Old Fashioned Shoe Leather Reporting." *PressThink* (blog post), April 16, 2015. http://pressthink.org/2015/04/good-old-fashioned-shoe-leather-reporting/.

——. "The People Formerly Known as the Audience." *PressThink* (blog post), June 27, 2006. http://archive.pressthink.org/2006/06/27/ppl_frmr.html.

Rosenberg, Scott. *Say Everything: How Blogging Began, What It's Becoming, and Why It Matters.* New York: Crown, 2009.

Ryfe, David M. *Can Journalism Survive? An Inside Look at American Newsrooms.* Cambridge: Polity, 2012.

Saridou, Theodora, Lia-Paschalia Spyridou, and Andreas Veglis. "Churnalism on the Rise? Assessing Convergence Effects on Editorial Practices." *Digital Journalism* 5, no. 8 (2017): 1006–24.

Schlesinger, Philip. *Putting "Reality" Together: BBC News.* London: Constable, 1978.

Schudson, Michael. *Discovering the News: A Social History of American Newspapers.* New York: Basic Books, 1978.

——. *The Power of News.* Cambridge, MA: Harvard University Press, 1995.

——. *The Sociology of News,* 2nd ed. New York: W.W. Norton & Co., 2011.

Schudson, Michael, and Chris Anderson. "Objectivity, Professionalism, and Truth Seeking in Journalism." In *The Handbook of Journalism Studies,* ed. Karin Wahl-Jorgensen and Thomas Hanitzsch (New York: Routledge, 2009), 88–101.

Shane, Scott. "From Headline to Photograph, a Fake News Masterpiece." *New York Times,* Jan. 18, 2017. https://www.nytimes.com/2017/01/18/us/fake-news-hillary-clinton-cameron-harris.html.

Shapiro, Ivor, Colette Brin, Isabelle Bédard-Brûlé, and Kasia Mychajlowycz. "Verification as a Strategic Ritual: How Journalists Retrospectively Describe Processes for Ensuring Accuracy." *Journalism Practice* 7, no. 6 (2013): 657–73.

Sherwood, Merryn, and Penny O'Donnell. "Once a Journalist, Always a Journalist? Industry Restructure, Job Loss and Professional Identity." *Journalism Studies* 19, no. 7 (2018): 1021–38.

Shoemaker, Pamela J., and Stephen D. Reese. *Mediating the Message in the 21st Century: A Media Sociology Perspective,* 3rd ed. New York: Routledge, 2014.

Sigal, Leon V. *Reporters and Officials: The Organization and Politics of Newsmaking.* Lexington, MA: D.C. Heath and Co., 1973.

Singer, Jane B. "Out of Bounds: Professional Norms as Boundary Markers." In *Boundaries of Journalism: Professionalism, Practices and Participation,* ed. Matt Carlson and Seth C. Lewis (London: Routledge, 2015), 21–36.

——. "Still Guarding the Gate? The Newspaper Journalist's Role in an On-Line World." *Convergence* 3, no. 1 (1997): 72–89.

——. "Who Are These Guys? The Online Challenge to the Notion of Journalistic Professionalism." *Journalism* 4, no. 2 (2003): 139–63.

Skovsgaard, Morten, and Peter Bro. "Preference, Principle and Practice: Journalistic Claims for Legitimacy." *Journalism Practice* 5, no. 3 (2011): 319–31.

Smith, Anthony. "The Long Road to Objectivity and Back Again: The Kinds of Truth We Get in Journalism." In *Newspaper History: From the Seventeenth Century to the Present Day*, ed. George Boyce, James Curran, and Pauline Wingate (London: Constable, 1978), 153–71.

——. *The Newspaper: An International History*. London: Thames & Hudson, 1979.

Soloski, John. "News Reporting and Professionalism: Some Constraints on the Reporting of the News." *Media, Culture & Society* 11, no. 2 (1989): 207–28.

Sparrow, Bartholomew H. *Uncertain Guardians: The News Media as a Political Institution*. Baltimore, MD: Johns Hopkins University Press, 1999.

Starkman, Dean. "The Hamster Wheel." *Columbia Journalism Review*, Sept./Oct. 2010. http://archives.cjr.org/cover_story/the_hamster_wheel.php.

Starr, Paul. *The Social Transformation of American Medicine*. New York: Basic Books, 1982.

Stewart, Robert K. "The Exchange System and the Development of American Politics in the 1820s." *American Journalism* 4, no. 1 (1987): 30–42.

Sumpter, Randall S. "Daily Newspaper Editors' Audience Construction Routines: A Case Study." *Critical Studies in Media Communication* 17, no. 3 (2000): 334–46.

Tandoc Jr., Edson C. "Journalism Is Twerking? How Web Analytics Is Changing the Process of Gatekeeping." *New Media & Society* 16, no. 4 (2014): 559–75.

Tandoc, Edson C., and Cassie Yuan Wen Foo. "Here's What BuzzFeed Journalists Think of Their Journalism." *Digital Journalism* 6, no. 1 (2018): 41–57.

Thomson, Elizabeth A., Peter R.R. White, and Philip Kitley. "'Objectivity' and 'Hard News' Reporting Across Cultures: Comparing the News Report in English, French, Japanese and Indonesian Journalism." *Journalism Studies* 9, no. 2 (2008): 212–28.

Tong, Jingrong. "Journalistic Legitimacy Revisited: Collapse or Revival in the Digital Age?" *Digital Journalism* 6, no. 2 (2018): 256–73.

Toropin, Konstantin Valerievich. "Gawker, BuzzFeed, and Journalism: Case Studies in Boundaries, News Aggregation, and Journalistic Authority." Unpublished master's thesis, Hubbard School of Journalism, University of Minnesota (2016).

Tuchman, Gaye. *Making News: A Study in the Construction of Reality*. New York: Free Press, 1978.

——. "Objectivity as Strategic Ritual: An Examination of Newsmen's Notions of Objectivity." *American Journal of Sociology* 77, no. 4 (1972): 660–69.

Turow, Joseph. *Breaking Up America: Advertisers and the New Media World*. Chicago: University of Chicago Press, 1997.

Usher, Nikki. "Going Web-First at *The Christian Science Monitor*: A Three-Part Study of Change." *International Journal of Communication* 6 (2012): 1898–917, http://ijoc.org/index.php/ijoc/article/view/1404.

——. *Interactive Journalism: Hackers, Data, and Code*. Urbana: University of Illinois Press, 2016.

——. *Making News at* The New York Times. Ann Arbor: University of Michigan Press, 2014.

Vobič, Igor, and Ana Milojević. " 'What We Do Is Not Actually Journalism': Role Negotiations in Online Departments of Two Newspapers in Slovenia and Serbia." *Journalism* 15, no. 8 (2014): 1023–40.

Vos, Tim P., and Patrick Ferrucci. "Who Am I? Perceptions of Digital Journalists' Professional Identity." In *The Routledge Handbook of Developments in Digital Journalism Studies*, ed. Scott A. Eldridge II and Bob Franklin (New York: Routledge, 2018), 40–52.

Vos, Tim P., and Teri Finneman. "The Early Historical Construction of Journalism's Gatekeeping Role." *Journalism* 18, no. 3 (2017): 265–80.

Vos, Tim P., and Ryan J. Thomas. "The Discursive Construction of Journalistic Authority in a Post-Truth Age." *Journalism Studies* 19, no. 13 (2018): 2001–10.

Weaver, Paul H. "Newspaper News and Television News." In *Television as a Social Force: New Approaches to TV Criticism*, ed. Douglas Cater and Richard Adler (New York: Praeger, 1975), 81–94.

Weber, Max. *The Theory of Social and Economic Organization*, trans. A. M. Henderson and Talcott Parsons. New York: Free Press, 1947.

Weldon, Michele. *Everyman News: The Changing American Front Page*. Columbia: University of Missouri Press, 2008.

White, Hayden. "The Value of Narrativity in the Representation of Reality." In *On Narrative*, ed. W. J. T. Mitchell (Chicago: University of Chicago Press, 1980), 1–23.

Wiik, Jenny. "Identities Under Construction: Professional Journalism in a Phase of Destabilization." *International Review of Sociology* 19, no. 2 (2009): 351–65.

Witschge, Tamara. "Transforming Journalistic Practice: A Profession Caught Between Change and Tradition." In *Rethinking Journalism: Trust and Participation in a Transformed News Landscape*, ed. Chris Peters and Marcel Broersma (London: Routledge, 2013), 160–72.

Ytreberg, Espen. "Moving Out of the Inverted Pyramid: Narratives and Descriptions in Television News." *Journalism Studies* 2, no. 3 (2001): 357–71.

Zamith, Rodrigo. "Quantified Audiences in News Production: A Synthesis and Research Agenda." *Digital Journalism* 6, no. 4 (2018): 418–35.

Zelizer, Barbie. *Covering the Body: The Kennedy Assassination, the Media, and the Shaping of Collective Memory*. Chicago: University of Chicago Press, 1992.

——. "On 'Having Been There': 'Eyewitnessing' as a Journalistic Key Word." *Critical Studies in Media Communication* 24, no. 5 (2007): 408–28.

——. " 'Saying' as Collective Practice: Quoting and Differential Address in the News." *Text* 9, no. 4 (1989): 369–88.

——. "Where Is the Author in American TV News? On the Construction and Presentation of Proximity, Authorship, and Journalistic Authority." *Semiotica* 80, no. 1/2 (1990): 37–48.

Index

analytics: for aggregation, 131–32, 253n53; from audiences, 133–35; ethics of, 154–57; metrics for, 140–47, 246n51; psychology of, 136–39; for SportsPop, 130

Anderson, C. W., 9, 38, 41, 87, 140, 202

Apostles of Certainty (Anderson), 87, 202

Apple News, 6, 9. *See also* journalism; media; news

Arizmendi, Adrian, 160, 180–81

Atlantic Wire, 99, 119, 121

atomic units, 161, 167–75

attribution, 88–89, 123–24

audiences, 127; of aggregation, 136–39, 146–47; analytics from, 133–35; atomic units for, 161; clickbait and, 147–54; continuity for, 254n59; controversy for, 159–60; credibility for, 112–13; crime for, 169; as data, 245n37; ethics for, 205; headlines for, 177; humor for, 170–71; information for, 94, 121–22, 159, 172; of journalism, 154–55; metrics for, 250n23; of news, 175–82; organizational legitimacy for, 108; professionalism of, 156; psychology of, 33–34, 44–45, 119–20, 124, 152–53, 203–4, 231n18, 244n30, 245n45; reporting for, 204–5; speech for, 252n42; technology and, 171, 227n31, 247n2, 253n44; of Twitter, 129–30, 253n53; video for, 223n104

authority, 127; accuracy for, 91–92; in aggregation, 51, 84–85, 122–23, 195–99; for Circa, 255n6; in culture, 39–40; in digital news, 34; ethics of, 18–19, 191; identity and, 126–28; information and, 215n54; in journalism, 15–22, 38–39, 49, 72–73, 95–96, 130–31, 147, 161–62, 168–69, 187–88, 193–95, 228n36; knowledge and, 242n3; in narratives, 183–87;

psychology of, 204–5; in reporting, 83, 126; on YouTube, 256n8

automation, 5–6, 25

Baron, Martin, 11

BBC, 35, 46, 54–55, 66

beliefs, 256n11

Bentley, Daniel, 81, 181

Benton, Joshua, 22

Bernstein, Carl, 41

Bezos, Jeff, 11

Billy Penn, 31, 76, 79, 116, 198; CMS at, 241n75; editors at, 239n40; journalism at, 240n46; policy at, 89; SportsPop and, 233n40

blogs, 10, 25–26, 47, 57–58, 170; professionalism for, 113; psychology of, 237n16

Boczkowski, Pablo, 44–45

Boesman, Jan, 187

Boyer, Dominic, 9, 245n45

Brady, Jim, 31

breaking news, 7

Britain, 23

Buttry, Steve, 125

Buxbaum, Evan, 49–50, 82, 101

BuzzFeed: for culture, 27–28; ethics at, 70–71, 148; Huffington Post and, 117–18; journalism for, 185–86; psychology of, 69–70; sources for, 78–79. *See also* journalism; media; news

Calcaterra, Craig, 88, 237n16

Carlson, Matt, 16, 191–92

Christian Times Newspaper, 1–2

Circa: atomic units for, 170–75; authority for, 255n6; economics for, 241n62; editors at, 48–49, 110–11, 253n49; ethics at, 74; history of, 28–29, 188–89, 252n32; leadership at, 252n35; metrics for, 253n53; narratives for, 175–82, 198–99,

231n11; *New York Times* and, 122; policy at, 49–50, 72, 158–62, 164–65, 205, 247n2; psychology of, 253n44; SportsPop and, 185; technology for, 34

circulation, 204–7

citation, 52–53

clickbait, 33–34, 246n54; for aggregation, 244n30; audiences and, 147–54; ethics of, 84; history of, 246n51; psychology of, 129–33, 143

Clinton, Hillary, 1–2, 31, 164, 177

CMS. *See* content management systems

CNN, 7, 53–56, 159–60, 201–2. *See also* journalism; media; news

cognitive investment, 21

Cohn, David, 174, 176, 253n53

Columbus Dispatch, 2–3

comments, 135, 138–39

comments, on social media, 62–64

commercial logic, 198–99

communication, 100, 107, 167

confirmatory phone calls, 62–63, 78–81, 205

conservative social news. *See* Social Post

conspiracy theories, 14, 44, 195

content management systems (CMS), 172, 241n75

continuity, 253n49, 254n59

controversy, 61, 70–71, 86, 159–60; in feature stories, 179–80; scandals, 165, 184

Cook, Timothy, 97

copy editors, 64

copyright, 223n105

corroboration, 78, 79–80

Costera Meijer, Irene, 187

Cowley, Stacy, 105, 146

creativity, 121

credibility, 46–47; in aggregation, 60; for audiences, 112–13; for blogs, 57–58; of CNN, 201–2; *Deciding What's True* (Graves), 202; from

ethics, 198; in journalism, 80–81; organizational legitimacy and, 110–11; politics of, 187–88; psychology of, 197, 223n105, 256n11; in social media, 50–51; of sources, 199–200; in U.S., 228n28; web traffic as, 70, 144–45

crime, 165, 169

critics, 12, 16–17

culture: of aggregation, 66, 109–10, 149–50; authority in, 39–40; beliefs in, 256n11; Billy Penn and, 31, 116; BuzzFeed for, 27–28; of editors, 49–50, 62, 82, 101, 159, 175–76; epistemology in, 257n15; of Germany, 9; headlines for, 190; immediacy for, 64–65; of journalism, 103, 176, 237n16, 240n56, 247n74; knowledge for, 17–18; media and, 228n36; narratives about, 249n13; of news, 253n52; of politics, 10; professionalism in, 195; psychology of, 16, 18–19, 23–24, 229n48; of reporting, 12–13, 103–4, 219n100, 236n9; scholarship on, 219n100; of social media, 137–39; at Social Post, 66–67, 141–42, 185; technology for, 212n23, 223n104; of U.S., 32, 199–200, 205–6, 214n35; of VidNews, 117, 126, 239n42

curation, 7–8. *See also* aggregation

cycles, 27–28, 68–69

Dalrymple, Jim, II, 77, 88

data: audiences as, 245n37; professionalism and, 219n100, 223n105; public opinion of, 144–45; real-time data, 143–44; from social media, 231n8; for sources, 229n46; structured data, 169, 182

Deciding What's True (Graves), 202

democracy, 16–17, 20

Denton, Nick, 26

second-hand evidence gathering, 85–86; of sensationalism, 152–53; of shortcuts, 75–78; for sources, 233n39, 234n58; for SportsPop, 139, 235n68; technology and, 67, 230n6; of television, 149; at VidNews, 74; of web traffic, 151–52; yellow journalism, 167–68

ethnographic work, 219n100

Europe, 9–10, 187

events, 178–79, 198, 252n43

evidence: aggregation and, 57–60; of corroboration, 79–80; documentation as, 42; empirical evidence, 41; for information, 45–46; for news, 35–37; in reporting, 59; scholarship on, 59–60; second-hand evidence gathering, 57–60, 85–86; sources as, 46–51; verification of, 43–44, 192, 229n43

excerpts, 124

exchange editors, 22–23

experience, 98–99, 125–26

expertise. See professionalism

eyewitnesses, 83

Facebook, 67, 72–73, 135, 137–38, 148–49. See also social media

facts. See evidence; information

fake news, 4, 14–15, 44, 202, 210n13; media and, 201–2; post-truth, 257n15; psychology of, 2, 199–200

feature stories, 179–80

Fishman, Mark, 41–42, 227n26

foreign news, 253n49

France, 25

Galligan, Matt, 171, 253n53

Galtung, Johan, 68–69

Gawker, 26, 119, 121

Geller, Pamela, 2

Germany, 9

Godler, Yigal, 59–60, 206

Google News, 9; automation by, 5–6, 25; for journalism, 66–67; metrics for, 183; Social Post and, 194; for sources, 36, 53–54, 63. See also journalism; media; news

gossip, 26

Graves, Lucas, 202

Hallin, Daniel, 23

hard news, 182

Harris, Cameron, 1–4, 6, 206–7, 209n1

headlines, 177, 190, 247n70

hedging, of information, 235n64

hierarchies: in aggregation, 107–8; in journalism, 46; in organizational legitimacy, 230n6

history: of aggregation, 22–28, 168–69, 225n5, 238n19, 239n42; of blogs, 25–26; of Circa, 28–29, 188–89, 252n32; of clickbait, 246n51; email newsletters, 256n11; of ethics, 109–10; of immediacy, 240n56; of journalism, 38, 236n9, 250nn20–21; of local news, 228n28; of media, 167, 190; of metrics, 140–41; of narratives, 161–62; of reporting, 9–10, 17–18, 91; scholarship in, 164; of social media, 147–49; of technology, 6; of television, 134–35; of U.S., 200–201; yellow journalism, 167–68

Hollywood Reporter, 79, 101–2

Holovaty, Adrian, 169

Huffington Post, 117–18. See also journalism; media; news

Huh, Ben, 170, 182

humor, 170–71

Hyatt, Abraham, 79, 89, 111, 177

hybrid ethnography, 219n100

hyperlinks, 25, 45–46, 88, 123–24, 194

hypotheses, 40–41

identity, 120–22, 126–28; aggregation and, 98–99, 240n46; professionalism in, 15–22, 39, 96–98, 103–8, 114–19, 192, 205, 217n69, 238n33

imitation, 15

immediacy, 64–65; for aggregation, 73–75, 176–77; economics of, 204–5; history of, 240n56; in policy, 180–81; as professionalism, 99–103; real-time data, 143–44; of social media, 81; of Twitter, 67–68

inferiority. *See* insecurities

information: aggregation of, 36, 80–81, 142–43; for audiences, 94, 121–22, 159, 172; authority and, 215n54; for critics, 16–17; economics and, 19; for editors, 55–56; epistemology of, 193; evidence for, 45–46; fake news and, 4; hedging of, 235n64; in journalism, 37, 163, 227n26; knowledge and, 39; from media, 4; for news, 37–46, 230n6; online information, 44; policy for, 74, 222n101; politics of, 256n11; primary sources for, 56; public opinion and, 211n18; technology for, 24–25, 81–85; verification of, 77

Ingram, Mathew, 8

insecurities, 95, 108–13, 127, 222n101

institutional forces, 227n31

interactive journalism, 13, 219n100

international news, 51–57, 86

interpretation, 187–89

interviews: editors and, 28, 36–37; ethics of, 79; with *New York Times*, 219n100; observation and, 41–42; organizational legitimacy and, 223n105; politics of, 222n101; professionalism in, 228n40; scholarship on, 34–44; with sources, 45, 63–64

investigative journalism, 11, 40–41

Jacobs, Ronald, 165

Jarlbrink, Johan, 228n36

Jindal, Bobby, 159–60, 178, 181

journalism: accuracy in, 27–28; aggregation and, 89–90, 93–96, 166–67, 190–92; audiences of, 154–55; authority in, 15–22, 38–39, 49, 72–73, 95–96, 130–31, 147, 161–62, 168–69, 187–88, 193–95, 228n36; at Billy Penn, 240n46; blogs as, 47; breaking news in, 7; for BuzzFeed, 185–86; comments for, 138–39; communication in, 100, 167; creativity in, 121; credibility in, 80–81; culture of, 103, 176, 237n16, 240n56, 247n74; democracy for, 16, 20; for digital news, 219n96; economics of, 11, 106, 131, 136; editors for, 35; *The Elements of Journalism* (Kovach/Rosentiel), 40; epistemology of, 43–44, 114–15; ethics of, 33–34, 37–38, 150–51, 163–64, 195–96, 223n105, 244n30, 256n5; in Europe, 187; events for, 252n43; experience in, 125–26; Google News for, 66–67; hierarchies in, 46; history of, 38, 236n9, 250nn20–21; hypotheses in, 40–41; identity and, 119–22; information in, 37, 163, 227n26; insecurities in, 222n101; interactive journalism, 13, 219n100; interpretation in, 187–89; investigative journalism, 11, 40–41; judgment in, 121–22, 136–37; knowledge for, 203–4; metajournalism, 197; mythology of, 127; observation in, 41–42; opinions in, 42–43; organizational legitimacy in, 118; performativity in, 252n42; policy for, 120–21; politics of, 96–97, 110; precision journalism, 226n16; professionalism in, 6–7, 23–24,

58, 93–96, 144, 183–84, 224n106, 242n3, 242n83; psychology of, 12, 18, 69, 134–35, 178–79, 189, 218n89; public opinion and, 4–5, 135, 156–57; reporting and, 9–10; scholarship on, 19, 65–66, 82, 115, 119, 126, 140–41, 149, 216n64; shortcuts in, 75–78; shortform journalism, 167–70; for Social Post, 111–12; technology for, 165–66, 245n45, 256n7; uncertainty in, 235n64; value of, 119–20; yellow journalism, 167–68

judgment, 68–73, 90–91, 121–22, 136–37, 141–42, 145–46

Keller, Bill, 11, 108
Kielbowicz, Richard, 22–23
Kirkland, Sam, 8
Klein, Ezra, 11
knowledge: in aggregation, 193–95; authority and, 242n3; for culture, 17–18; epistemology of, 215n54; fake news and, 14–15; identity and, 97; information and, 39; for journalism, 203–4; knowledge work, 192; Pew Research Center for, 8–9; production of, 12–15, 60, 194–95; psychology of, 20–21; in reporting, 126–27; scholarship on, 21–22
Kovach, Bill, 40
Krewson, Chris, 79, 101–2

LaForge, Patrick, 78–79, 86
language, 7–8
leadership, 107, 252n35. *See also* authority
legacy media, 2–3, 31, 32
Lippmann, Walter, 40
live streams, 82–83
local news, 228n28
Lule, Jack, 165

macro narrative, 164–67
marginality, 14
McCreery, Scotty, 152–53
McGill, Meredith, 22
media: critics of, 12; culture and, 228n36; economics of, 135, 139, 155–56; epistemology in, 39; fake news and, 201–2; gossip for, 26; history of, 167, 190; information from, 4; legacy media, 2–3, 31–32; online information for, 45; politics for, 25–26, 31–32, 186; psychology of, 108–9; in publication, 8–9; scholarship on, 83–84, 165; technology for, 148, 206; television, 35, 131–32, 228n38; trust in, 257n13; VidNews in, 29–30. *See also* fake news; social media
meso narrative, 164–67, 181–82, 185, 188
metajournalistic discourse, 193–94, 197, 199
metrics: for aggregation, 141–42; for analytics, 140–47, 246n51; for audiences, 250n23; for Circa, 253n53; ethics of, 132–33, 154–56, 231n8, 245n37; for Google News, 183; history of, 140–41; of organizational legitimacy, 150–51; of social media, 129–30
micro narrative, 164–67, 185–86
millennials, 31
Mindich, David, 167
Mitchell, Bill, 25–26
mobile apps, 6, 28–29, 171, 250n23
monotony, 101–3
muckraking, 167–68
Murdoch, Rupert, 108, 168
mythology: of journalism, 127; of narratives, 249n12; of news, 164–67; of reporting, 86–87, 90, 225n5

Nadler, Anthony, 156

narratives: for aggregation, 162, 188–89, 242n78; authority in, 183–87; for Circa, 175–82, 198–99, 231n11; about culture, 249n13; history of, 161–62; mythology of, 249n12; for news, 158–67; social media in, 185–86

news: advertising and, 26; advertising for, 201–2; atomic units in, 167–70, 167–75; audiences of, 175–82; blogs for, 10, 170; breaking news, 7; in Britain, 23; circulation of, 204–7; continuity in, 253n49; culture of, 253n52; cycles of, 27–28, 68–69; discovery as, 65–68; economics of, 25–26; evidence for, 35–37; Facebook for, 67; foreign news, 253n49; in France, 25; hard news, 182; information for, 37–46, 230n6; institutional forces for, 227n31; international news, 51–57, 86; judgment of, 68–73, 141–42; local news, 228n28; macro news, 164–67; meso news, 164–67, 181–82, 185, 188; micro news, 164–67, 185–86; mobile apps for, 6, 250n23; mythology of, 164–67; narratives for, 158–67; newsmaking, 9; news organizations, 46–48, 171, 174–75; newsroom, 103–8; newswork, 193, 219n100; newsworthiness, 68–73, 90–91, 160–61; politics of, 81; production of, 162, 197–98, 204–7; professionalism in, 211n21, 249n13; publication of, 5–6, 77–78; for public opinion, 70–71; recycled news, 8–9; Reddit for, 228n39; scholarship on, 163, 206–7; secondary news, 90–92; social media as, 1–2, 125; social news, 30; sources for, 76; for SportsPop, 50, 104; technology for, 226n16, 252n32; on television, 228n38; Twitter for, 28, 100–101, 158–59; uncertainty and, 61–65; value in, 244n30; verification of, 90. *See also* digital news; fake news

newspapers. *See specific newspapers*

New York Times, 105; aggregation at, 237n12; Circa and, 122; ethics of, 134; interviews with, 219n100; NYT Now, 105, 146, 219n100, 237n12;organizational legitimacy for, 197; policy at, 185; reporting at, 238n33; scholarship on, 75; sources for, 78–79; technology for, 146. *See also* journalism; media; news

Obama, Barack, 180

objectivity, 40–41, 111–12, 138, 167, 249n10

observation, 41–42

online information, 44, 45

online media, 10, 24–27

opinions, 42–43

organizational legitimacy, 105–6; for audiences, 108; credibility and, 110–11; ethics for, 111–12, 128; hierarchies in, 230n6; interviews and, 223n105; in journalism, 118; metrics of, 150–51; for *New York Times*, 197; politics of, 199–200

Orso, Anna, 116

outrage, 138, 139

Park, Robert, 17, 167, 182

perceptions, 108–13

performativity, 252n42

Perry, Katy, 82

Pew Research Center, 8–9

Philadelphia Inquirer, 76

plagiarism, 124–25, 223n105

policy: for aggregation, 5–8, 46, 64–65, 68–69, 151–52, 186–87, 204–7, 233n37; at Billy Penn, 89; at Circa, 49–50, 72, 158–62, 164–65, 205, 247n2; for digital news, 4–5, 32–33;

226n16, 252n32; for *New York Times*,
146; professionalism and, 256n11;
sources and, 233n37

Telegraph, 35–37

television, 35, 131–32, 134–35, 149,
228n38

terrorism, 174–75

theory. *See* scholarship

Trautman, Ted, 178–79

Trump, Donald, 1–2, 31, 43, 176–77,
199–202

trust, 39–40, 46–47, 50, 201, 229n48,
257n13

truth, 2–3, 4, 257n15

Tuchman, Gaye, 71, 201

Twitter: for aggregation, 230n6;
audiences of, 129–30, 253n53;
immediacy of, 67–68; for news,
28, 100–101, 158–59; reporting on,
54; for sources, 82–83; trust for,
50; TweetDeck application for, 66,
69, 100–101, 230n6. *See also* social
media

uncertainty: in aggregation, 199–204,
258n23; in digital news, 200; in
journalism, 235n64; news and,
61–65; psychology of, 85–90,
199–204

United States (U.S.): aggregation in,
98–99; credibility in, 228n28; culture
of, 32, 199–200, 205–6, 214n35;
editors in, 175; Europe and, 9–10;
history of, 200–201; politics in, 1–2;
public opinion in, 109–10; trust in,
229n48

USA Today, 52–54. *See also* journalism;
media; news

Usher, Nikki, 43–44, 75, 99–100,
219n100

value, 119–26, 244n30

verification: in aggregation, 75–78, 84;
confirmatory phone calls for, 78–81;
corroboration as, 78; of evidence,
43–44, 192, 229n43; of information,
77; of news, 90; policy for, 42–45,
59–60, 73–76; in reporting, 77; from
social media, 233n40; sources and,
77–79, 258n23

video, 223n104, 253n52, 256n8

VidNews, 29–30; culture of, 117, 126,
239n42; editors at, 70, 93–96;
ethics at, 74; policy at, 47, 184–85;
reporting for, 35, 254n56; Social Post
and, 111, 233n39; sources for, 51–57

Villard, Oswald Garrison, 24

Vox media, 11

Washington Post, 11. *See also*
journalism; media; news

Weber, Max, 16, 18

web traffic: as credibility, 70, 144–45;
economics of, 26–27, 246n54; ethics
of, 151–52; for social media, 155; for
Social Post, 231n10; for SportsPop,
73–74, 102, 146

Wink, Shannon, 239n40

wire services, 24, 46, 52–53, 172, 175,
182, 253n52

yellow journalism, 167–68

YouTube, 2, 54–55, 256n8. *See also*
social media

Zelizer, Barbie, 82–83

CPSIA information can be obtained
at www.ICGtesting.com
Printed in the USA
LVHW110350101019
633723LV00002BA/3/P